The Developmental Psychology of Music

DAVID J. HARGREAVES

Department of Psychology
University of Leicester

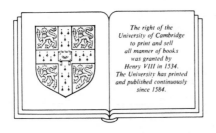

The right of the
University of Cambridge
to print and sell
all manner of books
was granted by
Henry VIII in 1534.
The University has printed
and published continuously
since 1584.

CAMBRIDGE UNIVERSITY PRESS

Cambridge
London   New York   New Rochelle
Melbourne   Sydney

Published by the Press Syndicate of the University of Cambridge
The Pitt Building, Trumpington Street, Cambridge CB2 1RP
32 East 57th Street, New York, NY 10022, USA
10 Stamford Road, Oakleigh, Melbourne 3166, Australia

First published 1986

Printed in Great Britain at the
Bath Press, Avon

British Library cataloguing in publication data
Hargreaves, David, *1948–*
The developmental psychology of music.
1. Music appreciation   2. Music –
Psychology
I. Title
780'.1'5   MT6

Library of Congress cataloguing in publication data
Hargreaves, David, 1948–
The developmental psychology of music.
Bibliography.
Includes index.
1. Music – Psychology.
2. Developmental psychology.
3. Child psychology.   I. Title.
ML 3830.H23 1986   781'.15   86–13660

ISBN 0 521 30665 5 hard covers
ISBN 0 521 31415 1 paperback

SE

THE DEVELOPMENTAL
PSYCHOLOGY OF MUSIC

CONTENTS

PREFACE

Music psychology has probably never been in a healthier state than as at present: the explosion of research over the last decade or so has meant that specialised tributaries of the main stream are beginning to emerge. My own empirical research with children made me realise that one of the most prominent tributaries might be called the developmental psychology of music, and this book represents my attempt to delineate it. I started serious work on the project whilst on study leave at the Center for Music Research at Florida State University, in autumn 1983; I am very grateful to the British Academy for providing the financial support for this visit, and to all those in Tallahassee, especially Vincent Kantorski, Clifford Madsen, Wendy Sims, and Jack Taylor, who made it so enjoyable.

Working in a large school of music in the U.S.A. was a new experience for me, and it put a new perspective on my view of the relationship between music psychology and music education. It became increasingly obvious that there was a clear-cut job to be done; whereas pedagogical practice in the sciences has a firm foundation in developmental psychology, it seemed to me that the equivalent foundations for music education were nowhere explicitly set out. Once started, the project grew and grew, and went well beyond the boundaries that I originally had in mind. The final product contains a good deal of what might be called cognitive and social psychology of music, and the contents inevitably reflect my own interests and attitudes. There is a fairly strong and critical emphasis on the usefulness of different theories in explaining empirical data, and this reflects the influence of Neil Bolton during my years as an undergraduate and postgraduate student. The approach is that of the experimental psychologist, and my own research interest in the aesthetic aspects of musical development will be apparent.

This interest has been developed in collaboration with my colleagues in the

Leicester Aesthetics Research Group, which had the good fortune to receive financial support from the Economic and Social Research Council between 1983 and 1985 (ESRC grant C0023 0085, which is gratefully acknowledged). Julia Berryman, Kate Castell, Andrew Colman, and Karl Teigen shaped my thinking and research: and perhaps the greatest influence upon us all was that of Wladyslaw Sluckin, the founder of the group, whose death in May 1985 leaves a gap that will be impossible to fill. Władek read one of the chapters of this book, and made some characteristically penetrating and helpful suggestions; I would have liked him to have seen the result. I am also very grateful to Rosamund Shuter-Dyson and to John Sloboda for their comments on certain chapters; to Arnold Hargreaves and to Liz Ockleford for providing information; to Nic Trower for help with word-processing; and to Penny Carter and Chris Lyall Grant of CUP, with whom it has been a pleasure to work. My greatest debt is to Linda, Jonathan, and Thomas Hargreaves, for their long-suffering support during the writing. Linda made comments on several of the chapters, and tried her best to put my ideas straight on some of the educational issues; Jonathan and Thomas gave me permission to use their songs and drawings, which I gratefully acknowledge.

Every effort has been made to obtain permission to reproduce copyright material, and I should like to thank all those authors and publishers who have granted it: detailed acknowledgements appear in the captions.

D.J.H.
November 1985

1

The developmental
psychology of music

Introduction

This book is an attempt to define and describe a newly emerging field of study: the developmental psychology of music. It represents the confluence of the disciplines of developmental psychology and music psychology; both of these, of course, constituting parts of the subjects of psychology and music, as well as of education. All these terms are labels of convenience for agreed areas of knowledge. They are to a certain extent arbitrary, and susceptible to change and obsolescence as knowledge advances. It could indeed be argued that this is a good thing, since the imposition of artificial subject boundaries in educational institutions and curricula can often impede the cross-fertilisation of ideas by which any discipline proceeds. I have therefore deliberately cast my net widely: my account will be overinclusive rather than underinclusive.

'Developmental psychology' has been virtually synonymous with 'child development' for many decades, although the increasing emphasis upon a 'life-span' approach (e.g. Ambron and Brodzinsky, 1979) means that behavioural changes in adulthood are now receiving more attention. The research to be described in this book has been carried out on adults, as well as on children and adolescents. 'Music psychology' is better thought of as a collection of loosely related topics than as a coherent discipline with any integrated conceptual or empirical framework. I hope to show that it is possible to develop a conceptually viable developmental psychology of music by bringing together these two concerns.

There are two main motives behind this enterprise. The first is to acknowledge and map out the considerable amount of healthy, vigorous research activity that has taken place in both fields over the last decade or so. Developmental psychology is one of the most active and rapidly expanding areas of contemporary psychology; the British Psychological Society's

Developmental Psychology Section is one of its youngest and biggest sections, for example, and the *British Journal of Developmental Psychology* was launched in 1983. Similarly, music psychology is experiencing a renaissance after many decades in the doldrums. It is now apparent that the complexities of musical creation, performance, and experience are becoming amenable to the increasingly sophisticated techniques and instrumentation of contemporary psychology. This is illustrated by the appearance of a variety of recent textbooks, as well as by the appearance of two journals in the early 1980s – *Music Perception*, and *Psychomusicology*.

My second motive arises from a consideration of the relationship between educational theory and pedagogical practice in the arts subjects as compared with the sciences. In junior school mathematics and science, for example, there is a considerable body of developmental as well as instructional theory that underlies the curriculum. Piaget's theory springs immediately to mind: there are several mathematics teaching programmes that are explicitly based on Piagetian principles, and that specifically employ some of Piaget's own experimental tasks (e.g. Fletcher and Walker, 1970; Nuffield Foundation, 1972; Harlen, 1975). Although music teaching (and indeed teaching in other arts subjects) forms an equally important part of the curriculum, there is no equivalent body of developmental theory upon which teaching practices are based.

Keith Swanwick, a prominent British music educator, has argued that music educators 'badly lack any kind of conceptual framework . . . we have no *rationale* that bears examination and stands up well against the views of different pressure groups' (1979, pp. 5–6). A recent British conference on arts education expressed a similar concern that 'Unless curriculum design and assessment are based on a clear conception of development it is difficult to see how either could be the outcome of coherent planning or stand up to public evaluation' (Ross, 1982, p. vii). Ross's series of edited books on *Curriculum issues in arts education* represents an attempt to forge a theoretical framework, and the founding of the *British Journal of Music Education*, in 1984, should provide a major lead: but there is still a very long way to go.

It is of considerable interest in this context to compare the position of music education in the U.S.A., where it is a thriving and well-established field of study in its own right, with that in the rest of the world. In Great Britain, as can be seen from the quotations above, we can distinguish fairly easily between the (theoretical) psychology of music and the (practical) pedagogical study of the best ways to teach music to children. There is a yawning gulf between the two, and the term 'music education' is clearly reserved for the latter. In the U.S.A., however, the term is used much more generally to apply to both the theoretical *and* the practical domains. North American 'music education' has a great deal of overlap with North American 'music psychology', as a glance at the contents of the leading U.S. *Journal of Research in Music Education* will quickly illustrate.

Despite the efforts that have been made in the pages of journals such as this, there are virtually no coherent psychological theories of the specific developmental processes underlying children's musical perception, cognition or performance. This book will attempt to draw some of the strands together.

The perspective of music psychology

The psychology of music, or music psychology, has recently produced an offspring known as 'psychomusicology'. The editor of *Psychomusicology* suggests that this new label 'encourages a re-examination of the nature of human response to music . . . it provides a new point of reference for inquiry that has existed at the extremities of such other areas as audiology, psychology, acoustics, musicology, and music education. The essential variable distinguishing psychomusicology from many of these other areas is *context*: the sensory, structural and expressive dimensions which contribute to a *music event*' (Williams, 1981, p. 3). Whichever label we use, the discipline remains something of a backwater as far as the mainstream of psychology is concerned. It is not taught as a component of most psychology degree courses in Great Britain or the U.S.A., for example.

There is no reason why music psychology should remain an isolated area within psychology, as its subject-matter overlaps with most other aspects of the discipline. It includes neurological and physiological investigations of the biological bases of music perception, and hemispheric lateralisation studies; acoustical and psychophysical studies of the mechanisms of auditory perception; cognitive psychological studies of such topics as auditory representation and coding, melodic perception and skilled musical performance; psychometric analyses of musical ability and its development; developmental studies of the acquisition of musical skills; social psychological investigations of the aesthetic and affective aspects of music listening; behavioural analyses of the learning of music; 'applied' studies in the fields of therapy, education, and industry, and so on. This list is by no means exhaustive, but it conveys the point that the richness and complexity of musical phenomena can be approached on all psychological levels.

The increasing theoretical and methodological sophistication of psychological research means that these complex phenomena *can* now be investigated; and there has been a consequent upsurge in the level of research activity. Apart from the emergence of the two new journals that were mentioned in the previous section, a new textbook on some aspect of music psychology has been published almost every successive year since 1978. Davies's (1978) *The psychology of music* was the first text to reflect the growing influence of cognitive psychology; and Radocy and Boyle's (1979) *Psychological foundations of musical behavior* is explicitly behaviouristic in its approach, as the title indicates. Hodges' (1980) *Handbook of music psychology* is an edited collection of detailed research reviews written by experts in their specialist fields. It is almost certainly the single most comprehensive guide to music psychology up to 1980, and includes Eagle's valuable historical review of textbooks and journals, 'An introductory perspective of music psychology'.

Shuter-Dyson and Gabriel's (1981) *The psychology of musical ability* is the second edition of a work first published by Rosamund Shuter under the same title in 1968; this quickly became known as the most authoritative guide to tests and psychometric research in music. The second edition contains two additional chapters, by Clive Gabriel, on 'Cognitive psychology and music', and 'Lateralisation studies'. Deutsch's (1982) *The psychology of music*, another collection of specialised reviews by experts, has a strong bias towards the acoustical, psychophysical and cognitive aspects of the field, and has been widely acclaimed by researchers in these areas. Sloboda's (1985) *The musical mind* and Howell, Cross and West's (1985) *Musical structure and cognition* are the most recent additions.

This very brief survey of the recent textbooks should convey the healthy state of music psychology that now exists. It is easy to detect the increasing prevalence and importance of cognitive approaches within the discipline, and I shall outline their scope later in this chapter. Crozier and Chapman (1984), whilst acknowledging that no one psychological explanation will ever be able to deal with the arts in all their complexity, nevertheless suggest that the study of central cognitive processes holds out the promise of much greater integration of theories of art than has hitherto been possible. I agree: but would add, in the case of music, that microscopic, 'bottom up' studies have tended to predominate. Although these form an important part of the developmental psychology of music, there are other aspects of the field that have been less adequately dealt with. I hope that this book will go some way towards redressing the balance.

The perspective of developmental psychology

The field of developmental psychology has undergone some dramatic changes over the last few decades. In the 1920s and 1930s, some research effort was devoted to the collection of normative data on the typical behaviour of children at different ages: the emphasis of this work was *descriptive* rather than *explanatory*, and it led to the compilation of sets of developmental norms such as those of Gesell (1940) and Bayley (1968).

There was a general decline of interest in child development in the 1940s and 1950s, as the major developments in psychology were taking place in other areas of the subject: but several lines of theoretical development were nevertheless influential. Two of the most important of these were the 'grand theories' of human development proposed by Piaget and Freud. There has been a dramatic revival of interest in Piaget's theory in the last two decades, such that it is now by far the most powerful single influence on contemporary developmental psychology; it will form the basis of Chapter 2 of this book. Freud's psychosexual stage theory, according to which libidinal energy is discharged at different parts of the body (erogenous zones) at different stages of development, has had much less of an impact on contemporary thinking, largely because it proved impossible to operationalise and verify.

A third major theoretical influence was that of behavioural psychology: this took the form of a body of research on what became known as 'child-rearing practices' (see review by Danziger, 1971). The typical approach was to look for correlations between ratings of parental behaviour on dimensions such as 'punitiveness' or 'permissiveness', and of children's behaviour on dimensions such as 'dependency' or 'aggression' (see e.g. Sears, Maccoby and Levin, 1957). The view implicit in these studies was that socialisation was a one-way process in which parents 'shaped' their children, without any appreciable influence being exerted in the opposite direction. Although the more recent formulations of social learning theory have departed radically from this point of view, it remains true to say that the early behavioural explanations of socialisation had no *specific* account of developmental processes: development was simply seen as the gradual accumulation of an increasingly complex 'reinforcement history'.

The tremendous revival of interest in child development over the last two decades has, I would suggest, three major features. The first is a new view of the child as an *active* agent in its own socialisation. Parent–child relationships, for example, are now seen as reciprocal systems in which the child influences the parent just as much as the parent influences the child: it is impossible to study one influence without the other. Closely related to this is the second feature: as in other areas of psychology, there is an increasing emphasis on what might be called a 'cognitive' approach. Whereas the early behaviourists held that the proper scientific study of psychology was restricted to observable events, and that this ruled out phenomena occurring in the 'black box' of the mind, contemporary cognitive psychologists have developed ways of getting inside the 'black box'. In the case of parent–child relationships, for example, researchers (e.g. Richards, 1974) have investigated the phenomenon of *intersubjectivity*. This refers to the shared 'constructions of meaning' that are created when the child interprets the actions of the parent, which are in turn based on the parent's interpretations of the child's behaviour.

The third feature of current developmental psychology is an enormous increase in methodological sophistication, in two main respects. First, advances in our understanding of developmental research strategies have meant that many of the problems associated with the use of the traditional cross-sectional and longitudinal designs can now be overcome. Schaie's (1965) *sequential* methods of analysis, for example, incorporate the important distinction between *age* effects, *cohort* (i.e. historical generation) effects and *time-of-measurement* effects. These effects have frequently been confounded in developmental research employing longitudinal or cross-sectional designs:

but the confounding is avoided in contemporary life-span research based on sequential methods. Secondly, recent technological developments have had a profound impact on developmental research methodology. The development of microcomputers and videorecorders, in particular, has meant that large amounts of multidimensional data obtained from observations of children can be stored and manipulated with ease, and at relatively low cost. Complex behavioural phenomena that would previously have been beyond the reach of psychological instrumentation can now be tackled; and this has given rise to some new research emphases.

The most striking of these is the proliferation of research on the *origins* of behaviour in infancy. It is now quite clear that babies do not live in the 'blooming, buzzing confusion' that was described by William James in the early days of psychology. The sophistication of infancy researchers now enables them to show how complex and elaborate are the predispositions and 'pre-wired' abilities that the newborn brings into the world (see e.g. Bower, 1982). Closely allied to this is the increasing emphasis upon an 'ecological' approach to research (Bronfenbrenner, 1975). Early studies tended to concentrate almost exclusively on the child's relationship with its mother, and to ignore the complex network of social relationships that might encompass the father, siblings, other family relations, caregivers, and so on. It is only fairly recently that developmental psychologists have started to look beyond the mother–child relationship; there is now an increasing number of studies of relationships with fathers (e.g. Pedersen, 1980), siblings (e.g. Dunn and Kendrick, 1982), and others. The range and flavour of current research reflecting this emphasis is conveyed well by the volumes in the Fontana/Open Books Developing Child series. Recent titles include *Children's friendships* (Rubin, 1980), *Fathering* (Parke, 1981), and *Day care* (Clarke-Stewart, 1982).

The behavioural phenomena of composition, performance and participation in music and the arts are probably as complex and potentially intractable as any that have been mentioned so far, though there are signs that developmental psychologists are getting to grips with these as well. The cognitive-developmental approach, stemming from the work of Piaget, has predominated: this has stimulated empirical research on symbolism and representation in children's play, language and drawings, as well as in music.

The musical perspective

Musicians, musicologists, music theorists, and those working in other branches of music all have their own perspectives on the subject-matter of this book. Some musicians, along with other artists, have been hostile to the scientific study of their activities on the grounds that any attempt to analyse the complex phenomena involved will necessarily trivialise and/or misrepresent them. It has also been argued, perhaps with some justification, that experimental procedures can themselves modify and distort the phenomena that are under investigation.

Davies (1978), whilst acknowledging that many musicians have a more down-to-earth view of their craft than the layman might believe, suggests that music has 'acquired a supernatural or mystical quality which tends to make any analysis of these activities seem sacrilegious' (p. 16), and that things such as 'good taste', 'sensitivity', and 'musical understanding' are thought of by some as 'magical properties of some sort of musical priesthood' (p. 15). He argues, as would any psychologist, that the scientific investigation of these phenomena ought to 'demystify' them, making them comprehensible to any non-musician.

It would be interesting to know what proportion of musicians still *do* hold the view that their subject is best left unsullied by empirical investigation: I suspect that this proportion is on the decline. This suspicion is borne out by the fact that several university music departments in the U.S.A. now teach research design and methodology as a regular part of their course work. The senior author of a text entitled *Experimental research in music: Workbook in design and statistical tests* (Madsen and Moore, 1978), for example, is based in a school of music which places a considerable emphasis on empirical investigation. It may well be that the view expressed above will ultimately seem just as out of date as the poet Keats' objection to physicists' investigations of the colours of the rainbow.

Although scientific methods can be applied to musical phenomena with just as much validity as they can to physical objects, there are some crucial differences about the subject-matter that must be borne in mind. Most musical 'laws' are man-made, culture-bound and therefore subject to change: and in this respect they contrast sharply with 'natural' laws such as those in, say, the field of physics. It follows that most research questions about the effects of music are essentially *normative*, rather than *factual* (Berlyne, 1971).

This argument has wider implications. The work of ethnomusicologists such as Blacking (1973) demonstrates that it is by no means clear that a universal phenomenon of 'music' can be identified. What constitutes 'music' in any given cultural group depends on the social context and function of the behaviour in question. There are considerable variations in the processes by which people make sense of, or 'construct' a melody, for example: and this is true *within* a given cultural group, as well as *between* different groups. The experiences, ideas, and emotions conveyed by music are culturally relative, as are the tonal structures and symbols themselves.

Most of the research that has been carried out in music psychology, which forms the basis of this book, has been rooted in the tradition of Western (mainly European) tonal music. The ethnomusicological perspective compels us to recognise that this is only one musical tradition, albeit a major and influential one: and thus that the explanations of musical behaviour that we develop are not necessarily universal. Elsewhere in this book, I complain that psychologists have woefully neglected the 'mundane', or 'lay' aspects of musical experience. They have dealt largely with serious 'art' music, which is a minority interest relative to the many different forms of 'folk', or popular music. This constraint must be seen in the wider cross-cultural context: most of the research to be described in this book has its limits prescribed by the parameters of Western tonal music.

The great, abstract issues which have concerned musicians, philosophers and art theorists for some decades pose formidable problems for the researcher; but there is every hope that they may not be intractable. Empirical research has already made a significant and unique contribution to three complex, interrelated problems, namely the meaning of music, and its relationship with emotion, and with language.

The massive question of the meaning of music has received a good deal of attention from aestheticians and philosophers, and some distinct theoretical positions have been developed. Perhaps the most fundamental distinction is that between *absolute* and *referential* musical meaning (see Meyer, 1956). Some theorists (e.g. Hanslick, 1891; Schoen, 1940) have maintained that musical meaning is absolute in the sense that it is intrinsic to the sounds themselves, without reference to any external or extra-musical phenomena. Meyer also suggests that absolute musical meaning may be either *formalist*, that is, based on the listener's perception and understanding of the formal structure of the music, or *expressionist*, that is, based upon the emotions and feelings aroused in the listener by its structural properties. The *referentialist* position, in contrast, is that musical meaning is derived from the extra-musical and contextual associations of the sounds. Some sociologists (e.g. Shepherd, 1977a) take an extreme form of this position, arguing that music represents a vehicle by which the 'meanings of society' might be expressed.

Other theorists have made similar distinctions, sometimes using different terms (e.g. Coker's (1972) *congeneric* and *extrageneric* meaning, and Schwadron's (1967) *isolationist* and *contextualist* viewpoints). These viewpoints are not necessarily incompatible: a piece of music can convey both types of meaning in different ways. Meyer (1956) points out that some confusion arises because these distinctions apply to two different kinds of musical meaning. In the case of *embodied* meaning, the piece and the listener's reaction to it are both musical: this refers to the musical expectations aroused by music events, which are the province of the musicologist. The psychologist is more concerned with *designative* meaning, that is, with non-musical reactions to a piece (e.g. verbal and sensory responses). These distinctions are confusing and overlapping: but empirical methods, fortunately, can help to clarify them. The distinctions can be built into techniques for analysing people's responses to music (see e.g. Hargreaves and Colman, 1981).

Inextricably linked with the meaning of music is its relationship with emotion. Meyer's concept of the embodied meaning of music, for example, hinges on the *expectations* that are aroused in the listener. As a result of people's accumulated knowledge of musical pieces, styles and idioms, different musical events arouse expectations as to what is likely to follow: and these expectations depend on the characteristics of the music, as well as on the experience of the listener. Part of the art of the composer is to create and relieve tension by controlling these expectations; and Meyer proposed that emotional reactions result from their violation – 'Affect or emotion felt is aroused when an expectation – a tendency to respond – activated by the musical stimulus situation, is temporarily inhibited or permanently blocked' (1956, p. 31). Meyer (1967) went on to explore the relationships between his theory and information theory, which is concerned with the precise specification of the amounts of information conveyed by stimuli, and with the corresponding levels of uncertainty, or expectation, that they convey to the perceiver. It is easy to see why this approach is potentially of great value to the experimental psychologist, as it offers the possibility of precise stimulus control in a very complex response domain. The field of experimental aesthetics follows this approach, and I shall return to it later.

Other theorists have taken quite different views. The musicologist Cooke (1959), for example, regards emotion as an essential *part* of the meaning of music, rather than as a detached 'response' to a 'stimulus'. The philosopher Langer (1953) presents another account which is based on the distinction between *discursive* and *presentational* symbols. The former have fixed definitions, and are translatable: scientists use discursive symbols such as numbers, for example. In contrast, the presentational symbols of the artist do not have fixed definitions; they are untranslatable from person to person, such that we can only understand the elements of a work in the context of the work as a whole. Langer's theory has not been universally accepted: but one of its most useful applications has been in the field of music. She sees music as a form of presentational symbolism that can convey complex emotional meanings: music is *about* emotion, as well as able to convey it. Langer maintains that the fullest expressions of the emotional aspects of human experience are to be found in the symbols of art.

The boundaries between philosophy, aesthetics, psychology, linguistics, and music itself are considerably blurred in investigations of high-level questions such as these. One substantial area of empirical research which cuts across the boundaries is that on the everyday language that people use to describe their reactions to music. Topics that have been investigated include descriptions of the major and minor modes; verbal associations between key signatures and colours; the relative effects of variables such as pitch, tempo, harmony, and rhythm on adjectival descriptions of music; psychoanalytic symbolism and the expression of tensions in music, and so on. This area has been reviewed by Farnsworth (1969), and I shall return to it in Chapter 5. More recently, Durkin and Crowther (1982) have investigated the language that children use about music, focussing on children's developing use of multi-meaning terms such as 'up', 'down', 'high', and 'low'.

This leads to a consideration, in more general terms, of the complex relationship between language and music. The composer Leonard Bernstein (1976) has pursued the interrelationships between musical discourse and linguistic theory from a musician's point of view: and Sloboda (1985) has undertaken a detailed comparison from the cognitive psychological viewpoint, referring to musical *phonology* (the characterisation of basic sound units), *syntax* (the rules governing the combination of these units), and *semantics* (the meanings associated with sequences of these units). The perception of a melody, for example, might be explained in the same way as the linguist explains a sentence. The central idea is that there are musical equivalents of the 'surface' and 'deep' structures of language, such that musical elements, and the hierarchical rules for their combination and processing, are stored in memory.

Sloboda draws a number of parallels between language and music: his central comparison is between the theories of the linguist Noam Chomsky and the musicologist Heinrich Schenker, which are essentially concerned with describing the *structures* of language and music respectively. Researchers such as Sundberg and Lindblom (1976), Longuet-Higgins (1978), and Lerdahl and Jackendoff (1983) are developing increasingly sophisticated models of the generative rule systems, or 'grammars' of musical structures, and are beginning to draw on the techniques of artificial intelligence research. There seems to be little doubt that musical memory is based upon stored rule systems such as these, but it is by no means clear as yet how the rules are best defined. Only time and further research will tell how far the linguistic analogy can be taken, though there can be little doubt that music theorists, linguists, and psychologists have a great deal to contribute to one another.

Psychological approaches to musical development

Although the days of 'grand', all-embracing theories in psychology have long since gone, such that there is now much more common agreement about the proper concerns and boundaries of the subject, there is nevertheless a considerable diversity of modes of explanation. I shall draw from psychology those theoretical approaches which have something to say about musical development, and assess what their potential contributions might be. I have made no attempt to present an original theoretical model by forming a conscious synthesis of the different approaches; but any one person's view of, or 'angle' on, a particular field will inevitably reveal its own assumptions and emphases. In other words, my own theoretical perspective on the developmental psychology of music will become apparent during the course of the book, and I shall try to make this perspective explicit by drawing the main arguments together in the final chapter.

The formulation and evaluation of theories is a vital part of any scientific enterprise. Theories are structures, or frames of reference, that enable us to organise facts and to see them in perspective. They guide the direction of research: and are susceptible to change according to the results of that research. Philosophers of science are concerned with the characteristics of different kinds of theories and models; and Marx and Goodson (1976) have shown how these vary in their underlying view of the relationship between theory and data. Such theorists suggest that an effective theory should have *breadth*, in being able to explain a reasonably wide range of behavioural phenomena; *testability*, in that it should be capable of being proved or disproved by empirical methods; *parsimony*, or directness, in that it should not depend too heavily on hypothetical constructs and assumptions in achieving its breadth of application; and *fruitfulness*, in the promotion of further research (and of its own consequent development).

I shall try to bear these criteria in mind in assessing the different theoretical contributions to musical development. Some of the theories come into direct conflict with one another on certain issues, and not on others. Different theories operate on different levels of explanation, so some have more general applicability than others. They focus on different aspects of behaviour, and may well use different terminologies to define behavioural events. Since psychology is still a relatively young science, it might well be argued that we need all the theories we can get, and this applies to the explanation of musical development just as it does to human behaviour in general.

My strategy in this section will be first to describe the nature and scope of developmental theories, concentrating on those which are potentially applicable to music. I shall then look in more detail at those approaches which *have* been applied to musical development: some of these are specifically developmental, and some are not.

The nature and scope of developmental theories

There are some excellent recent textbooks which have the common aim of reviewing and evaluating the main theories of human development (e.g. Lerner, 1976; Miller, 1983; Thomas, 1985). A comparison of their contents confirms the point above that any one reviewer's account of a given field reveals his or her own preconceptions and biases. These three authors vary widely in what they consider to be worthy of inclusion as a developmental theory, and in the organisational perspective that they give to each theory.

I pointed out earlier that three theoretical influences have been predominant in the historical development of developmental psychology: and that two of these are the 'grand' theories of Sigmund Freud and Jean Piaget. These are 'grand' in the sense of being comprehensive, large-scale attempts at explaining what Miller (1983) calls the 'big picture' of psychological development, and also in that each represents the life's work of a single man. Freud's theory has little to say about the details of musical development, though some psychoanalytic explanations of artistic creativity, which will be outlined in Chapter 6, are still useful and illuminating.

Piaget sees the child as a 'mini-scientist' who is continuously and actively seeking to make sense of his environment. This is accomplished by forming concepts, or what Piaget calls *schemes*. These schemes form the internal framework that the child uses to assimilate new knowledge and experiences: and the schemes themselves change in the process. The theory is essentially *cognitive-developmental*: it is cognitive in that schemes are hypothetical, internal constructs, and it is developmental in that it is primarily concerned with age-based changes in the organisation of these constructs. Other notable cognitive-developmental theorists include Lawrence Kohlberg, who has concentrated on the explanation of sex-role stereotyping (Kohlberg, 1966) and moral reasoning (Kohlberg, 1976); and Jerome Bruner (Bruner, 1966; Bruner, Olver and Greenfield, 1966), who has formulated a specific theory of instruction as well as a more general account of child development. In Chapter 2 I shall consider cognitive-developmental explanations of general artistic development, as well as specific applications to music.

The third major influence upon developmental psychology has been that of learning theory, or reinforcement theory, which essentially views human development as the accumulation of behavioural responses to environmental stimuli, learnt as a result of differential patterns of reinforcement. This approach has had a significant impact on the explanation of musical development, as well as on the practical aspects of music education: and I shall return to it later in this chapter. There are two further approaches that are potentially of use in explaining musical development: theories of the *principles of development*, and *perceptual-development theory*.

Two German–American psychologists, Kurt Lewin and Heinz Werner, were concerned with establishing the main principles by which development proceeds, in animals as well as in humans: and their approaches were similar to one another in various respects. Lewin (e.g. Lewin, 1942) used *topological* concepts in developing his 'field theory' of behaviour. These concepts, such as *life space, region, boundary, valence,* and *locomotion,* are used to identify the forces that act at any given time to make the child behave in a certain way. The main influence of Lewin's theory has been upon social psychology; and it has stimulated a field of research which has become known as *ecological psychology* (e.g. Barker, Kounin and Wright, 1943). This is based on the detailed investigation of the specific environments, or *behaviour settings,* which people inhabit. Ecological psychologists, like ethologists, stress the overwhelming importance of studying behaviour in its natural habitat.

Werner's influence has primarily been upon developmental psychology, and some of his work was specifically concerned with musical development. He proposed (e.g. Werner, 1961) that development proceeds according to what he called the 'orthogenetic principle'; this involves gradual developmental increases in the twin processes of *differentiation* and *integration.* The very young child's view of a set of objects, such as animals, is seen as *global, diffuse,* and *undifferentiated*; she may refer to everything that has four legs and a tail as 'doggie'. As she gets older, she begins to *differentiate* between subgroups of animals, such as dogs, cats, and rabbits; she also is able to *integrate* them into a hierarchy so that she understands the label 'animal' can be applied to all, and

(a)

(b)

Fig. 1.1 *Children's vocal reproductions of piano melodies (reproduced from Werner, 1961)*

that the set of 'animals' is different from the set of 'plants'. An important aspect of the orthogenetic principle is that it overcomes the long-standing argument as to whether development is *continuous*, that is, whether it proceeds without any discernible stages, or whether it is *discontinuous*. 'On the one side, the orthogenetic principle in *overall terms* . . . necessarily implies continuity. On the other hand, concrete forms and operations, novel functions and structures "emerge", and in this respect changes are discontinuous' (Werner and Kaplan, 1963, pp. 7–8).

Werner applied this principle to musical development in some studies of children's melodies; the results of his own research, as well as those of his colleague Brehmer, are summarised in Werner (1961). Investigations of spontaneous melodies produced by children aged from two to five showed, in line with the orthogenetic principle, that the melodies of the younger children were more diffuse and global; the notes tended to be simply strung together in unrelated sequences. Those of the older children, however, showed both differentiation and integration in that theme and variations were distinct; the melodies were made up of several phrases organised into something approaching a 'key'; that is, they possessed a tonal centre.

Brehmer's research used a different methodological approach in that it was concerned with children's vocal reproductions of piano melodies. Brehmer found the younger children were more likely to produce errors of reproduction, and that these errors represented shifts towards more diffuse melodic patterns. The complexity of the melody to be reproduced was also found to affect the number of errors; Motif I in Figure 1.1(a) was reproduced inaccurately by 35 per cent of a 6–9-year-old sample, whereas the equivalent figure for Motif II was 76 per cent. Motif II was most commonly rearranged by the 'inaccurate' subjects into one of the two melodies shown in Figure 1.1(b). Werner discusses the characteristics of these reproduced melodies, and concludes that their 'more primitive and less articulated organization' is primarily shown in terms of their 'expression of the quality-of-the-whole', and their 'homogeneity of direction and parts'.

There are two theoretical approaches to perceptual-cognitive development which centre on the *information content* of stimuli. *Information-processing theory* is a fundamental part of the increasingly influential approach of cognitive psychology, to which I devote the next section. The *perceptual-development theory* of Eleanor J. Gibson (e.g. Gibson, 1969) takes a quite different theoretical view of the information that is conveyed to the listener by perceptual stimuli. Gibson's concern is with the overall informational characteristics of a given stimulus array rather than with its analysis into component parts, or 'bits'. Her view is that objects are perceived directly, such that there is no need for the postulation of internal cognitive constructs such as 'processing mechanisms': this is a controversial claim to make in the prevailing climate of opinion.

Gibson sees perceptual development as the process of learning to extract information that is present in the stimulus itself, that is, 'what is already there', rather than as one in which the child supplies additional meanings, or constructions. Children can only take in a limited amount of information at any one time, and must therefore use certain strategies in order to reduce the amount that a stimulus contains: these strategies become increasingly efficient with age. A melody within a given piece of music might not be perceived as such on first hearing, for example: the child's developing ability to recognise it is based on the increasing accuracy of discrimination between invariant and variant features. The sequence of pitches represents the essential (invariant) character of the melody: this remains recognisable even when the variant features, such as key signature, tempo, instrumentation, and so on, are changed. Similarly, adults' gradual comprehension and appreciation of a new orchestral work proceeds by the direction of attention to the relational information it contains – to the overall patterning of its variant and invariant features.

Gibson specifically proposes three mechanisms by which these develop-mental changes occur. First, there is increasing correspondence between what the child perceives and what information is present in the stimulus: perception becomes more exact, or 'differentiated'. Secondly, children's attentional strategies become more efficient: they become increasingly able to attend to the essential, relevant aspects of a stimulus, and to ignore the irrelevant aspects. Thirdly, children's 'information pickup' becomes more efficient, or economical: this is accomplished by identifying distinctive features in stimulation, by extracting invariants from it, and by recognising progressively larger units of perceptual structure.

Gibson's is a 'narrow' theory of a specific aspect of development rather than a general developmental theory: it emphasises that humans are active perceivers of information, and it stresses the importance of the particular environment, that is, the ecological context within which perceptual development occurs. It seems potentially well suited to the explanation of musical development: the example above shows how Gibson's concepts of abstraction, filtering, and selective attention can be readily applied to melodic perception. Bartlett (1984) has developed a specifically Gibsonian theory of melodic memory which is based on the 'pickup' of melodic invariants, and on the proposal that melodic events function as units in memory. It is not appropriate to go into Bartlett's theory in detail here, but it *is* worth pointing out that this theory is directly opposed to those cognitive psychological theories of melodic perception which are based on internal organisational rules. Cognitive psychological theories have become very influential in music psychology: and the next section will outline the main features of the approach from which they derive.

Cognitive psychology

The term 'cognitive' has unfortunately become so widely used in present-day psychology that, in a sense, it has almost ceased to mean anything at all: there are books on cognitive social psychology, cognitive behaviour therapy, cognitive neuropsychology, and so on. There are considerable overlaps between the approach of 'cognitive psychology' in this broad sense, and several others reviewed in this chapter. I shall use the term in a more restricted sense to refer to the topics that used to be grouped together under the heading 'human performance'. They include perception, language, thinking, memory, learning, attention, and skills: and there is now little doubt that these topics form the central core of modern experimental psychology.

The emphasis of cognitive psychology is upon the internalised rules, operations, and strategies that people employ in intelligent behaviour just as much as on the external behavioural manifestations of these processes. This emphasis has taken the form of research on topics such as people's internal representations or mental images of the world, and the particular symbol systems that they employ; on perceptual processing mechanisms; and on the internal planning of behaviour sequences. These constructs are of course hypothetical: they represent models of behaviour which are essentially *functional*, rather than anatomical or physiological. However, they may well be isomorphic with physiological functioning, and the cognitive psychologist ultimately would like to be able to demonstrate some degree of causal interdependence between the two types of explanation.

A fundamental feature of cognitive psychology is *information-processing theory*: the influence of computer and information technology is readily apparent, so we could think in terms of a 'systems analysis' of human behaviour. This essentially mechanistic view of man is complemented by, and contrasts with, a strong European structuralist influence within cognitive psychology. Piaget's concept of the *scheme*, for example, could be thought of as a basic 'building-block' for internal cognitive structures. Other cognitive psychologists have postulated very similar constructs: Neisser's (1976) *schemata*, for example ('cognitive structures that prepare the perceiver to accept certain kinds of information rather than others', p. 20), are very similar to those of Piaget. Scheme-based theories have been developed in areas of psychology as diverse as gender-role stereotyping (e.g. Bem, 1981) and the development of children's singing (see Chapter 3).

Information-processing theory studies the flow of information through the human cognitive system. Various processes are carried out between the *input* to the system (usually a stimulus), and the *output* from it (e.g. a behavioural response, long-term memory trace, or decision). These include the encoding of information into a form which can be dealt with by the system, which might involve filtering, or selective attention to different features of the input; its transformation into some kind of mental representation; its storage in different kinds of memory system; and its comparison with information already held in memory. These processing mechanisms are directly analogous to those used by the computer in taking in, processing, storing, and outputting information. Some psychologists adopt the analogy loosely, whereas others (e.g. in artificial intelligence research) are concerned with the precise simulation of human thought processes in computer programs.

Miller's (1956) well-known paper 'The magical number seven, plus or minus two' was an important landmark in the field, suggesting that humans are limited to retaining approximately seven items in immediate memory, and that these items could be 'chunks' containing further coded information. Broadbent's (1958) *Perception and communication* developed the idea of a limited capacity channel for processing information, incorporating the selective filtering of information between the proposed short-term and long-term memory stores. Broadbent used flow charts to describe these processing mechanisms, and theorists like Atkinson and Schiffrin (1968) have developed more elaborate versions of these to describe the different *stages* of processing. A more recent trend (e.g. Cermak and Craik, 1979) has been the analysis of *levels* of processing alongside stages.

As far as music is concerned, the application of this approach has led to a concentration on certain key topics, sometimes generically referred to as 'musical processing'. A glance at Deutsch's (1982) text, for example, which clearly and explicitly exemplifies this approach, reveals a preponderance of studies of psychophysical and psychoacoustical aspects of tones, intervals and scales; of melodic perception and memory; of internal representations of the structure of pitch in terms of hierarchical levels of abstraction and categorisation; and of neurological aspects of music perception. Sloboda (1985) considers the nature of the internal representations, and 'the things they allow people to do with music', to be the central subject-matter of the cognitive psychology of music. He also cautions that work on the topics listed above, which has by now taken on the nature of a research *paradigm*, is limited in the extent to which it reflects what goes on in real-life music listening: and that researchers should therefore guard against becoming constrained by the features of the (albeit flourishing and successful) paradigm of music perception.

Cognitive psychologists have not primarily been interested in developmental questions, although some of these have cropped up. Miller (1983) provides a clear account of the general trends that have emerged from what she calls the 'diverse, multifaceted enterprise' of studying information processing in children. Research has centred on the development of memory in children, and its relation to logical reasoning, problem-solving, and knowledge acquisition; and on developmental changes in the ways in which children consciously and unconsciously represent information. Development is conceived, from this point of view, in terms of the acquisition of particular cognitive skills, and of increases in the capacity and rate of processing. Although some specific attempts have been made to explain the mechanisms of development, for example, in terms of self-modification through feedback (Klahr and Wallace, 1976), it is by no means clear what new insights these might add to the long-established Piagetian concepts of assimilation and accommodation.

Correspondingly, there has been relatively little interest in musical development; with one or two notable exceptions (e.g. Dowling, 1982), the majority of studies have used adults, rather than children, as subjects. There is no simple reason why this should necessarily be the case; it is simply that the cognitive approach has led towards certain topics in music, and that these have tended not to have any particular developmental orientation. There is no reason why a cognitive psychologist might not study the perception of melody in children; but one who did would be more likely to be interested in aspects of melodic processing that might equally well be found in adults, than in formulating a specifically developmental explanation.

It is clear that cognitive psychology has considerable potential for the explanation of musical phenomena, and that it has been extended so far to a relatively narrow range of topics. Serafine (1983) has taken this first point to its limit in asserting the primacy of 'thinking in or with sound' over the properties of the sound itself: 'I . . . favor the term "musical thought" over "music" ' (p. 156). There can be no doubt that musical meanings *are* mental constructions of the listener, but to describe them *exclusively* in these terms renders uncertain the status of the music itself, that is, 'what is there'. It is hardly surprising that Serafine's provocative article has aroused the ire of music theorists and others (e.g. Marantz, 1985; Brody, 1985), who have severe misgivings about the way in which the cognitive psychological approach might constrict and misrepresent the insights of their own disciplines. Are their own formal analyses of musical structures just that, or are they implicitly analyses of mental constructions, that is, of cognitive processes? Only further collaboration between workers in both disciplines will enable us to tell.

Learning theories

Learning theory, or reinforcement theory, has its origins in the behaviourism of J.B. Watson (e.g. Watson, 1924). One of the central tenets of behaviourism was that psychology should be purely concerned with overt, externally observable behaviour, and not with conscious states. Introspection was declared redundant: and the philosopher's age-old 'mind–body' problem was correspondingly regarded as a non-issue. In its purest form, the learning theory approach asserts that all behaviour can be explained in terms of the laws of operant and classical conditioning (see Kimble, 1961). The environment is essentially seen as a massive complex of *stimuli*: behaviour as a similarly complex network of *responses*: *reinforcers* as stimuli which affect the emission of responses: and *learning* as the associations, or couplings, that are formed between stimuli and responses. This view is essentially *reductionistic*, and *mechanistic*: behaviour is seen to be learnt as a result of environmental events, which can further extinguish and modify it. Development is accordingly seen as the gradual accumulation of a *repertoire* of responses, which proceeds according to the individual's *reinforcement history*.

Different variants of this basic position were subsequently developed by theorists including Guthrie, Hull, Skinner, Spence, Tolman, and Thorndike (see Bower and Hilgard, 1981, for a full account). All of these developments occurred in North America, and Miller (1983) has pointed out that the history of learning theory and the history of American psychology were virtually synonymous until the 1960s. Additional explanatory constructs such as *stimulus generalisation* and *discrimination*, *chaining*, and *secondary reinforcement* were introduced in order to enable more sophisticated explanations to be derived from the basic laws of conditioning: and Bijou and Baer (1961) proposed a specifically operant analysis of development. It became apparent to many learning theorists that the full complexity of human development could not be explained in terms of simple learning principles without the introduction of some more *mentalistic*, or *cognitive* constructs. As I pointed out earlier, behavioural research on 'child-rearing practices' ran up against the central and inescapable problem that socialisation is not a one-way process in which children maintain a passive role: children actively 'shape' their parents just as much as vice versa, and an adequate theory needs to take this two-way process into account.

The outcome of this issue was the development of *social learning theory*, which has its roots in the principles of reinforcement, but which also draws upon psychoanalytic insights as well as on cognitive and social psychology. Dollard and Miller's (1950) *Personality and psychotherapy* and Bandura and Walters' (1963) *Social learning and personality development* were important landmarks in its development, and Bandura's (1977) *Social learning theory* is probably the most sophisticated recent statement. Miller (1983) has undertaken a detailed comparison of Bandura's account with traditional forms of

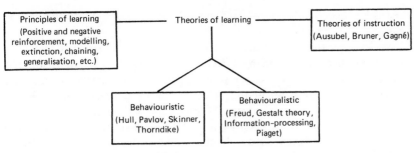

Fig. 1.2 Varieties of 'theories of learning'

learning theory. She clearly shows how modern social learning theory takes into account the social context of learning: how it deals with the cognitive processes that mediate complex learning, such as imitation, identification and modelling: how it explains observational learning, that is, that which occurs without the actual *performance* of the model's behaviour: and how it incorporates *reciprocal determinism*, that is, the two-way process mentioned above in which people's behaviour influences their environment at the same time as vice versa. All of these were irreconcilable problems for traditional learning theories: modern social learning theory seems to overcome them, and to have much more potential for integration with cognitive approaches like those of Piaget and the information-processing theorists.

Theories of learning and theories of instruction It should be clear already that even within psychology, the field of learning theory is a large and complex one in which terminological and conceptual confusion abounds. The confusion is compounded when educators and others attempt to apply the theories in their own fields. In this section I hope to clarify some of these problems by making some distinctions between different uses of the term 'theory of learning'. Figure 1.2 summarises these distinctions; this shows that there are at least three different such uses, each with its own level of specificity and range of applicability. The first distinction is that between *theories* of learning and *principles* of learning. Research carried out in the behavioural tradition over several decades has produced well-established *principles* of the mechanisms of behavioural change which are extensively used in clinical as well as educational settings. These are essentially principles of reinforcement which are based on the laws of classical and operant conditioning. As mentioned in the previous section, they include the operation of positive and negative reinforcement, schedules of reinforcement, modelling and behaviour shaping, extinction, immediate and delayed reinforcement, stimulus discrimination and generalisation, chaining, and so on. *Theories* of learning, on the other hand, utilise these principles in different ways according to some preconceived view of the nature of human learning. Thus it is quite possible to apply the principles of learning in practical situations without holding any particular theoretical viewpoint. We shall look at their application to music learning in the next section.

Amongst the theories of learning, we can now make our second distinction, which has been proposed by Greer (1980), between *behaviouristic* and *behaviouralistic* theories. Greer proposes that 'Behavioristic theories are concerned with lawful predictions of the relationship between behavior and the environment. Behavioralistic theories look at the behavior and the environment in order to describe internal processes' (p. 19). In the first category are those theories in which the principles of learning are applied most directly, namely those of Hull, Skinner, Spence, Watson, and others, which were mentioned earlier. Within the second category Greer includes Gestalt theory, Piaget's theory, Freud's psychodynamic theory applied to learning, information-processing theories of learning, and so on, all of which explicitly involve some form of internal mediating processes. This second category includes theories that I have elsewhere labelled 'cognitive', which illustrates that the term 'learning theory' is capable of very wide usage. Bandura's (1977) version of social learning theory is presumably an intermediate case which is essentially 'behaviouristic' in its orientation, yet which invokes 'behaviouralistic' constructs in explaining learning.

The third distinction is that between theories of *learning* and theories of *instruction*. Broadly speaking, we can think of the former as 'pure' explanations of the essential processes of learning, and of the latter as the application of these explanations to complex, real-life human learning in settings like the classroom. 'Theories' of learning in this sense of the term tend to have no specific explanation of developmental processes except insofar as the individual's reinforcement history becomes progressively more extensive and complex with age. Theories of instruction, on the other hand, must necessarily deal with developmental processes as an inherent concern; and they tend also to be 'behaviouralistic' in their orientation.

Accounts of these latter theories, of which the most prominent are those of Bruner (1966), Ausubel (1968), and Gagné (1977), are available in textbooks of educational psychology (e.g. Patterson, 1977); it is not appropriate to dwell on them here. Gagné's *Conditions of learning* is one of the most widely quoted sources, in which he specifies and describes eight different types of learning: stimulus learning, stimulus-response learning, chaining, verbal association, discrimination learning, concept learning, rule learning, and problem-solving. Taxonomies such as this, and Bloom's well-known *Taxonomy of educational objectives* (Bloom, 1956; Krathwohl, Bloom and Masia, 1964) have been adopted by music educators as the foundation for prescriptions about teaching methods.

Behavioural approaches to music learning The learning theory approach is almost certainly that which has had the widest practical application in the field of music learning. Applications have been made in the fields of behaviour therapy, music therapy, and programmed instruction, for example, as well as in the classroom: we shall look at some applications to music education in Chapter 8. In the most general and neutral terms, we could say that behavioural techniques have been used to 'modify musical behaviour' in various practical settings; and this has largely involved the application of the *principles* of learning rather than of any particular learning *theory*.

A good deal of the research in this field emanates from the work of C.K. Madsen, R.D. Greer and their associates (see e.g. Madsen, Greer and Madsen, 1975; Greer, 1978, 1980): a seventeen-point summary of the main empirical findings is detailed by Tunks (1980). In his review of operant research on music learning over a ten-year period, Greer (1978) points out that most of the work has been concerned with either *motivation* or *affect*. I shall defer a consideration of the latter until Chapter 5, when behavioural studies of responses to music will be compared with several other methodological and theoretical approaches. Suffice it to say here that the operant approach leads to a conception of affect as *reinforcement value*, and to the adoption of direct behavioural measures of listening preference, that is, of 'free operant selection behaviour'. This has some distinct advantages as well as some disadvantages, as we shall see later.

There are two main types of operant research on motivation: that in which music is itself used as a reinforcer, that is, in which it acts as the independent variable, and that which looks at the effects of other reinforcers on musical behaviour, that is, in which this behaviour represents the dependent variable. Studies of the first type have shown that listening to music can reinforce children's performance on tasks such as verbal and mathematics learning (e.g. Madsen and Forsythe, 1973); and that music instruction and performance can also act as effective reinforcers of various academic and social skills (e.g. Greer, Randall and Timberlake, 1971; Madsen, Dorow, Moore and Womble, 1976).

Studies of the second type have investigated the effects of a variety of extrinsic reinforcers on music learning. Teacher approval/disapproval has clearly been shown to have a powerful influence on student attitudes, and on the control of 'off-task behaviour' (e.g. Forsythe, 1975; Murray, 1972), and programmes have been devised to train teachers in the systematic use of approval and other behavioural techniques (e.g. Greer and Dorow, 1976). Other extrinsic reinforcers that have been investigated include food rewards, grades, progress charts and tokens; research has also been carried out on the use of modelling techniques and systematic desensitisation of anxiety in instrumental performance teaching (see review by Greer, 1978). Successive approximation, or *shaping* techniques have also been shown to improve performance in basic musical skills such as pitch discrimination (Fullard, 1975) and notational symbol learning (Eisenstein, 1976).

Some music educators, especially outside the U.S.A., might feel hostile towards this neutral, impersonal, and essentially atheoretical approach to their craft: but the main question must presumably be 'do these methods work?' I shall return to this question in Chapter 8.

Experimental aesthetics

The study of aesthetics, which concerns the creation and appreciation of art and beauty, has been approached in two distinct ways. 'Speculative' aesthetics is concerned with high-level, abstract questions such as the meaning and nature of an art; parts of philosophy, art history, and art criticism form its province. 'Empirical aesthetics', on the other hand, is the scientific study of the component processes of appreciation. The two approaches differ in their view of the suitability of the scientific method; about what constitutes a work of art; and about what can strictly be defined as an 'aesthetic response'.

In psychology, the field of experimental aesthetics very clearly adopts the empirical approach. Gustav Theodor Fechner, one of the founding fathers of the discipline, characterised it as 'aesthetics from below' in his *Vorschule der ästhetik* in 1876. By this he meant that the starting-point must be the rudimentary building-blocks of aesthetic preferences, such as likes and dislikes for simple shapes, colours, sounds, geometrical forms, and so on. Fechner considered that an understanding of these rudimentary mechanisms would eventually lead to an 'aesthetics from above', that is, to a consideration of the broader questions of speculative aesthetics.

Fechner attempted to test theories such as that of the 'aesthetic mean', according to which beauty was considered to be associated with the absence of extremes: sounds might be most pleasing when they are neither too strong nor too weak, for example. His approach was to assess people's preferences for different colours, visual patterns, and auditory stimuli. For example, subjects were presented with different-shaped rectangles in order to test the famous 'golden section' hypothesis that the ratio of 0.62 between the lengths of the longer and shorter sides may have unique, even divine, aesthetic properties. The results from studies in this tradition over the next few decades were generally inconclusive, and interest in these questions lapsed, though there are some signs of a contemporary revival (e.g. Boselie and Leeuwenberg, 1984).

Another body of early research along related lines similarly failed to fulfil its promise. Eminent scholars such as Binet (1903), Bullogh (1921) and Myers and Valentine (1914), for example, were concerned with the establishment of characteristic individual modes of aesthetic appreciation, or 'apperceptive types'. These were intended as descriptions of reasonably stable and consistent aspects of behaviour, and so were presumably akin to dimensions of personality. I shall look at them in detail in Chapter 5: here again, we shall see that contemporary research (e.g. Machotka, 1982) has a renewed interest in some of the early questions.

After a pronounced slump in the 1940s and 1950s, experimental aesthetics gained new impetus from the work of Daniel Berlyne (e.g. Berlyne, 1974) in the mid-1960s. Berlyne uncompromisingly adopted a neo-behaviouristic, psychobiological approach, which gave rise to what he called the *new experimental aesthetics*. Two central features of Berlyne's explanation are the emphases on *arousal* as the major determinant of aesthetic response, and on the *collative properties* of stimuli. Berlyne held that art objects produce pleasure by manipulating the level of arousal of the observer: and that they do this by means of their collative properties, such as their complexity, familiarity, and surprisingness. In other words, the observer 'collates' information from different aspects of the stimulus: and the resulting level of arousal determines the likelihood of further exploration of that stimulus.

Berlyne also proposed that the 'hedonic value', or pleasingness of a stimulus is related to the observer's level of arousal according to an *inverted-U-shaped* curve. We like those things best, according to this curve, that produce in us an intermediate level of arousal. The inverted-U function has its origins in the work of the founding father of experimental psychology, Wilhelm Wundt; and its various developments will be discussed in detail in Chapter 5. Berlyne's own empirical research investigated the effects of varying collative stimulus properties, and it revived interest in the whole field which remains unabated today.

Though the emphasis has been upon visual stimuli, perhaps because they are relatively easy to work with in the laboratory, a certain amount of research has also been carried out using auditory and musical stimuli. As in cognitive psychology, of which experimental aesthetics could be considered to be a part, most of the research has not had a specifically developmental orientation, although many studies have used children as subjects. Those parts of experimental aesthetics that specifically contribute towards the developmental psychology of music are covered in Chapters 2 and 5.

Research in experimental aesthetics is currently in a healthy state; the approach 'from below' is beginning to tackle some of the questions that Fechner saw as arising 'from above' with a reasonable degree of sophistication. Its range and scope has become fairly wide, as it includes responses to everyday objects which are perceived in an artistic or aesthetic context as well as those to 'pure' works of art. A pile of bricks could be (and indeed has been) considered to be an aesthetic object in some settings, for example, but is likely not to be so to a building-site worker. Experimental aesthetics tries to encompass both of these responses: it has a unique contribution to make to speculative aesthetics in that it casts its net to incorporate everyday, or mundane, likes and dislikes.

Psychometric approaches
Psychometrics, the theory and practice of psychological testing (sometimes also known as 'individual differences' or 'differential psychology'), continues to exert a powerful influence on psychological thinking (see e.g. Anastasi, 1982). It has met with a considerable amount of hostility from various

quarters (see Hargreaves, 1974), and has been an unfashionable area for research in psychology over the last twenty years or so. Nevertheless, psychological tests continue to be administered widely (often, in this day and age, by microcomputers) in the fields of educational, clinical, and industrial psychology, and they are particularly prevalent in the U.S.A. By far the most common tests are those of intelligence, and the IQ test has had a long and controversial history. Many of the areas of contention have concerned the ways in which the tests have been used rather than their contents, and professional bodies such as the British Psychological Society and the American Psychological Association have consequently developed rigorous codes of practice for their use.

Psychological tests are essentially sets of standardised procedures for comparing people with respect to certain aspects of behaviour: individuals are usually assessed by comparing their test performances with some normative level, derived from a representative sample of the population that the test is aimed at. The most common type of reference measure is the *age norm*: individuals' test performances are compared with the typical scores of other subjects of their own age. It is probably for this reason that there is a close link between psychometrics and developmental psychology. Establishing age norms on a given test involves consideration of the relevant developmental issues, especially on tests designed specifically for children. A considerable amount of research evidence concerning developmental processes in music has been gained from psychometric studies, and we shall draw on this body of literature in Chapters 3 and 4.

Musical ability testing probably forms the largest single area of the psychology of music, and the field has been surveyed by many authors (e.g. Farnsworth, 1969; Lundin, 1967; Davies, 1978). Probably the most comprehensive account is Shuter-Dyson and Gabriel's (1981) *The psychology of musical ability*, which is the second edition of a text originally published under the same title by Shuter alone (Shuter, 1968). The field has been reviewed so comprehensively in these sources that there is little point in any duplication here; what follows is a brief outline of the major issues in the field, particularly those with developmental implications. The central question throughout is whether the assessment of musical ability presents its own unique problems, or whether it presents specific cases of the general problems facing psychometrics as a whole.

There are formidable problems involved in formulating precise definitions of central concepts such as 'musical ability', 'musical aptitude', and 'musicality'; in practical terms these problems revolve around a given test's *validity*. The validity of a test is the extent to which it measures what it is supposed to measure; it is normally assessed in terms of the correlation between a group of subjects' scores on the test, and their performances on a measure of some *criterion variable*. Criterion variables include measures of attainment in education or in the work situation; ratings by experts or peers;

the performances of subject groups known to be expert on the skills being tested: and subjects' performances on other similar tests of the same variable. Criterion variables are notoriously difficult to establish in the case of general intelligence, since experts have been unable to agree on a precise definition of the concept. The well-known suggestion that 'intelligence is what intelligence tests measure' is operationally useful, though of course wholly circular.

Criterion variables are generally much more easy to specify in the case of musical ability tests, such that test validity is not so problematic: typical criteria might be assessments of instrumental performance, or of written or aural skills. We can distinguish between three basic types of test in music. Tests of musical *ability*, or *aptitude*, are designed to assess an individual's potential for skilled musical behaviour regardless of previous musical learning or experience. They might in a sense be called 'musical intelligence tests', and a wide variety of them is available. Some of the best-known and most widely used include Seashore's (1960) *Measures of musical talents*, Bentley's (1966) *Measures of musical abilities*, and Gordon's (1965) *Musical aptitude profile*. Tests of musical creativity also fall into this broad area, and I shall return to these in Chapter 6.

Secondly, tests of musical *achievement* are designed to assess the individual's knowledge of or attainments in music, such as performance skills, or understanding of musical theory. Some well-known tests of this type include Colwell's (1970a) *Music achievement tests*, the *Iowa tests of music literacy* (Gordon, 1971) and the *Aliferis music achievement test* (Aliferis, 1954). Thirdly, tests of *attitudes* towards music can be divided into two types. The first type elicit information about people's *interest* in music; such scales have been devised by Gaston (1958) as part of a general assessment of 'musicality', as well as by Hevner and Seashore (see Farnsworth, 1969). The second type might be called tests of *preference*, which are also sometimes referred to as tests of 'taste', 'appreciation', 'sensitivity', and so on. I shall take a detailed and critical look at these, and particularly at the problem of their validity, in Chapter 5.

There are three broad issues facing those who devise tests in these areas, and the content and form of different tests reflect different theoretical positions with respect to these issues. The first, and by far the most intractable, is the age-old 'nature/nurture' question about the relative influence of hereditary and environmental factors on ability. Anastasi's famous paper (1958) traces the history of this question, which continues to rear its head in various psychological and educational contexts, and which has profound implications for social policy. The majority of contemporary psychologists adopt some form of *interactional* model that is explicitly based upon the reciprocal influence of biological and social factors, so that the question of nature versus nurture does not arise as such. Archer and Lloyd (1975), for example, working in the field of sex differences, regard the genotype as providing 'a flexible plan, but not a fixed blueprint, for the developmental process. The final outcome would be determined by interaction with environmental conditions prevailing at each successive moment in the process' (p. 168).

In the field of musical ability, some authors (e.g. Seashore, 1938) have taken a strongly hereditarian view, whilst others (e.g. Lundin, 1967) have opposed this, emphasising instead the importance of environmental factors. Studies of famous musical families such as the Bachs may lend support to the view that musical abilities involve a greater genetic component than other abilities involved in general intelligence; but Shuter-Dyson and Gabriel's (1981) comprehensive review of all the genetic studies provides no clear support for this view. Even the highly specialised 'absolute pitch' capacity possessed by some individuals has become 'demystified' of late in the sense that no clear evidence has been found for a strong genetic influence upon it, and in that the dividing line between 'absolute' and 'relative' pitch is by no means clear-cut. I shall return to this particular question in Chapter 4.

The second major issue concerns whether there exists a general dimension of musical ability on which individuals differ, which implies that its component skills are highly intercorrelated, or whether there is little relationship between individuals' relative standing on these component skills. The same question has been asked about general intelligence (see e.g. Vernon, 1979); and many factor analytic studies have been carried out in attempts to resolve the issue. Broadly speaking, there is an American research tradition culminating in the work of Guilford (1967) that takes the latter position, and a British tradition, of whom Vernon is one of the main exponents, that favours the notion of a 'general intelligence' of which more specialised abilities form interrelated parts.

Shuter-Dyson and Gabriel (1981) have reviewed the factorial research on musical ability, and this has led them to propose a speculative application of Horn and Stankov's (1982) model of 'auditory and visual factors in intelligence', which tends to emphasise the interrelationships between different functions rather than their independence. Shuter-Dyson and Gabriel conclude that 'While recognising the contribution of the various musical elements to music listening and performance, we have emphasised the importance of the interrelations and coordination that music requires' (p. 76). In other words, the evidence seems broadly to support the notion of 'general musical ability', or 'musical intelligence'.

The third issue is one that surfaces repeatedly in all branches of music psychology: should the stimulus materials used in tests and experiments consist of real-life music, or should non-musical materials, such as electronically generated tones, be employed? Briefly, the former approach has the advantage of 'ecological validity', whereas the latter has the advantages of relatively less cultural bias, and of a greater potential for experimental control. This question has been debated at length in different contexts (see e.g. Davies, 1978), and is taken up in Chapter 5 in relation to studies of music listening. The short answer is, of course, that both musical *and* non-musical materials should be employed alongside one another in order to capitalise on the advantages of both approaches; and there are also ways of combining the two, as we shall see later.

In conclusion, it seems that the broad outcome of psychometric research on 'musical intelligence' is similar to that on general intelligence with respect to the three major theoretical issues. As far as the *practical* issues of children's music are concerned, there can be no doubt that the outcome of research in this area is of considerable importance. Studies have been carried out on the effects of music teaching and instrumental practice, on the use of tests in selection for musical instruction, on the effects of the home and school environment on musical development, on racial and social class differences in musical ability, and so on. Scores on different kinds of tests are widely used as the dependent variables in such investigations, since they enable intergroup comparisons to be made with some degree of standardisation.

Social psychology

It has been suggested that 'there are almost as many different definitions of social psychology as there are social psychologists', and that 'we are all social psychologists' in the sense that we are constantly engaged in the subtleties and complexities of social interaction in everyday life. Both of these semi-jocular suggestions make it clear that the scope of the subject is extremely wide. Eiser's (1980) 'textbook' definition of social psychology as 'the scientific study of human social behaviour' (p. xiii) is one that few psychologists would dispute – though many sociologists have a markedly different conception. Like 'cognitive', the adjective 'social' is used so widely that it can sometimes appear to mean very little, though the key feature of the phenomena that it describes is *social influence*. Social psychology is concerned with the influence that people have upon the behaviour and attitudes of others. There is a substantial degree of overlap between social and developmental psychology, which is increasing as developmental psychologists (a) more explicitly take account of the social context of their experimental procedures, and (b) become increasingly concerned with specifically social aspects of development (e.g. friendship formation). 'Developmental social psychology' is a term which has fairly recently been coined to describe the interface between the disciplines, and it is gaining in currency.

In 1969, Paul R. Farnsworth published the second edition of his *Social psychology of music*. Farnsworth used the adjective 'social' to indicate his emphasis on what he called the 'cultural determinants' of musical behaviour as distinct from its 'biological and physical bases' (p. 4). Although this was an important and pioneering book, only three of the ten chapters (on 'Language aspects of music', 'The nature of musical taste', and 'The measures of musical taste') could really be said to cover specifically 'social psychological' topics. Apart from the introductory chapter, the remaining chapters deal with 'the basic underpinnings of musical structure' (three chapters), 'musical ability' (two chapters), and 'applications to industry and therapy' (one chapter). This reflects the point above that the adjective 'social' has an extremely wide usage, and Farnsworth employed it in its most general sense.

Chapter 7 of this book is devoted to social psychology and musical development: as we shall see there, it is easy to distinguish between the broad sociological perspective upon social influences on musical development, and the more specific approach of experimental social psychology. The former is concerned with explaining the macroscopic influences of large-scale social institutions, such as the media, the school, and social class, and is thus led to broad theoretical issues such as the 'mass culture debate', as we shall see. The latter has a much more microscopic concern with the detailed mechanisms of social influence, which gives rise to experimental studies of prestige and propaganda effects, small-group influences upon individuals' responses to music, and so on. The focus of these studies has been upon attitudes towards and preferences for music, though the potential scope is far wider than this.

Konečni (1982) has surveyed the experimental social psychological research, covering in particular his own studies of small-group social influences on emotional states, mood, and musical preference. He complains that research on musical preference has largely ignored the immediate social context of the listening situation: 'More-or-less active listening to music has become fully imbedded in the stream of daily life of ordinary men and women. People listen to music while working, talking, eating, engaging in sexual intercourse. That this fact has been ignored by psychoaestheticians, and that they have continued to think of preference as a process largely unrelated to social situations, is quite remarkable' (p. 500). Konečni also points out that the social and technological changes that have taken place in recent years have meant that music of every type is now readily available to a very large number of people, and that the variety of listening situations is therefore extremely wide. His review makes it clear that this whole area is virtually virgin territory: the social psychology of music is a ripe and potentially very fruitful field for investigation.

Plan of the book

This preliminary attempt to map out a new field of study is bound to lack comprehensiveness, and to have many loose ends. My hope is that this initial attempt may inspire others to build upon the framework that is presented here, and thus to develop the developmental psychology of music. It is certain that any one person's view will be idiosyncratic, and shaped by his or her interests, preconceptions and biases; I therefore offer no apology for my own. There is a strong emphasis on theory throughout, reflecting my view that empirical 'facts' are of little use unless they can be organised into some kind of explanatory framework. The framework serves to generate and guide research, and it is subject to constant change in the light of the new 'facts' that emerge from that research.

I have deliberately adopted a general policy of overinclusiveness rather than underinclusiveness in relation to my subject-matter, ranging widely over psychological research that is relevant to musical development as well as over that which is specifically devoted to it. I have interpreted my 'developmental' task from a broad 'life-span' perspective, including a good deal of research on adults as well as on children. I have also tried my best, insofar as the research literature permits me, to consider music itself in the widest possible terms. I expressed the view earlier in this chapter that a good deal of research in music psychology has tended to restrict itself to Western tonal music, and in particular to European 'art' music. Since most people do not listen to this music for most of their listening lives, it is easy to see that such research is unrepresentative of the real world. My argument is that music psychology must consider its subject-matter in all its forms, 'classical' or 'popular', ethnic or Western, old or new, good or bad, if it is to possess scientific validity. This seems to be an obvious point, but a cursory look at the musical stimulus materials used in studies reported in the field's learned journals soon shows that it is one worth making. The point is closely related to that raised in the previous section about the importance of the social context of music listening. It also relates to the complaint that a good deal of research in this field is essentially unbalanced in the sense that those psychologists who carry it out have a woefully incomplete knowledge of the day-to-day concerns and attitudes of working musicians, as well as of music theorists. Davies (1978) and Sloboda (1985) have both made valiant efforts to redress this balance, but most of the research that they review nevertheless reflects primarily psychological rather than musical concerns.

Chapter 1 has set the scene for our enterprise, and has given plenty of clues about the contents of the remaining chapters. Chapter 2, 'Children's thinking and musical development', outlines the cognitive-developmental approach, and especially Piaget's theory, in some detail: music is considered in relation to other aspects of artistic development. This, along with Chapter 1, can be regarded as providing the theoretical basis for some of the later chapters. Chapters 3 and 4 draw on cognitive psychology, learning theory and on the psychometric approach in tracing the course of musical development in preschool and school-age children respectively.

A broader approach to development across the whole life span is taken in the rest of the book. In Chapter 5, 'Development of responses to music', the focus is upon the aesthetic aspects of musical development. Research in this area draws upon cognitive, social, psychometric, behavioural and other approaches, and has a good deal of practical significance for real-life music listening. The emphasis shifts from the listener to the composer and the performer in Chapter 6, 'Creativity, personality and musical development'.

The problems of musical creativity are considered here from the point of view of creativity and personality as a whole. This is a fascinating, complex and extremely difficult area for research: most of the work so far has been theoretical and introspective rather than experimental, though some empirical advances are being made within the cognitive and psychometric traditions.

Chapter 7, 'Social psychology and musical development', is related to Chapter 5 in its focus upon aesthetic issues, and follows on developmentally from Chapters 3 and 4 in its consideration of social influences upon teenage and adult music preferences. Theories and empirical research which derive from the broad sociological perspective, as well as from the more microscopic approach of experimental social psychology, are compared and evaluated. In Chapter 8, 'Developmental psychology and music education', different conceptions of 'music education' are examined, along with their main practical features, and the links with developmental theory are explored.

2

Children's thinking and musical development

Some psychologists would argue that if we can understand how children think, we can probably understand most other aspects of their behaviour. This is the basis of the 'cognitive-developmental' approach; and the figure largely responsible for its predominance in today's child psychology has been Jean Piaget. A good deal of contemporary research on musical development is rooted in theories of children's thinking: Piaget's theory is by far the most influential of these, and I shall consequently devote the main body of this chapter to it.

We start with an outline of the basic concepts of genetic epistemology, that is, of Piaget's developmental psychology, and very briefly outline his account of developmental stages. Most relevant to musical development are the second and third of these: and so we look next at symbolic development in the second, pre-operational stage. In particular, studies of symbolic play and drawing throw a good deal of light on parallel musical developments. The transition into the third, concrete operational stage has probably received more research attention than any other aspect of Piagetian theory: and we look at this in terms of the acquisition of conservation. Research on 'music conservation' is of particular interest to us here, and I question and evaluate the validity of this Piagetian analogy. There are several well-trodden paths of criticism of the theory which I consider next. One of Piaget's main critics with respect to artistic development has been Howard Gardner, and I devote some attention to the alternative theory that Gardner proposes. The chapter closes by looking at theoretical accounts of developmental stages in aesthetic appreciation, and at empirical research on children's sensitivity to artistic styles.

Piaget's theory

The amount of literature *on* Piaget, as well as that *by* him, is immense: this section will be confined to those parts of that literature most relevant to children's music. No attempt will be made to describe the theory in detail: many textbooks have been written which do this job in different ways. Amongst these I would single out Boden's *Piaget* (1979) and Piaget and Inhelder's own introductory book *The psychology of the child* (1969) as providing the best general introductions.

A good deal of the Piagetian research that has been carried out by experimental psychologists over the last twenty years or so has been fairly critical of the theory. The special volume of the *British Journal of Psychology* (1982) which was edited by Peter Bryant in honour of Piaget after his death in 1980 gives a good idea of the continuing importance of the theory in modern developmental psychology, as well as of the critical way in which many researchers view it. Piaget's account of what children can and cannot be expected to do at different ages has also been widely assimilated into different school curricula and educational programmes (see e.g. Schwebel and Raph, 1973; Varma and Williams, 1976). One important effect of this account has been that children in any given stage have not been considered to have sufficient cognitive maturity to attempt the tasks of the next stage, so that there may be no point in starting them on such tasks until they have reached an appropriate level of developmental 'readiness'. Now this has probably been the single most contentious point in the whole of Piagetian theory, perhaps because it has the widest educational implications. A great deal of research effort has been devoted to trying to prove that young children *can* do things that Piaget's theory predicts they should *not* be able to do. Let us outline the background to Piaget's theory before returning to his empirical research.

Genetic epistemology

Piaget never trained as a psychologist: his interest in children's thinking was a joint outcome of his grounding in biology, and his wide-ranging interests in philosophical problems. His ambitious application of a biological model of development to the problems of epistemology resulted in a lifetime's work on the origins (genesis) and development of children's thinking. Piaget called this enterprise *genetic epistemology*; the term 'mental embryology' might also have been appropriate.

Piaget saw logic as an essential part of the organisation of thinking, and the concept of an *operation* was central to this. Piaget proposed that the intrinsic features of logic have their origin in the activities of the subject. Thought operations are derived from the actions we perform upon objects in the outside world, and so thought is an internalised form of action. This view enabled Piaget to explain how development tends towards increasingly abstract and logical forms of thinking, such that similar sets of logical rules

develop in all children. Bolton (1972) has proposed that Piaget's operational-
ism enables him to overcome, or at least side-step, the ancient philosophical
conflict between rationalism and empiricism. The child gradually acquires the
logical rules of adulthood by an accumulation of experiences which derive
from actions performed on the environment.

Piaget proposes that *equilibration* is the mechanism by which the
acquisition of logical thinking occurs. Cognitive structures are seen as
'unstable' in relation to new objects and experiences, and the tendency to
equilibrate towards more stable states is a kind of intrinsic 'cognitive drive'
which motivates exploration. The environment is a constant source of
feedback, which guides the tendency to explore: and the developmental stages
represent successive levels of stabilisation, or adjustment to it. There is a
permanent tendency towards equilibrium *within* cognitive structures, and
also *between* those structures and the environment. This makes it clear that
Piaget's theory is based on the (biological) idea of *adaptation* to the
environment: adaptation is seen as taking place via the twin processes of
assimilation and *accommodation*. We assimilate new objects and events that
we encounter in our environment: we accommodate to these objects and
events by changing our ways of thinking about them; and our thinking moves
to a new level of equilibrium as a result. Assimilation and accommodation are
indissociable aspects of any developmental acquisition; as in biological
nutrition, that which is taken in (Piaget used the analogy of cognitive 'food',
or 'aliment') becomes part of that which takes it in.

The basic 'building blocks' of cognition are *schemes*, or *schemata*. In a
baby, a scheme might be a co-ordinated set of actions such as those involved in
sucking different objects. The baby soon learns, by trial and error, that some
objects are more suckable than others! Piaget would say that the objects are
assimilated to the sucking scheme; and that because of this differentiation
between them, the scheme accommodates to take account of their properties.
Cognitive development is thus seen as the increasing differentiation and
complementary integration of the framework of schemes, which is mobile and
functional. Schemes in older children are still essentially co-ordinated sets of
operations, but here they exist at a higher, more abstract level. The
mathematical thought processes involved in the inference that $A = C$ if both
$A = B$ and $B = C$, for example, represent an important and fundamental
example of such a scheme, as we shall see later. Piaget's early use of schema
(plural-schemata) as the generic term for all such structures was gradually
replaced by scheme (plural-schemes). In this later usage, the former term takes
on the more specific connotation of a literal (e.g. visual) representation.

Probably the best-known aspect of Piaget's theory is his proposal that there
exist four major, qualitatively different *stages* of cognitive development
through which all children pass. The sensori-motor stage (ages 0–2) is divided
into six substages, which move from the primitive use of reflexes in early
infancy through to the beginnings of internal representation, or symbolism.

Symbolic development provides the essence of the second, pre-operational stage (ages 2–7): this is sometimes divided into the pre-conceptual (ages 2–4) and the intuitive (ages 4–7) subperiods. A major 'revolution' in the child's thinking occurs around the age of seven, with the transition into the concrete operational stage; and the acquisition of formal operational thinking, which represents the final stage, occurs at the age of eleven or so.

Symbolic development in the pre-operational stage

The acquisition of what Piaget calls the semiotic or symbolic function in the pre-operational stage is a major developmental milestone. Assimilation provides that which is *signified*: and accommodation produces the (internal) *signifiers*. There are two types of the latter: *symbols* are signifiers which resemble the signified in some way, such as a visual image of an object; *signs* are arbitrary signifiers which bear no such resemblance, such as words. During most of the sensori-motor period, signifiers and signified are seen as undifferentiated: differentiation begins towards the end of this stage. The full-scale symbolic function, which is at its height in the preschool period, manifests itself in five forms, namely deferred imitation, verbal evocation, the mental image, symbolic play, and drawing. I will describe the first three of these very briefly, and then discuss symbolic play and drawing in more detail.

Deferred imitation refers to the reproduction of an action sequence after it has occurred: Piaget (1951) quotes the example of his daughter's imitation, some 12 hours later, of a playmate who got into a terrible temper, screamed, and stamped his foot. Verbal evocation is the spoken equivalent of this; the child says 'meow' after the cat has disappeared. The mental image is what Piaget calls an 'internalised imitation'; it does not appear to have any behavioural manifestation.

Symbolic play In many ways, symbolic or make-believe play captures the essence of the pre-conceptual subperiod. Play is a vital part of children's lives; in a very loose sense, it could almost be thought of as 'what children do'. We have all seen, and in the past ourselves enjoyed, playground games of doctors and nurses, cowboys and Indians, and so on; and play is also an important feature of children's music-making. This is also true of adults: many composers and improvisors have stressed the importance of play in their musical creativity, and some of their introspections are reported in Chapter 6. In spite of this ubiquity, psychologists have found it surprisingly difficult to formulate a precise definition of play. It has been suggested that play behaviour is an end in itself, and therefore lacks purpose; that it is spontaneous; that it gives pleasure; that it lacks organisation. All of these are true of certain forms of play, but do not in themselves form adequate or comprehensive definitions. Several theories of play attempt to explain its precise nature and functions (see e.g. Herron and Sutton-Smith, 1971; Bruner, Jolly and Sylva, 1976). It would not be appropriate to cover these here: I shall confine myself, following the theme of this chapter, to Piaget's account of the role of play in cognitive development.

This is expounded in full in *Play, dreams and imitation in childhood* (Piaget, 1951). Play and imitation are explained in terms of the balance between assimilation and accommodation; play behaviour is defined as that which is characterised by a predominance of assimilation, in the sense that new toys, people, situations and so on are incorporated into existing schemes. Imitation, on the other hand, is characterised by a predominance of accommodation in the sense that the child's thinking is subordinated to models provided by the outside world.

The general philosophy underlying most preschool playgroups and nursery schools is that children 'learn through play'; Piaget's theory perhaps provides the best account to date of how they might do so. There are strong arguments against an uncritical acceptance of this philosophy, however. Smith (1978) expresses the view that children may not always learn from play *as such*; it might be other aspects of the play environment, such as contact with adult helpers or other children, that give rise to any learning that occurs. Smith has reviewed the numerous experimental studies of the effects of play on cognitive abilities such as problem-solving and creativity, and has carried out such research himself (e.g. Smith and Syddall, 1978; Simon and Smith, 1983; Smith, 1984). Although many studies have found positive transfer effects, it seems clear that this is a field in which adequate experimental controls, for example, for experimenter effects, are extremely important as well as difficult to implement. Different forms of play promote different forms of learning, and current research is trying to identify these interconnections with some degree of precision.

Piaget suggested that the symbolic play of the pre-operational period gives way to 'games with rules' in the later stages of development. These rules can be institutional or spontaneously created, and their acceptance is seen as one important way in which the child's socialisation culminates in the adult's objective, rationalistic outlook. As part of a broader critique of Piaget's theory of play, Sutton-Smith (1966) disagreed with this latter suggestion: he proposed that play does not 'drop out', but becomes increasingly internalised as games on the one hand, and as an expressive system (fantasy, daydreams and ruminations) on the other. Piaget's (1966) reply to this was that play diminishes with age only in the sense that it becomes more adapted to reality. In other words, 'play' in a general sense differentiates during the course of development, whereas 'children's play' in its strictest sense, which exhibits 'the deformation and subordination of reality to the desires of the self', does in fact diminish. As we shall see in Chapters 3 and 6, music-making in children and adults incorporates play in *both* of these respects.

Drawing The study of children's drawing has a long history, and a good deal of normative data has been collected over the years (see e.g. Eng, 1931;

Kellogg, 1969; Lowenfeld and Brittain, 1975). There has been a sudden increase of interest and research activity in this field over the last decade or so, particularly within cognitive psychology (see e.g. Butterworth, 1977; Freeman, 1980). This has resulted in a general trend away from what might be called a 'product-oriented' and towards a 'process-oriented' approach to the study of drawing, which has direct implications for the study of musical development.

The early normative studies gave rise to various accounts of developmental stages in children's spontaneous drawing which differ in detail, but which are essentially quite similar. There is general agreement that the *scribbling* of preschoolers becomes more articulate and controlled up to the age of three or four or so, and that scribbles give way to what might be called *preschematic* drawings in the early school years. Preschematic drawings are characterised by what Lucquet (1927) called *intellectual realism*: the child apparently 'draws what he knows, not what he sees'. This results in phenomena such as 'transparencies', as when the drawn man's head is visible through his hat, or his legs through his trousers; or 'turning over', when two visual perspectives are incongruously combined in the same drawing (e.g. the four legs of a table are depicted as emerging from the corners of an aerial view of its top). Schematic drawings emerge in the later school years, that is, up to the age of ten or so; these exhibit an increasing degree of internal organisation, though they retain certain non-realistic features. 'Air gap' drawings, in which the elements of landscapes are ordered on the page in relation to ground and skylines, but in which a visually unrealistic 'gap' appears, are a good example of these (see Hargreaves, Jones and Martin, 1981). Schematic drawings gradually give way to *visually realistic* drawings in adolescence.

Research attention has centred on the second of these four stages: do young children really draw only 'what they know' in an egocentric fashion, and in what sense can these drawings be said to contain 'errors'? Piaget's view is that 'Drawing is a form of the semiotic function which should be considered as being halfway between symbolic play and the mental image. It is like symbolic play in its functional pleasure and autotelism, and like the mental image in its effort at imitating the real' (Piaget and Inhelder, 1969, p. 63). Piaget draws heavily on Lucquet's (1927) account of drawing: the concept of intellectual realism is congenial to Piagetian theory because it embodies the interaction between internal schemes and imitative accommodations. In more down-to-earth language (Piaget's terminology is notoriously dense and cumbersome), children's drawings are of immense interest to the developmental psychologist because they provide direct access to the child's view of the world through her attempts to reproduce it.

The 'product-oriented' approach is to collect normative data about the features found in drawings produced at different ages, and then to evaluate any given drawing by comparison with these norms. In the well-known Goodenough-Harris *Draw-a-man test* (Harris, 1963), for example, drawings

Fig. 2.1 The 'tadpole man' drawing

of men and women are scored according to a scheme in which up to 73 and 71 points respectively are awarded according to the number and realism of the features present. The child's level of 'intellectual maturity' is then assessed by reference to the normative score for his or her chronological age. The conception of 'intellectual maturity' used here is very similar to general intelligence, and Harris reports high correlations with a variety of standard IQ tests.

Let us explore the implications of this approach, and contrast it with the process-oriented one, by considering the universal 'tadpole man' drawing. An example of this is shown in Figure 2.1: all children are consistently found to reproduce such drawings of people at the age of two or three or so. In the context of the *Draw-a-man test*, the tadpole man represents an immature, undeveloped and essentially faulty conceptual scheme which gradually drops out with increasing age. Does this imply that children think that the body is not differentiated from the head, or that arms and legs grow out of people's heads? There are several problems inherent in such a view (see Freeman, 1972, 1976; Hargreaves, 1978): perhaps the most fundamental is the massive oversimplification involved in making direct inferences about cognitive *competence* from measures of drawing *performance*. Apart from the general level of conceptual knowledge that children have about the class of objects being drawn, which is presumably what represents 'intellectual maturity', we need to consider their *internal models* of those objects (cf. Barrett and Light, 1976); the plans, strategies or *programmes* that they formulate in organising drawings; and also the *production skills*, including the motor skills and the artistic conventions, that they employ. Drawing 'errors' could derive from any one of these levels, or from interactions between them, and it seems premature to assume that they necessarily originate at the deepest conceptual level.

Process-oriented research attempts to identify these intermediate processing mechanisms, and a common research technique has been to give children drawing-completion tasks which are organised so as to violate common 'faulty' strategies. Freeman (1975), for example, provided preschool children with pairs of circles, one vertically above and touching the lower, which were designed to represent the head and trunk of a person respectively. The ratio of the areas of the two circles was systematically varied in each of ten such pairs, and subjects were asked to attach arms and legs to each. Freeman found that children who spontaneously produced conventional men in a pretest remained consistent in attaching arms to the trunk: but that for those who spontaneously produced 'tadpole men' in the pretest, the tendency to attach arms to the head was a function of its size in relation to the trunk. These 'tadpole drawers' 'correctly' attached the arms to the trunk when it was significantly larger than the head, but reverted to their 'tadpole' strategy when it was significantly smaller.

This shows that common drawing 'errors' can be eliminated by varying task demands. Freeman argues that the fact that 'tadpole drawers' were ready to drop this strategy when the task rendered it inappropriate indicates that such 'errors' of representation may well arise from production or programming deficiencies rather than from curious or inadequate conceptual schemes. In some respects, they resemble so-called 'virtuous errors' in language development: the child who says 'I rided my bike' is applying the past tense rule in a perfectly logical and appropriate fashion, but the utterance is of course 'wrong' by adult standards. Drawing errors such as transparencies, turning over, and other superimposition and omission effects may be explained better in terms of the constraints children impose upon themselves within their own production rules than as a consequence of conceptual immaturity. The emphasis of current process-oriented research is upon identifying and cataloguing these rules, and observing developmental changes in their use (see e.g. Goodnow, 1977).

The study of musical representation is less well developed than this, but the signs are that it is likely to follow a similar direction. We shall see in Chapter 3 that some recent research on the development of children's singing is elaborating the idea that 'outline songs', or 'song frames', may be directly analogous to 'tadpole'-type drawings in some respects. Spontaneous songs have not typically been thought of as 'faulty' in the same sense, presumably because there is no musical equivalent to a realistic or 'correct' visual representation; but the postulation of *production schemes* for song (e.g. Dowling, 1984) is in line with the arguments adumbrated above. There is also some interesting new research on children's representations of music in drawing, which I shall discuss in Chapter 4.

The acquisition of conservation

The biggest and most controversial area of Piagetian research is that on the transition from the pre-operational to the concrete operational stage. Piaget proposed an elaborate account of the logic of concrete operations which is expressed in terms of the complementary structures of *groups*, *groupings*, and *lattices* (see e.g. Flavell, 1963). This is not the place to discuss these, but we should at least be aware of some of the general features of concrete operational thinking. They are best described in the practical context of the acquisition of *conservation* abilities, which have been studied in many realms of young children's mathematics, including number, volume, classification, space, distance, time, and speed. Piaget's conservation tasks are probably the best known of all his practical demonstrations; and they are the main means by which his theory has been applied to music.

In the first part of a typical number conservation experiment, for example, the child is shown two identical rows of counters, each arranged in a straight line. She is asked 'Are there more in this row (*experimenter points to one of the two rows*) or more in this row (*experimenter points to the other row*) or are there the same number in each row?' Children of all ages ought to answer this question correctly; it acts as a 'baseline' against which the second part is judged. If a child gave the wrong response for any reason, the experimenter would be justified in removing her from the subject sample. In the second part, the experimenter spreads out one of the rows of counters so that it becomes a longer straight line, and the question is repeated. According to Piaget, pre-operational children ought now to answer incorrectly, replying that there are more counters in the longer row. Piaget argues that they do not possess *number invariance*, that is, the concept that the number of counters remains the same no matter how the spatial array is changed. It is only when they progress into the concrete operational stage, at the age of seven or so, that they are likely to answer this second question correctly.

In the third part of the experiment, the counters are put back into their original array, and the question is asked once again. The concrete operational child should give the correct response in all three stages of the experiment; but Piaget predicts, interestingly, that the pre-operational child should answer correctly once again in part three even though she gave the wrong response in part two. He proposes that thinking must display *reversibility* in order to be truly concrete operational. The child must be able to realise that a transformation can be reversed such that the display returns to its initial state; that is, that the different *states* of a display are explicitly related to the *transformations* of it. Number invariance specifically involves a synthesis of *seriation* and *class inclusion*. To have fully achieved conservation of number, said Piaget, the child must have grasped the underlying concepts of how objects can be *ordered* according to some given dimension, such as size, and how they might be *classified*, or grouped in different ways. The ability to count is not necessarily evidence of number invariance: the child may simply be 'parroting' a list of verbal labels, learnt by rote in the same way as a nursery rhyme might be.

The mastery of seriation involves another important general acquisition, namely the ability to make *transitive inferences*. To arrange three unequal rods, A, B, and C in order of their length, for example, the child must combine the knowledge that (for example) A ⟩ B and that B ⟩ C, and make the transitive deductive inference that A ⟩ C. The ability to make such an inference without a direct visual comparison between A and C necessarily involves concrete operational thought. Another essential feature of such thought is *decentration*: Piaget proposes that the child acquires the ability to recognise the interdependence of two variables without *centring* on either one of them. In one of the well-known volume conservation tasks, for example, liquid is poured from the second of two identical containers into a third, differently shaped container. The pre-operational child typically answers, incorrectly, that the amounts of liquid in the first and third containers are different, usually centring on either the height or the breadth of the liquid in them. The concrete operational child perceives that height and breadth co-vary, jointly determining volume, and thus answers correctly that there is the same amount of liquid in the two containers.

As I have said already, the detailed application of this part of Piaget's theory to different areas of primary mathematics has had a profound effect on curriculum sequencing, and a great deal of research effort has been devoted to attempts to show that the pre-operational-age children may be able to show concrete operational competence under certain conditions. One common theme has been that Piagetian tasks rely too heavily on children's verbal responses, such that apparent cognitive failures may in fact stem from inappropriate language use, and a body of research has arisen on the *non-verbal assessment* of conservation (see Miller, 1976). Other studies have investigated the effects of *training* on conservation task performance (e.g. Goldschmid, 1968): success in the training of conservation abilities may be interpreted as undermining the validity of the stage theory. Now many of the studies in these two areas *have* been able to show conservation-type abilities at an earlier age than Piaget would predict: but does this mean that the theory is wrong? Piaget would claim that these results represent merely *pseudoconservation*; whilst the children may have got a specific short-term set of questions correct in a given study, there is no evidence that the experimental effects generalise to the full range of abilities required for concrete operational thinking, nor that they possess any long-term stability.

Two other lines of research have attempted to make rather more fundamental critiques than this; both are based on the proposal that genuine operational competence is present at a much earlier age than Piaget suggests by virtue of quite different theories of the underlying cognitive processes. The research of Jerome Bruner and his colleagues at Harvard University in the 1960s (e.g. Bruner, Olver and Greenfield, 1966) was based on a quite different view of the relationship between thinking, language, and the environment. They placed much more emphasis than Piaget upon the role of environmental objects and situations in *moulding* thought; for Piaget, the development of similar logical structures inexorably takes place more or less regardless of the precise content of that which is assimilated during the course of development. The Harvard researchers collected cross-cultural data to support their case, and this broadly confirmed the findings of other cross-cultural Piagetian research. Generally speaking it seems that Piagetian stages *can* be identified in children in non-Western societies, though there is a greater degree of age- and task-related variation in performance than the theory would predict (see Modgil, 1974).

Bruner also had an alternative view of the acquisition of conservation which was based on the idea that it occurred through the child's 'primitive sense of identity' of the task material before and after transformation rather than through an internalised cognitive operation. Pre-operational children's errors were seen as arising from their confusion by misleading verbal and perceptual aspects of the tasks, rather than from logical incapacity. The thrust of this argument, if not its detail, is in some ways similar to that of Bryant (1974). Bryant proposed a radical alternative theory whose premise was that pre-operational children *can* and *do* make logical inferences; that cognitive development proceeds as a progressive series of inferences made about the relationships between objects and their environmental backgrounds, or frameworks.

Whilst there is some degree of empirical support for these alternative theories, neither can be said to have invalidated or replaced that of Piaget. Though young children can be shown to possess operational competence under certain experimental circumstances, the fact is that they do not spontaneously display it in most of their everyday activity. This idea that the *context* of the child's thinking might influence its quiddity leads us to a new, important, and rapidly growing area of theory and research which has become known as *social cognition* (see e.g. Butterworth and Light, 1982). Light (1983) has undertaken a thorough conceptual analysis of the different ways in which the term can be used in relation to Piagetian theory, and some of the empirical research in this new field has investigated children's performance on conservation tasks.

An important landmark in this literature is Donaldson's book *Children's minds* (1978). Donaldson reports some recent work which demonstrates that the social context of the test situation is inextricably linked with the cognitive content of it. In the typical Piagetian conservation experiments described above, for example, the 'experimenter' asks the (child) 'subject' various standard questions; the child has certain expectations as to how she should behave, built up from her past experience of similar test situations. Rather than responding solely to the literal wording of the questions she is asked, she reacts to a whole conglomerate of different sources of information: to non-verbal signals, subtle cues and hints, and, perhaps most important, to the *perceived* motives and intentions of the experimenter. In other words, she constructs an explanation of the situation which is based on what Donaldson calls 'human sense'. Donaldson's view is that psychological experimenters, as well as teachers and educators, pay too little attention to children's use of 'human sense' in everyday life. This puts an interesting new perspective on Piaget's well-known view that children's thinking is essentially *egocentric*; that they are unable to take the point of view of others. Piaget held that egocentricity manifests itself in various ways, such as the inability to appreciate the visual perspectives and the social roles of others; this view has also been subjected to critical empirical scrutiny in recent years (see e.g. Cox, 1985).

In one well-known experiment (McGarrigle and Donaldson, 1975), children's performances on standard versions of conservation tasks in which the transformations of the materials were *intentionally* carried out by the experimenter were compared with conditions in which the transformations were made to appear *accidental*. This latter aim was accomplished by the ingenious device of introducing a 'naughty' teddy bear who disrupted the proceedings to the apparent displeasure of the experimenter. When the transformation was made to appear to be outside the control of the experimenter in this way, pre-operational children produced many more conservation responses than they did under normal conditions. McGarrigle and Donaldson concluded that Piaget's neglect of the social context of the text situation had led him to seriously underestimate the child's cognitive abilities; and this result has generally been borne out in subsequent replications (see Bryant, 1982; Donaldson, Grieve and Pratt, 1983). To put this another way, we could say that it is the *experimenter* who displays egocentricity in certain important respects.

Social cognition research emphasises the interdependence of the cognitive and the social aspects of development, which have in the past been studied without reference to one another. A parallel distinction is that between cognition and affect: this has been present in psychological thinking for many years, and it is equally artificial. There are signs that these barriers are beginning to break down, with the growing realisation that cognitive development embodies changes in the social and affective domains, and vice versa. This point is particularly relevant to our understanding of artistic development, since works of art are probably more capable of eliciting complex aesthetic, affective, and cognitive responses than are stimuli in any other domain.

Music conservation The pioneer in this field, who has continued to explore it more extensively than any other researcher, is Marilyn Pflederer Zimmerman of the University of Illinois. She has devised a range of 'musical conservation' tasks which are analogous to Piaget's non-musical tasks; let me illustrate them by means of a typical example: 'conservation of melody under deformation of duration values'. In the first version of this task (Pflederer, 1964) children were first played a four-bar phrase from Bartok's *For children* (1946), followed by the same phrase played in augmentation (i.e. with each note doubled in time value). The children were told a story about the dancing of a little girl and her jolly grandfather, and asked two questions: which dance tune was for the little girl and which was for the grandfather? Was the grandfather's dance tune the same as the little girl's or was it different? The children were allowed to hear the tune as many as four times, and 'conservation of melody' was inferred if both questions were answered correctly.

A correct response to the second question was defined as the recognition by the child that the two melodies are both 'the same' *and* 'different' in certain respects: and this is crucial to an understanding of what Pflederer Zimmerman means by 'music conservation'. The rationale is that the pre-operational child should *either* say that the two versions of the tune are 'the same' by recognising some kind of melodic gestalt, *or* that they are 'different', in this case with respect to note durations: this is seen as equivalent to 'centring' in the standard Piagetian tasks. In concrete operational thinking children become able to 'decentre'; this is interpreted in the musical tasks as the ability to recognise the constant aspects of the melody when one of its properties is varied.

This task was developed as part of Pflederer Zimmerman's doctoral research, the first published details of which appear in Pflederer (1964). In this paper nine such tasks are described, not all of which were employed in subsequent research. In each case, one aspect of the musical material (the 'foil') was varied whilst another ('property conserved') was held constant. The 'foils' included 'durational values', 'tonal pattern', 'varying pitches', 'pitch level', 'rhythm pattern', 'rhythmic and harmonic accompaniment', and 'key of accompaniment'; the properties conserved included 'meter', 'rhythm pattern', 'melody', 'tonal series', 'tonal pattern', and 'tonality'. Broadly speaking, the results from this pilot research supported Piagetian theory. Pflederer Zimmerman found that her eight 8-year-old subjects were generally able to appreciate that two versions of a melody differing in meter, tonal, or rhythmic patterns were in some sense 'the same' as well as 'different', whereas her eight 5-year-old subjects were not.

This study suffers from several methodological shortcomings, though we should remember that the tasks were being piloted in a fairly exploratory manner. The number of children was much smaller than one would normally expect in a study of this kind, and (perhaps for this reason) there was no real attempt at a comprehensive statistical analysis of the results. The use of well-known music as test material raises problems of familiarity and cultural bias, and we can see from the description above that there is a certain amount of terminological confusion surrounding the definition of the different tasks (e.g. what are the differences between 'melody', 'tonal pattern', and 'tonal series'?). Nevertheless, this research made a variety of potentially fruitful suggestions as to what a musical conservation task might be, and laid the foundation for quite a number of subsequent studies.

In a later study (Pflederer and Sechrest, 1968), the exploratory research was modified and refined. All the musical material was once again from Bartok's *For children*, and children aged 5, 7, 9 and 13, numbering 198 in all, were tested. The children were played four phrases from the music, each of which was paired with seven 'systematic deformations', as well as with an exact repetition of itself. The seven deformations involved changes in the instrument, tempo, harmony, mode, rhythm, contour, or interval of the phrases. The children were asked whether the original phrase and the deformed version of it were 'the same', 'different', or 'same in some ways and different in others'; as in the previous study, the last of these three responses was taken to represent conservation. Once again, Piagetian theory was apparently supported by the results; the authors give copious examples of typical 'non-conservation', 'intermediate', and 'conservation' responses to these tasks produced by children of different ages. Some examples from the 'harmony deformation' task are quoted in Table 2.1.

Pflederer Zimmerman has continued to conduct research along these lines (e.g. Webster and Zimmerman, 1983) and her efforts have stimulated others to do likewise: the whole area of work has recently been reviewed by Serafine (1980) as well as by Tunks (1980). Generally speaking, success on 'music conservation' tasks does seem to improve with age, and there may be a plateau at the age of nine or so. Conservation of tonal patterns seems to appear earlier than that for rhythmic patterns, and deformations of instrumentation, tempo, and harmony are recognised earlier than those of mode, contour, and rhythm. Several researchers have investigated the effects of training; some (e.g. Pflederer Zimmerman and Sechrest, 1970; Serafine, 1975) have found that 'music conservation' abilities cannot be trained in pre-operational-age children, which could be interpreted as supportive of Piaget's position, whereas others (e.g. Botvin, 1974; Foley, 1975) have found that they can. At the risk of overgeneralisation, I would like to suggest that Piaget's theory receives general support from the empirical research in this area, and that the validity of the 'music conservation' tasks is generally accepted, at least in the field of music education.

Pflederer (1967) formalised the theoretical basis of the tasks by proposing five 'conservation-type laws' for the development of musical concepts. These are all based on the notion that children gradually acquire the capacity to recognise the invariant aspects of a melody irrespective of variations in other

Table 2.1 *Typical 'non-conservation', 'intermediate', and 'conservation' responses to the 'harmony deformation' task*

Five-Year-Olds.

Nonconservation: Different, because one is playing with a whole bunch of keys and the other is only playing with two. (Were they the same in any way?) No.

Conservation: The second one was chords. The first one didn't have chords. (Were they the same in any way?) Well, the song was the same and the piano was the same.

Seven-Year-Olds.

Nonconservation: Different. They were using more fingers than the first one. (Were the songs the same in any way?) No.

Intermediate: That's different because they played the piano. They played the piano with the other instruments. (Were they the same in any way?) Yes, the song was, but, um, some of the music in the middle wasn't because, um, the piano was playing.

Conservation: If they took off the four, and then it would be the same.

 They had a low note after each note. They could be the same at the end if they took away the low notes.

 Well, it's just a little different. They had another new note after the other one. (Was there anything the same about them?) Not exactly. Just the notes if they didn't put the new . . . it would be the same if they didn't put the chord in it. Yeah, I think it would be the same.

Nine-Year-Olds.

Nonconservation: In the middle of the second song they started to play two hands together. (Were the songs the same in any way?) No.

Intermediate: The second one was played with two hands and the first one with one hand. (Were they the same in any way?) I don't know.

Conservation: They were the same song, but two people were playing it. (What is that called?) A duet. They were the same. It was played with chords, but it was the same in the melody.

Thirteen-Year-Olds.

Nonconservation: Well, that's still played by the piano and they added some chords to it. I'd say it's a little bit higher than the first one. (Are the tunes the same in any way?) No.

Table 2.1 (*cont.*)

Thirteen-Year-Olds. (*cont.*)	
Intermediate	It's different because on every third note they played a chord or an interval. They played more than one note. (Were the tunes the same in any way?) The first notes were the same. It was different because it didn't play the same amount of notes. (What do you mean by that?) It played three notes and then it moved, the last one had more of a chord.
Conservation:	Most of it was harmonized; otherwise it was the same. (What was the same?) Well, the second one was the same as the first with harmony put in.
	They add chords to that one. Otherwise it would be the same.

Reproduced from Pflederer and Sechrest (1968) by permission of M. Pflederer Zimmerman and Council for Research in Music Education.

properties. Briefly, the five laws are *identity* (e.g. variation of instrumentation without note changes), *metrical groupings* (variation of note values within measures, meter remaining constant), *augmentation and diminution* (doubling or halving of note values), *transposition* (variation of pitch by playing in a different key) and *inversion* (substitution of lower tones for higher tones whilst maintaining essential melodic or harmonic characteristics).

Despite this theoretical elaboration, there are almost certainly some fundamental divergences from Piaget's general theory that call into question the validity of the concept of 'music conservation'. In a traditional Piagetian task the child sees some transformation of the material in front of her and is questioned about its effects; the transformation is then reversed such that the material returns to its initial state, and the questions are repeated. The musical tasks differ from this in that *the child does not observe the transformations*. Because musical events are ordered in the dimension of time, such that two versions of a melody cannot be attended to simultaneously, the child can never be certain that the second version of the melody she hears was in fact derived from a first version. She may perceive them as having distinct identities, never initially having been equivalent. Similarly, the essential property of *reversibility* is missing from the musical conservation task in that the child is never able to observe the reverse transformation of the melody to its original state. In other words, it is by no means clear that the cognitive processes involved in arriving at 'correct' responses to these tasks are those which characterise concrete operational thought.

Gardner (1973a) points out that 'there is a sense in which *any* change in a musical stimulus makes it different and that, as a consequence, analogies with Piaget's research are forced' (p. 194). The two forms of the melody, in other words, are not equivalent in the same sense as are the two rows of counters in the traditional number conservation task. Furthermore, it could even be that conservation abilities are not being tapped at all in these studies, but rather some form of melodic recognition memory of the kind that is measured in musical ability tests. Serafine (1980) suggests that the musical task of recognising 'theme and variations' may be an equally valid interpretation of what is involved; and Pflederer Zimmerman implicitly accepts this point in referring to conservation-*type* laws and responses. Shuter-Dyson and Gabriel (1981) make an interesting comment on this point in relation to Pflederer and Sechrest's (1968) study. Alongside the seven thematic deformation conditions was a control condition in which each original tune was paired with itself. Since this was the only task on which the 5-year-old subjects performed relatively well, whereas the 8-year-olds did better on all the tasks, it seems likely that whatever abilities *are* involved in the tasks must be more than mere recognition memory.

The operational definition of 'music conservation' in these studies is inherent in the response that the two forms of the stimulus are both the same and different in certain respects. Strictly speaking, of course, the latter response is the only correct one: the two versions of the melody are objectively different. An important general point here, as in the social cognition research mentioned earlier, is that the form of the question could determine the child's response. Another general point which applies to Piagetian research as a whole is that age is not a 'pure' independent variable. If performance on Pflederer Zimmerman's tasks is found to improve with age, this *may* demonstrate the acquisition of music conservation; but this is only one possible interpretation. The result could derive from parallel developmental improvements in memory and attentional capacity, perceptual and perform-ance skills, verbal expressiveness, or other confounding capabilities.

One way of investigating this kind of question is to manipulate different aspects of the experimental situation, and to see if the result persists: some of our own research has investigated the effects of changes in the musical stimulus material. Crowther *et al.* (1985) gave a Pflederer Zimmerman-type pitch transposition task to 5-, 7-, 9- and 13-year-old subjects, in which eight new types of musical material were used alongside the original Bartok phrases. We found that 'conservation' responses were more frequent in the older children, and with the more familiar types of musical material. Hargreaves, Castell and Crowther (in press) confirmed both of these findings using familiar and unfamiliar tone sequences (very common nursery rhyme tunes and 'statistical approximations to music' respectively) in pitch transposition and rhythmic inversion tasks in a cross-cultural study of 6- and 8-year-olds in England and the U.S.A. The older children performed significantly better than the younger ones, and performance was generally higher with the familiar tunes. It is very likely that melodic recognition rather than 'conservation' underlies the processing of the very familiar tunes in this study; we speculate that unfamiliar melodies may be processed according to the contour relationships rather than the pitch-interval relationships between their notes.

This speculation is pursued in more detail and placed in a developmental context in Chapter 4: it originates from that body of research on melodic memory which is based on the information-processing approach (e.g. Dowling and Bartlett, 1981). This work has extensive theoretical overlaps and task similarities with 'music conservation' research, though as yet there has been virtually no interchange between the two fields. The theoretical clarification and task validation that is urgently needed in music conservation research may well be facilitated by such an interchange.

Evaluation of Piaget's theory

Four main lines of criticism have been levelled at Piaget's theory, and some of these have already been mentioned in the context of the conservation experiments. In broad terms, they refer to Piaget's *methodology*; to his *stage theory*; to his *adaptation model* of the process of development; and to his *logical model*. These psychological critiques of the theory run parallel to the main features of its application to educational psychology (see e.g. Brown and Desforges, 1979; Modgil, Modgil and Brown, 1983).

Piaget's own empirical data was collected by means of his so-called 'clinical method', which involved flexible, open-ended interviews with individual children. The reasoning behind their responses to questions such as those in the conservation tasks was probed and explored in detail, regardless of whether they were correct or incorrect. This method is open to the same criticisms that apply to all clinical techniques; because the questions are not standardised, and because their direction and interpretation depend on the subjective judgement of the tester, they do not meet the normal scientific standards of validity and reliability. Now Piaget never himself claimed to have carried out rigorous experimental tests of his theory, and his practical work is best regarded as illustrative. His tasks are demonstrations of parts of the theory rather than critical tests of it, and the methodological criticisms should be seen in this context. Proof of the validity of the theory nevertheless depends on data from properly designed and controlled experiments, even if Piaget could not necessarily have been expected to provide this himself.

Bryant (1974) discusses a methodological issue which is fundamental to the Piagetian enterprise, namely the potential problems of confounding involved in the use of age as an independent variable. He points out that in order to provide a conclusive demonstration of any age-based behavioural improvement, the psychologist ought to supply a control task which is similar to the experimental task in all ways *except* the aspect under investigation. Only if improvements with age are found on the experimental and *not* on the control task can conclusions be drawn about development. Bryant's own work on memory and verbal labelling effects in conservation tasks (e.g. Bryant and Trabasso, 1971) provides an excellent model of how such controls ought to be incorporated into Piagetian experiments.

Piaget's stage model is of central importance in educational applications of the theory; if school curriculum sequences are to be based on a Piagetian model of what children can be expected to do at different ages, it is crucial that the stages exist as coherent sets of operations in the way that the theory suggests. In other words, there should be evidence of the *internal consistency* of stages, such that their essential properties are manifest in performance regardless of the specific task. The evaluative research on the acquisition of conservation that was outlined earlier (on non-verbal assessment, effects of training and social context, cross-cultural influences, etc.) is crucial here; and though my own general conclusion was that children under normal, everyday circumstances *do* tend to think in the way that Piaget suggests, Brown and Desforges (1979) maintain that there is very little evidence for the logical coherence of stages. They suggest that Piaget is forced to fall back on intermediate or transitional stages, or to invent superfluous theoretical constructs such as 'vertical décalages' in order to account for low inter-correlations between measures of an operation within a particular stage, and consequently conclude that the stage model is inadequate.

The main educational application of Piaget's view of the process of development, that is, of his adaptation model, has been in providing a theoretical rationale for what might be called 'child-centred' teaching methods. If the child is internally motivated to achieve new levels of equilibrium, then the teacher's job is presumably to provide an optimal environment for self-paced learning; and this contrasts with traditional 'teacher-centred' methods in which the direction and pace of learning is set by the teacher. The teacher is expected to assess the child's level of 'readiness' for new learning experiences, and thereby to tacitly guide the child's own discovery of these experiences through active involvement.

The main objection to this has been that Piaget's central explanatory concepts, that is, assimilation, accommodation, and equilibration, are too vague and general to be of any specific use. In the educational context, Brown (1983) argues that the general exhortation that the learner should be 'active' leaves far too much unspecified in practical terms of classroom practice; an adequate theory should be able to provide details of the appropriate learning experiences. From the theoretical point of view, however, there seems little doubt that interactive models of the process of development have been successfully adopted in areas as diverse as sex-role stereotyping (e.g. Archer and Lloyd, 1982) and mothering (e.g. Schaffer, 1971); and Piaget's version may still be one of the most sophisticated.

Piaget's logical model implies that the direction of cognitive development is always towards increasingly articulate forms of logical thinking. This has been criticised because it appears to promote scientific activity to a higher status than 'ludic' or 'antic' activities: in other words, than those activities which are important in the arts. This critique forms the starting point of Gardner's theory, and so I shall defer its consideration until the next section.

Despite the immense volume of critical testing that psychologists have carried out on the theory, and despite Brown's (1983) gloomy conclusion that 'it does not seem that Piagetian theory is of direct assistance in the psychology of education' (p. 100), the fact is that researchers continue to test it, and that educators continue to formulate practical implementations. I think that this speaks for itself.

Gardner's theory

Gardner's (1979) critique of Piaget's logical model has two main strands. First, he regards the view of the 'competent scientist' as representing the 'end state' of cognition as surprisingly narrow. Mature cognition involves a good deal more than logical–rational thinking; and 'Piaget has consequently paid little heed to adult forms of cognition removed from the logic of science: there is scant consideration of the thought processes used by artists, writers, musicians, athletes, equally little information about processes of intuition, creativity or novel thinking' (1979, p. 76). Gardner's second point is that Piaget pays insufficient attention to the *content* of children's thinking. Piaget seems to view all environmental objects and situations as 'grist to the mill' of cognitive development regardless of their physical characteristics, the symbol systems they employ, their media of transmission, and their mode of response. This might at the very least lead to an oversimplified description of the course of cognitive development; but the problem may be more fundamental than this in that environmental variability might *shape* thinking, rather than merely providing 'resistances' for it to assimilate. This latter view is essentially the one voiced by Bruner and his Harvard colleagues, which I discussed earlier.

Gardner (1973a) suggests that artistic behaviour combines the *subjective* and *objective* aspects of life; aesthetic objects are the objective embodiment of subjective experiences, and they give rise to unique personal understandings in each individual. The arts also transcend the distinction between *affect* and *cognition*: aesthetic objects simultaneously produce patterns of thought and of feelings in the observer. Gardner builds these interdependencies into his proposal of three interacting 'systems' in development. The *making* system produces *acts* or *actions*, and this is seen most clearly in the creator or performer. The *perceiving* system deals with *discriminations* or *distinctions*: the critic is expected to excel in this respect. Finally, the *feeling* system gives rise to *affects*, which are most clearly seen in the audience member. The three systems are held to be present in all animal and human life, and development is conceived as a process in which the degree of interaction between them gradually increases, eventually reaching a point at which no single system can be considered in isolation from the other two.

Gardner's account of development centres on the child's acquisition and use of *symbols*. Symbols are organised into different *systems*, which can either be primarily *denotational* (e.g. numerical notation, where each number has a precise referential meaning) or *expressive* (e.g. abstract art, which has no precise reference to other aspects of experience). Some symbol systems can encompass works which display one, or the other, or both of these properties (e.g. language, dance, drama, drawing, sculpture, and of course music): systems also vary widely in the *precision* of their correspondence with different aspects of behaviour and experience, that is, in their 'notationality'. Gardner thinks that an important task of developmental psychology is to identify the nature of adult competences in specific symbol systems, to study the developmental changes which culminate in these, and to explain the relationship of these changes to cognitive development as a whole.

Symbolism is of course central to Piaget's account of the pre-operational stage, as we saw earlier, and so we need to consider carefully in what respects Gardner's approach is different. Both theorists agree that the most important early manifestation of symbolism is the infant's acquisition of 'object permanence', that is, the gradual recognition that objects still exist even when they go out of sight. Piaget's theory of the sensori-motor stage elaborates upon this in some detail, and a considerable amount of critical empirical research has been stimulated by it (see e.g. Bower, 1982). It is by no means clear that 'out of sight is out of mind', even at the age of four to five months.

Full-scale symbolic activity emerges towards the end of the sensori-motor period, and Gardner sees the preschooler's acquisition and use of words, drawings, make-believe, and other symbols as 'the major developmental event in the early years of childhood, one decisive for the evolution of the artistic process' (1973a, p. 129). Now Piaget would probably agree with the first part of this statement, but not the second. Gardner claims that by the age of seven, most children have achieved the essential characteristics of the audience member, artist and performer, so they can be considered to be more or less fully-fledged 'participants in the artistic process'. The implication is that Piaget's concrete operations and formal operations are not necessary for such participation; indeed, Gardner goes so far as to claim that 'The groupings, groups and operations described by Piaget do not seem essential for mastery or understanding of human language, music, or plastic arts' (1973a, p. 45). Gardner thinks that artistic developments can be explained *within* symbol systems, that is, without the need for any mastery of the underlying logical operations.

Gardner's own account of aesthetic development has just two broad stages. He proposes a 'presymbolic period' of sensori-motor development in the first year of life, during which the three systems unfold and differentiate, followed by a 'period of symbol use' from ages two to seven. Within the second period, the arbitrary elements of symbol systems become linked to specific artistic activities, that is, to the 'code' of the culture. These activities are explored and amplified, and the use of symbols becomes increasingly 'socialised' towards conventional notational systems. Towards the end of this period, children's work acquires 'a sense of competence, balance and integration' within symbol systems, and it is in this sense that they are regarded as 'participants in the artistic process'. The 'later artistic development' that occurs from the age of eight onwards involves further progressions in skill development, 'cognitive sophistication', critical acumen, self-consciousness, etc. (as well as certain regressions); but these achievements are not seen as being *qualitatively* any more advanced than those of the 'period of symbol use'.

Gardner may be overstating his case in some respects – some important musical developments take place after the age of seven, for example, as we shall see in Chapter 4 – but his view is a provocative and plausible one. There is nothing new in the emphasis on symbolic development, but the suggestion that artistic developments are medium- or symbol-system-specific, rather than showing general stage-related features, ought to be susceptible to empirical investigation. It may be difficult to carry out a 'crucial test' of this aspect of the theory (a) because the evidence in favour of it would essentially be negative, for example, that performance on one task was unrelated to that on another, and (b) because the empirical outcome would presumably be dependent on the particular symbol systems chosen for investigation. Winner *et al.* (1985) have nevertheless attempted to carry out such an investigation, which I shall discuss in the final part of this chapter.

Winner *et al.*'s study forms part of the work of Gardner's *Project Zero* group, which is based at Harvard University. The title was coined to convey how little was known about artistic development when the research programme started some fifteen or so years ago, and Gardner and his colleagues can take a good deal of credit for the substantial advances that have been made since then. Following the theoretical position outlined above, the Project Zero researchers have carried out experimental, cross-sectional and longitudinal studies of developmental changes within a variety of art forms; and a central organising theme of this work has been the development of sensitivity to artistic styles. Empirical studies have been carried out on style sensitivity in visual art (e.g. Gardner, 1970) and literature (e.g. Gardner and Gardner, 1971) as well as in music (e.g. Gardner, 1973b). Research has been carried out on topics including children's use of and preference for metaphors (e.g. Winner, Rosenstiel and Gardner, 1976); the development of song (e.g. Davidson, McKernon and Gardner, 1981 – see Chapter 3); numerical symbolism and children's counting (e.g. Shotwell, 1979); and the ability to distinguish fantasy from reality (Morison and Gardner, 1978). This list is by no means comprehensive, and I would refer the reader to Winner's (1982) *Invented worlds* for a coherent account of the psychology of the arts which is grounded in the Project Zero approach. The research on music, and also some of that on visual art, will be discussed in more detail in the last two parts of this chapter.

The development of aesthetic appreciation

Piaget's influence is easy to detect in studies of the development of aesthetic appreciation: age trends are frequently explained in terms of cognitive-developmental stages. Gardner, Winner and Kircher (1975), for example, carried out a broad-ranging investigation of children's conceptions of various artistic topics and media. They tape-recorded open-ended interviews with 121 4–16-year-olds in which each child was shown a picture, or read a poem, or played some music. The interview was pre-planned to include questions in seven areas, which concerned the source, production, medium, style, formal properties and evaluation of art, and its relation to the outside world. Using a Piaget-type 'clinical method', the interviewers probed and elaborated upon the child's initial response to what she had seen or heard.

Analysis of transcriptions of the tape recordings revealed that the children could be divided into three broad groups on the basis of their responses. Those of the youngest children (4–7-year-olds) were mostly *immature*: they were concrete and mechanistic in that they reflected a primary concern with the mechanics of producing a work, and the techniques involved in doing so. The responses of the older children (14–16-year-olds), in contrast, were mostly *mature*: they revealed an understanding of the complexities and difficulties of producing art works, of the stylistic differences between them, and of the properties of different artistic media. The children in the middle age group (8–12-year-olds) gave *transitional* responses which exhibited some of the features of immature and mature views, as well as some distinct features. Predominant amongst these was the conception of art as *striving towards realism*; children judged this by reference to external standards rather than to their own viewpoints. Transitional responses also showed a concern with standards of fairness, as distinct from the authoritarian rule-based orientation of immature responses; and they were often very literal, failing to move beyond the most concrete interpretation of the question.

This general developmental pattern surfaces over and over again in different parts of the Project Zero research on style sensitivity, as we shall see in the next section; Gardner (1972a) adopts an explicitly cognitive-developmental explanation of it, drawing on the work of Bruner and the Gibsons as well as on Piaget's theory. Another account of developmental stages in aesthetic appreciation which runs along very similar lines is that of Parsons (Parsons, 1976; Parsons, Johnston and Durham, 1978). Parsons draws most specifically on Kohlberg's theory of moral development, which itself derives from Piaget's work. Parsons describes four developmental stages and, like Kohlberg, examines different 'topics' within each stage. Parsons' work is largely based on studies of reactions to pictures; since the topics (such as 'semblance', 'subject matter', 'feelings' and 'colour') are specific to visual art, I will not discuss them in detail here.

Parsons suggests that in the first stage, between the ages of four to eight or so, the aesthetic qualities of an object are defined in terms of the child's own experience. One child's strong preference for a scene of farm life, for example, arose because the picture reminded him of his cowboy hat; Parsons suggests that children confuse what is perceptually present with what is not. Another feature of this stage is that taste determines judgement: 'what is good' is 'what I like'. I have investigated the relationship between these two features of aesthetic attitudes by comparing adults' 'quality' and 'liking' ratings of musical excerpts (Hargreaves, Messerschmidt and Rubert, 1980). The two are positively correlated in adults, as one would intuitively predict, but they are not conceptually equivalent: I found that musically untrained subjects were more likely to separate or 'fragment' the affective and evaluative components of their attitudes than were trained subjects.

Now Parsons is effectively saying that first stage children show no such fragmentation; and he also proposes that their aesthetic perception is *egocentric* in that they cannot distinguish others' views from their own. Rosenstiel, Morison, Silverman and Gardner (1978) provided some empirical support for this view by demonstrating that there was little variation amongst 6-year-olds' selections of pictures (art works by the masters) that they liked best, that were painted best, or that others would like best. Hart and Goldin-Meadow (1984), on the other hand, found that when asked to predict the likes and dislikes of familiar others (parents, siblings, and friends) for familiar art works (children's drawings of spaceships), children as young as three made different choices from the drawings they chose for themselves, and were able to provide consistent reasons for these differing choices. Hart and Goldin-Meadow suggest that the divergence from Rosenstiel *et al.*'s results was probably because the subjects in the earlier study may have assumed that the 'other' view to be predicted was that of the adult. Their apparently egocentric judgements may in fact have been non-egocentric judgements based on the idea that older individuals would be likely to choose the same drawings as themselves. The extent to which pre-operational children *spontaneously* behave as 'nonegocentric art critics' remains an interesting area for further exploration.

In Parsons' second stage, from eight years to adolescence or so, the child relies on sets of rules and conventions. Properties of art works are not dependent on one's own point of view, but are judged according to public rules; and their appeal depends on whether or not they adhere to these rules. Rules of *realism* are central; the degree of realism of a picture is the main criterion of its appeal so that abstract works are rejected, and photographs are judged superior to paintings. Parsons also proposes rules of *form*, pertaining to balance, contrast, grouping, etc., and rules of *subject-matter*. Certain types of subject-matter are considered to be appropriate for art works, whilst others (e.g. the unpleasant, the painful, or the tragic) are not. The parallel with Kohlberg's account of moral reasoning at this age is very clear; what is right is determined by what is allowed.

In the third stage, beginning at the onset of adolescence, the child acknowledges that a wide variety of possibly conflicting sets of rules might be used to evaluate art. Any subject-matter is considered to be acceptable; evaluations begin to be based on formal criteria, including style and composition, and it is acknowledged that different styles might employ different rule-systems. Although the emphasis on formal properties increases, judgements are still essentially *relative*: they are made by reference to the artist's intentions, or to the observer's personal opinion. It is only in the fourth stage that aesthetic qualities are thought of as publicly accessible qualities of the object itself, as completely independent of the characteristics of the observer.

Gardner, Winner and Kircher (1975) conclude that 'For the most part, findings about the arts seem to mirror the trends uncovered by Piaget, Kohlberg, and others in the cognitive-developmental tradition' (p. 74). There seems to be a problem here; how does this 'mirroring' relate to that part of Gardner's theory which goes against Piaget, in particular the suggestion that concrete operational developments are unnecessary for artistic participation? Should Gardner not predict that there are *no* clearly identifiable developments after the age of seven or so? Parsons (1976) also argues against the wholesale importation of Piagetian stages into the aesthetic realm on the grounds that this does not give sufficient acknowledgement to the autonomy and uniqueness of aesthetic experience.

I think that the answer to this apparent contradiction lies in the distinction between competence and performance, which seems to recur in discussions of the validity of stage models. Gardner's theory predicts that children should be capable of mature artistic reasoning by the age of seven, and he may be right; but the fact is that in most everyday situations they do not spontaneously display this ability. This is precisely the same point that I made about children's ability to make logical inferences, and their everyday tendency not to do so, earlier in the chapter.

Children's sensitivity to artistic styles

The definition of artistic style is part of the province of art historians and philosophers. It is a problem that has engaged their attention for many years; the connoisseur's perception of a given artist's style is extremely complex and sophisticated. It seems to be impossible to formulate general rules about the features of art works that determine style because these features can be specific to the artist, as well as to the artistic medium. In this section I shall look at some research on style sensitivity in the visual arts, since this is the medium in which most work has been carried out, before considering the question of musical style.

For most practical purposes the empirical psychologist needs an operational definition of style; the most common approach has been to treat style sensitivity as a form of concept formation. Gardner (1972a), for example, operationalises style sensitivity as the ability to group together works produced by one artist. This definition exists at a high, abstract level in that there is no specification of the defining attributes of the works themselves. It would be possible to work at an even higher level of generality; presumably many observers would be able to detect the family resemblance between the paintings of Renoir and Monet, for example, even though they might never have heard of the two artists, or of 'the impressionists', by name.

Several studies have investigated the development of stylistic sensitivity to paintings. Machotka (1966), in one fairly typical and often-quoted study, showed colour reproductions of paintings by artists including Renoir, Gauguin, Van Gogh, Toulouse-Lautrec and Picasso to 120 boys whose ages ranged from six to eighteen. He presented the pictures in sets of three, and asked the subjects to indicate which they liked best, which they liked least, and to give reasons for these choices. The responses were divided into twelve categories according to what aspect of the pictures formed the basis of the judgement (e.g. *content*; *realistic representation*; *clarity*; *harmony*). Machotka found that the younger boys (4–7-year-olds) tended to focus on colour and subject-matter; that the 17–11-year-olds concentrated on whether or not the pictures were realistic representations of their subject-matter; and that the appreciation of stylistic factors only gradually emerged in adolescence. Machotka's interpretation of these results was explicitly in terms of Piagetian stages, and it is consistent with Parsons' (1976) account, which was described in the previous section. The same pattern of results has emerged in other empirical investigations (e.g. Gardner, 1970).

Although it seems from this evidence that pre-adolescents are unlikely to classify pictures according to style, some studies have shown that they can be trained to do so. Gardner (1972b) reinforced subjects for sorting paintings by style rather than subject-matter in seven half-hour training sessions over the course of seven weeks; he found that all of his 10-year-old subjects, and most of his 7-year-olds, developed a high level of style sensitivity. Silverman *et al.* (1976) confirmed this result; they also found that a substantial proportion of their 10-year-old subjects consistently applied a multidimensional analysis after training, and that intensive exposure to a small set of distinctive styles was more effective in promoting this than was more superficial exposure to a wider range of styles. The results of these studies support the conclusion I made earlier about the apparent contradiction between the theories of Piaget and Gardner. Pre-adolescent children can reliably be trained to make fine stylistic discriminations amongst paintings, but under normal circumstances they tend not to do so.

There is no clear musical equivalent to the distinction between content and style in visual art, and this raises the question of how the Parsons-type approach might be applied to music. The problems of defining musical style are also formidable: a recent debate betwen Brody (1985) and Serafine (1983, 1985) leads to the conclusion that it is all too easy to treat any principle by which musical works can be grouped as one of 'style'. It is useful to make the distinction between *idiom* and style in music. As with visual art, style can exist at different levels of abstraction, referring to historical periods or to individual composers (e.g. 'the style of Mozart', 'the classical style', etc.); but idioms such as tonality cut across these. The tonal idiom is present in the works of Beethoven as well as in those of the Beatles, but the two are stylistically quite different.

Here again, the empirical psychologist needs to work out an operational definition; and Gardner (1973b) carried out a pioneering piece of research in which musical style sensitivity was defined as the ability to judge whether two fragments of music came from the same composition. He played pairs of musical fragments to 10 boys and 10 girls in each of 5 different age groups between six and nineteen: in half the pairs the fragments were drawn from the same work, and in the other half they were not. The pairs were matched for the presence or absence of a musical 'figure' against the stylistic 'ground', that is, a solo voice against an instrumental background. The children were asked to say whether or not the two fragments in each pair came from the same original piece. Gardner used classical pieces from four different periods, namely Baroque (e.g. Vivalidi, Scarlatti); Classical (e.g. Stamitz, Mozart); Romantic (e.g. Bruckner, Meyerbeer); and Modern (e.g. Bartok, Berg).

Age had a significant effect upon the accuracy with which pairs could be correctly identified as 'same'; the 6- and 8-year-olds made significantly more errors than the 11- , 14- and 18–19-year-olds, and there were no significant differences within these two broad age groups. Subjects in the two oldest groups also had a tendency to perform relatively better on those 'different' pairs whose members came from widely divergent eras. The most striking aspect of the results, however, was the general level of success on the task, even in the two youngest age groups. The 6-year-olds adopted a stringent criterion for 'same' judgements: they tended to rate most pairs as 'different', and to be unable to provide reasons for their judgements. The 8-year-olds were able to respond 'same' even when the two members of the pair did not sound continuous, and they tended to use extra-musical metaphors (e.g. 'peppy', 'churchy', 'like a horse race') to explain their judgements. The 11-year-olds obtained the highest absolute scores on the task; they were able to base their judgements on several different variables, frequently using instrumentation, rhythmic aspects, and texture. The tendency to speak in terms of musical 'schools' (e.g. 'baroque', 'jazz') only developed above this age, that is, in the 14–19-year-olds. Gardner suggests that these results illustrate a general developmental shift from responses to music in terms of subjective, personal experience towards those which are more analytic and objective. This fits in with the finding that musically untrained adults are more likely to respond in the former manner than those who have some training, as we shall see in Chapter 5.

Gardner restricted his study to the repertoire of classical music written between 1680 and 1960 so as to provide a reasonable degree of experimental control over the many dimensions which could have affected the results; but the corresponding disadvantage of this restriction is the lack of generality of the conclusions. It could well be the case that children's style sensitivity is greater for music that is more familiar to them, and better liked by them. Castell (1982) investigated this possibility by repeating Gardner's experiment with jazz and rock music (the Modern Jazz Quartet, Focus, and Pink Floyd) alongside classical pieces (Mozart, Munrow and Ravel), and also tried to make the task as lifelike as possible by embedding it in a plausible story. She constructed 'same' and 'different' pairs in the same way as Gardner, and asked groups of 8–9- and 10–11-year-olds to imagine finding a room full of musicians and musical instruments. 'You listen to what they're playing for a moment, like this (*first fragment played*) and then you go away for a while – when you come back they're still playing, like this (*second fragment played*). What I'd like you to tell me is whether or not the musicians are still playing part of the same piece.'

As predicted, all the children were more accurate when judging 'popular' than 'classical' pairs; and a surprising result was that the 8–9-year-olds were significantly better at the task than the 10–11-year-olds. This difference arose from the younger children's better performance on the 'popular' pairs: there was no difference for the 'classical' pairs. Now this is quite different from Gardner's finding that the 11-year-olds in his study were the most accurate. The divergence almost certainly derives from differences between the musical stimuli employed in the two studies. It does not arise from the *over*sensitivity to stylistic differences of the 10–11-year-olds in Castell's study, as she initially suspected, because they made more errors on the 'different' as well as on the 'same' pairs. Castell speculates that 'by the age of 11 children have formed very definite likes and dislikes in the field of current pop music, and cease to distinguish very much between pieces and styles that fall outside their chosen favourites . . . The 8–9-year-olds, on the other hand, were perhaps more "open-eared" as there might be less social pressure on them to like certain types of music and dismiss others' (p. 25). It is clear that taste has a strong effect on judgement here, and this has more general implications. When preferred styles are employed in experiments alongside the 'high art' works that are the most common stimuli in psychological research on the arts, the results may be quite radically different.

Let us conclude this section by looking at an ambitious study by the Project Zero group which differs from most of the others discussed so far in that aesthetic responses to three different art forms were investigated within the same experimental design. Winner *et al.* (1986) set out to discover whether the perceptual skills used in the arts generalise across art forms and aesthetic properties, or whether they are art-form- and/or property-specific. They devised tasks of sensitivity to three aesthetic properties (repleteness, expression, and composition) in each of three art forms (drawing, music, and literature), and administered these to 90 children at each of three age levels (seven, nine and twelve years). The tasks can be illustrated by a description of the three musical ones. The *repleteness* task requires the subject to select the correct (i.e. unaltered) one of two continuations of a target melody, when the other is varied in articulation, timbre, or dynamics. The *expression* task involves matching one of two fragments of musical pieces to the mood of a target piece, which can be 'happy', 'sad', 'excited', or 'calm'. The *composition* task requires the subject to select the correct one of two endings for an incomplete target melody, when the other is not compositionally balanced with it.

Winner *et al.* found a general improvement across all the tasks between the ages of seven and nine. There was no evidence for any generalisation of the ability to perceive either the same aesthetic property across art forms, or different aesthetic properties within the same art form. They interpret these results as showing that aesthetic perception develops 'property by property, and domain by domain'. This seems to support Gardner's position that aesthetic developments occur within symbol systems, so there is no need to postulate any general underlying cognitive processes like those of Piaget.

As I suggested earlier, the problem with this interpretation is that it is essentially based on negative evidence. There are various other possible reasons why no relationships were found between the children's performances on the different tasks in this study. It could be that the properties of repleteness, expression, and composition have quite different functions and meanings in the three art forms, such that their operationalisations in the experimental tasks were not comparable. It could be that the tasks were invalid measures of these properties; although Winner *et al.* were aware of this potential problem, and took care to calibrate their tasks against adult performances, there is no guarantee that the tasks were measuring what they were supposed to. Given the scale and diversity of the study, it would in a sense have been surprising if any generalities *had* emerged. These complaints aside, Winner *et al.* have performed a valuable and difficult service in collecting data; until others come up with evidence to the contrary, we must accept the conclusion that 'aesthetic perception appears to emerge as not one skill but many'.

3

Musical development in the preschooler

In Chapters 3 and 4 we deal with the foundations of the developmental psychology of music: the details of how children's perception and production of music proceeds with age. I shall approach this in terms of the different component skills involved in rhythm, pitch, melody, harmony, and so on. Research in these areas is patchy and rather piecemeal; some topics have been investigated in much more detail than others. In a sense, much of this work has been fairly atheoretical; the emphasis has been on the collection of normative data about musical development rather than on any consistent explanation of it. Having said that, however, there are some definite signs that cognitive psychology is beginning to formulate a consistent theoretical approach. Dowling's (1982) review 'Melodic information processing and its development', for example, incorporates a coherent account of how the cognitive structures and strategies underlying children's production and perception of melodies change with age. Dowling shows how a hierarchy of melodic features – pitch, contour, tonality, and interval size – appear in children's processing in a predictable developmental sequence, and suggests that this same hierarchy can be observed in adults. Dowling's approach is very welcome in that it represents a theoretical integration of some of the nebulous empirical findings which abound in this field, and I shall return to it later.

Shuter-Dyson and Gabriel (1981) provide a very useful summary of the major milestones in musical development. This appears as Table 3.1, which will serve as a useful reference point for the findings to be described in the next two chapters. I shall concentrate on the developments that occur up to the age of eleven or so: it would be impossible to cover these adequately in a single chapter, and so I have decided (rather arbitrarily and uncomfortably) to divide it into two on a chronological basis. Thus, Chapter 3 deals with musical development in infants and preschool children, and Chapter 4 traces

Table 3.1 *Milestones of musical development*

Ages	
0–1	Reacts to sounds.
1–2	Spontaneous music making.
2–3	Begins to reproduce phrases of songs heard.
3–4	Conceives general plan of a melody; absolute pitch may develop if learns an instrument.
4–5	Can discriminate register of pitches; can tap back simple rhythms.
5–6	Understands louder/softer; can discriminate 'same' from 'different' in easy tonal or rhythm patterns.
6–7	Improved singing in tune; tonal music perceived better than atonal.
7–8	Appreciates consonance vs. dissonance.
8–9	Rhythmic performance tasks improved.
9–10	Rhythmic perception improves; melodic memory improves; two-part melodies perceived; sense of cadence.
10–11	Harmonic sense becoming established. Some appreciation for finer points of music.
12–17	Increase in appreciation, cognitively and in emotional response.

Reproduced from Shuter-Dyson and Gabriel (1981) by permission of Methuen and Co.

developments after the age of five or so. We start by looking at the development of responses to non-musical and musical sounds from early infancy through the rest of the preschool period. The central part of this chapter is devoted to some recent and rapidly advancing cognitive psychological research on the development of song. Finally, we trace the development of rhythmic skills, which are amongst the first to emerge in the infant's response to music.

Early responses to sound and music

Responses to non-musical sounds
Many parents of newborn infants have an urgent practical interest in finding out what kinds of sounds will quieten crying. They form an eager, sleepless market for tape cassettes of swooshing, seaside noises of wind and water, and of everyday domestic clatter such as motors, washing-machines and vacuum-cleaners, which are advertised as sending babies off to sleep. Psychologists, audiologists, and others have made various suggestions as to what the essential characteristics of sounds with these properties might be. Studies of very young babies (up to one week of age) suggest that any sound is more calming than no sound at all (e.g. Brackbill, Adams, Crowell and Gray, 1966; Bench, 1969); and researchers seem to agree that most newborns can discriminate between sounds on the basis of numerous acoustic parameters, particularly *intensity* and *frequency* (cf. Eisenberg, 1976).

Bridger (1961), for example, played tones of set frequencies to 50 babies up to five days old. The tones typically produced physical movement and changes in heart rate; Bridger played them until the babies habituated, that is, until the tones ceased to evoke any response. At this point, tones of different frequency were sounded, such that any renewal of the responses must have indicated that the babies could discriminate between different frequencies. Using this technique, Bridger found that most babies could indeed make fairly fine discriminations between different frequencies. Birns *et al.* (1965) found that low frequency tones had a greater calming effect on crying than did tones of higher frequencies, and Eisenberg (1976) found that matched pairs of ascending and descending tonal sequences had a distinct arousing effect. The precise reasons for these effects are unclear, though the various hypotheses put forward include differential masking of some frequencies by the baby's own crying, and the tactile effects of some auditory sensations.

Another popular suggestion is that the *rhythmicity* of the sounds heard by infants may have an important bearing on the responses evoked. In particular, a powerful influence may be exerted by the mother's heartbeat, which is a predominant feature of the prenatal environment. It has often been suggested by laymen and musicians, as well as by some psychologists, that the putative 'primeval appeal' of some pop music may derive from its prominent rhythmic pulse, something like that of a human heartbeat. This is at its clearest in the dominant bass drum figures heard in a good deal of modern 'disco' music. Unfortunately, the evidence for the first part of this intuitively appealing hypothesis is equivocal. Brackbill *et al.* (1966) found that heartbeats were no more calming than were the sounds of a metronome and of a lullaby, for example, whereas Salk (1962) found that they were. Any investigation of infant behaviour at this age has to allow for considerable margins of error in the reliability of response measures, and in situational and other artefacts, as well as for the wide range of individual differences that is typically found. It seems very likely that such 'noise', or error variance, can account for the conflicting results.

By 11–12 weeks of age, babies can clearly distinguish the human voice from other sources of sound, and they seem to prefer it. In particular, the mother's voice is preferred to others by the age of 14 weeks or so. This ties in with other findings in the fields of attachment and parent–child interaction (see e.g. Schaffer, 1971; Richards, 1974). Studies of crying, smiling, direction of gaze and so on suggest that infants' initial, superficial attachment to any person gradually declines between the second and the seventh months, and is replaced by a sharply defined attachment to the mother. Fear of strangers also develops at around this time. The response to sounds thus becomes increasingly co-ordinated with other aspects of early social development.

Responses to musical sounds

Moog (1976) carried out a large-scale cross-sectional investigation of 'the musical experience of the preschool child' which is one of the few to attempt a systematic developmental description. Moog played six types of musical material to 50 children at each of ten different age levels between six months and five and a half years, which involved approximately 8,000 'tests' in all. The six types of material ('test series') were three well-known children's songs; three combinations of words and rhythm (words spoken rhythmically, words spoken with a changed rhythm, and 'nonsense-word rhythms'); 'pure' rhythms (played on percussion instruments); instrumental music (including Bruckner, a pop song and an original twelve-tone melody); 'cacophonies', such as string quartet recordings with various deliberate distortions; and non-musical sounds such as those made by a vacuum-cleaner, and by road traffic.

Moog's methodology was unstructured and open-ended rather than experimental–manipulative; he played tapes of the material described above to his subjects, and 'observed their responses'. It is difficult to ascertain exactly what observations and recordings were made by reading Moog's account, though the data largely consist of frequency counts of vocal and behavioural responses. Moog explicitly bases his research on the approach of genetic psychology (cf. Bühler, 1930; Werner, in Chapter 1). His book contains what is essentially a normative description of early musical development as it emerged from his own empirical results. We must be cautious about its status as a general developmental description, since it is essentially subjective and culture-bound: but it is nevertheless based on a much larger subject-sample than any comparable investigation. Moog also obtained some supplementary data from approximately 1,000 parents, and recorded examples of the subjects' own singing.

The results suggest that somewhere between three and six months, babies start to respond actively to music rather than to 'receive' it passively. They begin to turn towards the source of the sound, and to show manifest pleasure and 'astonishment'. Soon after this, music consistently produces bodily movements – often rhythmic swaying, or bouncing. At this early stage it seems unlikely that such movements are necessarily produced by more rhythmic types of music. The infant probably responds to the 'pure sound', and it is only at around the end of the first year that rhythmic aspects of music seem to have a distinct effect.

The next clear development in the first year of life is vocalisation to music; Moog distinguishes between musical and non-musical babbling. Non-musical babbling appears first, and is seen as the precursor of speech. It does not seem initially to relate to anything in the child's environment, and then only gradually becomes attached to specific people and things. Musical babbling, on the other hand, occurs as a specific response to music heard by the child. 'Babbling songs' consist of sounds of varied pitch, produced either on one vowel or on very few syllables; three such songs, produced at the age of eight months, are shown in Figure 3.1. Moog suggests that these early songs bear no resemblance to any other music heard by the child. They are not clearly organised according to any diatonic system; they seem to be

Fig. 3.1 Three 'babbling songs' by 8-month-olds (reproduced from Moog (1976) by permission of the author)

'rhythmically amorphous'; and the pauses in them occur according to the need to breathe, rather than according to any apparent rhythmic organisation.

Figure 3.2 shows a babbling song produced by my own elder son at the age of twelve months, that is, a few months later than the examples above. Whilst it has the same essential features, it also shows the beginnings of some later aspects of musical organisation. The pitch glissandi and downwards melodic lines described by Moog are clearly present, but the middle section also contains a discernible four-note figure, which is varied in repetition. Moog's

Fig. 3.2 *'Babbling song' by a 12-month-old*

illustration of babbling songs by children aged one to two (1976, p. 76) contains similar evidence of repeated figures. Psychologists must be very careful about their use of conventional tonal notation in transcriptions such as these. An ambiguous or indeterminate vocalisation could quite easily acquire spurious musical significance in the process of transcription itself. Moog went some way towards tackling this problem by devising a quarter-tone-based system, but the potential problem of assimilation to adult conventions is still present.

In the second year, Moog found a marked increase in the amount of active response to the test pieces. The number of different types of physical movement increases dramatically, including seesawing with one foot, nodding the head, raising and lowering the heels, moving the knees backwards and forwards, and so on. Children also show clear attempts to carry out 'dance movements' with other people, and there are some early signs of co-ordination between music and movement at about eighteen months or so: they begin to match their own rhythmic movements with those present in the music. This co-ordination can first be sustained only for limited periods of time, but these periods get longer as the child gets older. Moog reports that he could find no significant increase in this co-ordination between the third and fourth years. What does develop during this period, however, is the incorporation of music and singing into imaginative play. Piaget (1951) has pointed out that symbolic and make-believe play represent the essence of the preschool period; and music, particularly singing and round games, forms an important part of this.

Physical responses to music seem to decline during the later preschool period, Moog found that 3-, 4-, and 5-year-olds were increasingly likely to sit and listen attentively to music, rather than to make spontaneous movements in response to it. Although the *number* of movements decreases with age, their *variety* actually increases, as does the co-ordination between different movements into recognisable dance steps. It appears, in general, that children increasingly *internalise* their response to music, and employ it in the broader contexts of activities such as imaginative play, and forming social relationships (e.g. in dancing with others). Moog's account, though essentially descriptive rather than explanatory, provides a rich source of evidence illustrating this.

Whereas Moog was mainly concerned with a global description of the broad features of musical experience, some experimental studies have attempted to analyse how the component skills develop with age; the emphasis has been upon the perception of short, single-note melodies. Chang and Trehub (1977a) played six-note atonal melodies to 5-month-old babies, at the rate of 2.5 notes per second, 30 times in all. All the babies whose heart rates showed initial deceleration (i.e. a 'startle' response), followed by habituation to the melody (about one-half of the total) were then played either an exact transposition of the original melody (up or down a minor third) or a new arrangement of the transposition so that the initial contour was destroyed. Chang and Trehub found that the initial 'startle' response reappeared to the melody with the altered contour, but not to the transposition. This seems to indicate that babies of this age can recognise changes in melodic contour; and that overall changes in pitch level are not as salient. This conclusion should be drawn cautiously, since over half of the initial pool of subjects were excluded from the final sample because they failed to meet Chang and Trehub's habituation criterion. In a second study, Chang and Trehub (1977b) found that changes in the rhythmic pattern of the melody had the same effect as changes of melodic contour.

Subsequent research (Trehub, Bull and Thorpe, 1984) has looked in more detail at the precise kinds of melodic transformation that infants can recognise, including key transposition; altering of intervals with contour preserved; altering of the octaves from which individual notes were drawn with contour preserved; and octave changes with accompanying contour changes. These researchers conclude that 'infants treat new melodies or tone sequences as *familiar* if these sequences have the same melodic contour and frequency range as a previously heard sequence, and as *novel* if either the contour or range differs' (p. 829). Now this conclusion is very important from a developmental point of view. The idea that infants use a 'global processing strategy', based on melodic contour, precisely parallels that used by adults in processing atonal or unfamiliar melodies (see Dowling, 1982). It can also explain some of the findings which arise in research on melodic conservation, as we saw in Chapter 2. As children get older, they gradually abandon their use of fairly gross, 'global' processing strategies, and move towards the use of more subtle features such as tonality and interval size. This line of argument will be pursued in the next section, since the same features underlie early songs.

The development of song

Children's singing has probably received more attention than any other topic in the whole field of musical development. There are some well-known descriptive studies in the literature, particularly those of Werner (1961); those carried out by Moorhead and her associates at the Pillsbury Foundation School, California (e.g. Moorhead and Pond, 1978; Pond, Shelley and Wilson,

1978); and those of Moog (1976), which have already been discussed. Werner's research, which was touched on in Chapter 1, described the musical aspects of children's spontaneous melodies. Werner investigated aspects like the direction of melodic movement (ascending or descending), the role of repetition in overall forms or melodic 'gestalts', the length, range, and endings of melodies; and he proposed a theory of discrete developmental stages. The Pillsbury Foundation School was specifically set up in order to study the spontaneous expression and development of music. It was specially equipped with a wide variety of instruments (e.g. oriental, percussion, and Orff instruments), and the curriculum was designed to provide the maximum opportunity for children to develop their music-making in a spontaneous, unconstrained environment. This music was recorded systematically; and early songs play an important part of Moorhead and Pond's account of it.

More recently, there have been some detailed studies of the development of song which attempt to explain the underlying cognitive processes rather than merely to describe the surface features. Dowling's (1982, 1984) research, for example, forms an integral part of his broader account of the development of melodic information processing. His empirical description of the gradual move in early songs from a predominance of gross features such as melodic contour towards an incorporation of more precise features such as tonality and intervals runs parallel to his account of children's perception of the features of given melodies. As we shall see, many of the theoretical considerations which apply to spontaneously produced melodies can also account for developments in children's attempts to reproduce standard melodies. Dowling's research has a great deal in common, both theoretically and methodologically, with that of the Boston Project Zero group (e.g. McKernon, 1979; Davidson, McKernon and Gardner, 1981; Davidson, 1983).

Both of these research programmes take their methodological lead from research on children's language development, particularly that stimulated by the work of Roger Brown (e.g. Brown, 1973). Their approach is to record as much of the spontaneous output of a small number of children as is possible, comprehensively and naturalistically, over a long period of time. This broad-based approach is regarded as better suited to the rich complexity of unfolding song than a more focussed, nomothetic analysis might be. The most fundamental similarity between the two research programmes is their emphasis on describing the cognitive bases of early songs.

I shall draw quite heavily on these two programmes in my description of the development of song; and I shall also use some illustrative examples taken from unsystematic tape recordings of my own two sons, Jonathan and Thomas, who were born in December 1978 and July 1980 respectively. The rest of this section is in three parts. First, we trace the origins of song in the spontaneous vocalisations of young infants, and consider the emergence and mastery of what Davidson *et al.* (1981) term the basic *outlines* of song, up to the age of three or so. Next we shall look at the characteristics of what they call

na   na   na   na   na

Fig. 3.3 The hypothesised 'universal chant'

'first draft' songs, up to the age of about five and a half. Finally, we will consider some current theoretical accounts of the cognitive *schemes* that underlie the development of song.

Infant vocalisations and early outlines of song

One well-known observation about very early song is that there may exist a 'universal chant' which is produced by children of all cultures. This is characterised by the presence of the descending minor third, and also frequently includes the fourth (see Fig. 3.3). Such chants were observed by Moorhead and Pond (1978) and Gesell and Ilg (1943), and a common suggestion has been that they may be used by children when teasing others.

The idea of early artistic 'universals' across cultures is a provocative one. Leonard Bernstein (1976), in his search for a variety of such structural universals in music, proposed that the child's employment of *mi, sol,* and *la* in these chants is related to their position in the harmonic series, that is, as the fourth, second, and fifth overtones respectively in any given scale. This theory is intuitively appealing, but is as yet supported only by anecdotal evidence. Neither Moog (1976) nor Dowling (1984) found any evidence for the universality of the descending minor third in their data, and the cross-cultural evidence for it also seems to be weak (cf. Blacking, 1967). Dowling's data even prompt him to propose tentatively that the perfect fifth might occur more universally, but this remains an open empirical question.

Moorhead and Pond's data led them to make the distinction between *chants* and *songs*. Chants are evolved from speech; they are rhythmic, musically simple, repetitive, and very often associated with physical movement. They are essentially social, that is, produced more often in groups than by individuals; indeed Moorhead and Pond consider the chant to be the most primitive universal musical form, which primarily functions as an instinctive form of expression. Songs, on the other hand, are typically more complex and individual. Dowling's (1984) observations provide some recent confirmation of this distinction, although he found a relatively lower proportion of chants than that in Moorhead and Pond's data.

Observations of very young infants have shown that 'vocal play', the precursor of spontaneous song, begins at a very early age. Ostwald (1973) observed that babies explore the range of pitches accessible to their voices, and Revesz (1953) suggested that they attempt to imitate some of the pitches they hear. Kessen, Levine and Wendrich (1979) produced some sophisticated evidence for this. In their study, babies under six months old were trained to sing back pitches from the minor triad D-F-A after a few brief training

Fig. 3.4 *Spontaneous songs by 2-year-olds*

sessions. They were able to do this successfully two-thirds of the time, and many of their imitations were very nearly in tune. The authors also comment that the babies appeared to enjoy the task, and that they worked hard at it. In summary, it seems that infants of six months or so possess many of the prerequisites of music-making. They can vocalise, vary and imitate pitch, and detect changes in melodic contour.

These abilities are put to use in the construction of rudimentary songs by the age of twelve months or so. We saw this in Moog's (1976) description of 'musical babbling'; and the Boston Project Zero researchers have coined the term 'outline songs', which develop over the second and third years of life, to describe these early efforts. The idea is that children possess some conception of the basic form, or *frame*, of a song, without 'filling in' the details of precise pitch relationships, rhythm, and so on; these follow at a later stage. In this respect, outline songs are directly analogous to phenomena such as the 'tadpole man' in early drawings, which were discussed in Chapter 2. The 'tadpole man' reveals a clear 'outline' understanding of the human form: but the details within the outline, particularly the absence of a body, are not fully worked out.

The spontaneous songs of the 2-year-old tend to consist of brief phrases which are repeated over and over again. These phrases consist of notes with discrete pitches, and their melodic contours and rhythmic patterns remain more or less constant. The repetitions are likely to vary in pitch: the overall pitch level wanders, as do the interval sizes between the different notes. Figure 3.4 shows two very clear and basic examples of this typical pattern, which were produced by my two sons at the ages of 23 and 24 months respectively. The first (Fig. 3.4(a)), sung by the elder boy to the syllables 'gum-ba', consists of a two-same-note phrase that was repeated in a chromatically descending sequence. The second, sung by my younger son to the syllables 'lee-la', shows almost exactly the same pattern preceded by an ascending version of it. Dowling (1982, 1984) has also collected some examples of such early songs from recordings of a sample of twenty-one children, as well as of his own daughters. One 24-month-old sang the words 'Duck on my house', based on the contour of the 'E-I-E-I-O' phrase from 'Old Macdonald had a Farm', over a period of approximately two weeks. The melodic contour remained constant, and the pitch level and intervals between the notes were varied.

Fig. 3.5 *Spontaneous song by a 32-month-old (reproduced from Dowling (1982) by permission of Calla Dowling, W.J. Dowling, and Academic Press, Inc.)*

Figure 3.5 shows a rather more elaborate song that Dowling recorded by his own daughter at the age of 32 months: each note was sung to the syllable 'yeah'. It can be seen that this song incorporates repetitions of the same contour at different pitch levels. Figure 3.6 shows a spontaneous song by my elder son at the age of 42 months: similar contour repetitions can be seen here, as well as some early signs of harmonic organisation in the form of a major triad which recurs in the last few phrases. These observations illustrate how children exert increasing schematic control over their songs through repetition and variation; and how early songs form the basis for later ones. Dowling suggests that these processes are precisely parallel to those of syntax acquisition in language.

The research of the Boston Project Zero Group was based on a detailed longitudinal study of the songs of nine children between the ages of 1.6 and 6.6 (see Davidson *et al.*, 1981; Davidson, 1983). One aspect of the development of outline songs that emerges in clear detail from their data is that of the control of pitch and intervals: and this complements Dowling's account. From 12 to 18 months or so, children's songs are not based on discrete pitches: they are characterised by pitch glissandi that are produced within a single breath. (This does not imply that infants are *unable* to sing discrete pitches, of course: some evidence that they do possess this ability was mentioned earlier.) By the age of 19 months this ability, or competence, is matched by singing performance: children not only *can*, but also *do* typically begin to use discrete pitches in their songs, which appear as small intervals. Werner (1961) suggested that minor thirds are produced early on, and McKernon (1979) identified the early appearance of intervals even smaller than this. Of the intervals sung in the songs of McKernon's sample of 17–23-month-olds, 43 per cent were seconds, and the size of these intervals gradually increased with age. Major seconds, minor thirds, and unisons seem to be most common in the earliest songs, and minor seconds and major thirds are frequent by the age of two and a half, when fourths and fifths also begin to appear. Winner (1982) notes that, since the most common intervals in songs of all cultures are seconds and minor thirds (Nettl, 1956), there is a clear parallel with the songs of adults.

oh la la la lay _____ oh la _____ la la la

oh la _____ la la la oh la _____ la la la la la la la

Fig. 3.6 *Spontaneous song by a 42-month-old*

Although pitch is being organised in this way, songs at this stage tend to lack any consistent melodic or rhythmic organisation. Moorhead and Pond (1978) suggest that the melodies are not organised around any recognisable tonal centre; they remain atonal, with undulating rather than ascending or descending contours. They also suggest that rhythm, similarly, tends to be 'free and flexible', with no obvious consistent beat. Dowling (1984) disagrees with this, since many of the spontaneous songs in his own sample had a steady beat both within and between phrases. He further suggests that 'the adaptation of the speech rhythms of the words the child is singing to the beat structure of the song is the main source of rhythmic complexity in these songs' (p. 146). Only further empirical work will resolve disagreements such as this.

Towards the end of the second year, as we saw above, children begin to incorporate regular patterns into their songs. McKernon (1979) has demonstrated how one child gradually incorporated a regular rhythm into her singing of a standard song, 'ABC', between the ages of approximately 18 and 30 months (see Fig. 3.7, and also the description by Davidson *et al.* (1981)). At 19 months, the song's pitch range is narrow and the interval sizes are small: this resembles the early spontaneous songs that were described earlier. The words of the song are really all that define it at this stage, as they are assimilated to whatever melodic repertoire is already present. By the age of 23 months, we can see that some rhythmic organisation is present. The child recognises that the last note of A-B-C is longer than the first two, and that the L-M-N-O-P notes should be sung more quickly. By the age of 28 months, the rhythmic organisation is complete: the words are sung with the correct rhythm. After this, the correct contours and intervals quickly stabilise.

This is an interesting illustration of the way in which the child's singing gradually proceeds towards a song 'outline', or 'frame'. The process is precisely analogous to Piaget's account of the processes of assimilation and accommodation which were discussed in Chapter 2. The child *assimilates* elements of the environment, in this case rhythmic patterns presumably heard elsewhere, to existing musical schemes which we term 'song outlines' in this case. As a result of this assimilation the schemes themselves change: the child *accommodates* to them. Davidson *et al.* conclude that children 'seem to be developing a set of song-related expectations, a kind of "song frame", which structures their performance of standard tunes' (p. 305).

"ABC" at nineteen months

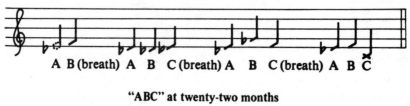

A B (breath) A B C (breath) A   B C (breath) A B C

"ABC" at twenty-two months

A B C A B C D H I J

"ABC" at twenty-three months

A B C A B C L M N O   P

"ABC" at twenty-eight months

A B C D E F G H I J Kee L M en-no   P

Fig. 3.7 Development of rhythmic organisation in early songs (reproduced from McKernon (1979) by permission of Jossey-Bass, Inc.)

The most interesting developmental question that arises from this view is how children's early song outlines gradually approximate towards 'correct' (i.e. cultural) melodic structures. One obvious clue lies in the degree of similarity, and interrelationship, between the child's versions of standard songs and their spontaneous songs. Davidson *et al.* note that those parts of the former that correspond most closely to the original model tend to appear simultaneously as parts of the child's spontaneous repertoire. They cite, as an illustration of this, the appearance of one child's spontaneous song based on the word 'Nanno' in her version of 'Ring around the rosy' (known in the U.K. as 'Ring-a-Ring-a-Roses'): this is shown in Figure 3.8. It shows the child's emerging ability to select melodic fragments from an increasingly large repertoire, and to match these with increasing accuracy to the components of standard models.

Spontaneous tune

Nan-no na Nan-no Nan-no na nan-no

Standard tune

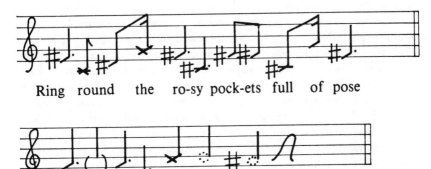

Ring   round   the   ro-sy pock-ets full   of   pose

ash-es   ash-es   every-body   fall   down!

Fig. 3.8 Interrelationships between spontaneous and standard songs (reproduced from McKernon (1979) by permission of Jossey-Bass, Inc.)

This matching and interchange between the elements of spontaneous and standard songs is very well illustrated by the occurrence of what Moog (1976) termed 'pot-pourri' songs. These are new songs made up of words, melodies and rhythms borrowed from others already in the child's repertoire; in a sense, they could be thought of as standard songs which are assimilated to the child's own spontaneous song schemes. Figure 3.9 shows a short song produced by my elder son at the age of 36 months; the resemblance of its two distinct halves to parts of 'Old Macdonald had a Farm' is obvious, and it is interesting that the second half (based on 'E-I-E-I-O') is pitched a tone lower than the first half.

Two months later the same son mixed phrases from 'Baa Baa Black Sheep' into his version of 'Goosey Goosey Gander' ('Goosey goosey gander / have you any wool?'), and also rearranged different phrases within the former nursery rhyme ('Baa baa black sheep / have you any wool? / one for the master and one for the dame / yes sir, yes sir, yes sir, yes sir'). At the age of 36 months his younger brother spontaneously sang an original set of words (probably inspired by a visit to see the Bayeux tapestry) to the tune of 'The Grand Old Duke of York' ('The children who was dead / who killed them in their eye / and then they were dead they couldn't get up / and they couldn't get up then

I   wan da on - ly   poo poo poo   pee pee   hee!

Fig. 3.9 Spontaneous song by a 36-month-old

they were down dead'). A year or so later, at the ages of 5.9 and 4.3 respectively, both boys tape-recorded a set of their own spontaneous 'pop songs' with original words (titles included 'Chew it', 'Dipping up and down again', 'Do you remember that cafe there', etc.). The songs, though original, were very clearly modelled on some common elements of pop music. Some of the phrases that recurred in them are shown in Figure 3.10: these contain typical dotted rhythms, syncopation, and stereotyped 'pop' lyrics.

These examples show various coalescences between standard and spontaneous songs; some could be thought of as 'failed', or inaccurate versions of the former, and others primarily as spontaneous songs which borrow heavily from the standard repertoire. According to the Boston group, the development of standard and spontaneous songs is roughly parallel at this stage, with a considerable proportion of common elements. With increasing age, standard songs tend to possess greater musical sophistication than do spontaneous ones (McKernon, 1979). The latter are thought to remain tonally disorganised even up to the age of four or so, and children tend not to repeat them or to try to teach them to others (Winner, 1982). Standard songs are seen as being much easier to memorise and repeat to others because they do possess some degree of tonal organisation.

Dowling (1984) disagrees with the view that standard songs exert a predominant influence on the development of the organisation of singing. He places much more emphasis on the integral role of spontaneous song patterns, citing instances of recurrences over time of distinctive tonal and rhythmic structures, even in the second year. His own evidence suggests that the child's memory for these spontaneous patterns tends to be poor, however; and he concurs with the view that 'pot-pourri' songs include those 'failed' versions of standard songs that are 'filtered through the child's own song-production system' (p. 150).

The mastery of the outline of a song, according to Davidson *et al.*, is fairly well developed by the age of three. In general terms, their suggestion is that the child by this stage is able to use her own internal schemes with sufficient flexibility and range in order to produce a recognisable representation of some entity in the outside world. They call this 'topological mapping', which represents the emergence of a 'second wave of symbolization' across all the artistic domains. It is represented in the development of outline drawings such as the 'tadpole man', as we saw in Chapter 2, and in the emergence of 'canonical stories' which might consistently contain an opening line, a middle section, and a close, as well as in the emergence of 'outline songs'. The symbolic mapping is described as topological because it captures the

Fig. 3.10 *Phrases from spontaneous 'pop songs' by 4–5-year-olds*

properties of outlines (enclosingness, proximity, relative size, and so on, in visual terms) rather than the precise details within these outlines. The incorporation of these details is correspondingly described as 'digital mapping', which I shall trace next in describing the development of 'first draft' songs.

Development of 'first draft' songs

By the age of five, children possess a wide repertoire of the 'standard' nursery songs of their culture, and they can perform recognition memory tasks better with these than they can with unfamiliar musical material (Dowling, 1982). A number of longitudinal studies have been carried out investigating the development of children's ability to accurately reproduce songs that are presented to them (e.g. Updegraff, Heileger and Learned, 1938; Moog, 1976; Petzold, 1966). There seems to be common agreement that words are learned first, followed by rhythm, contour, and intervals, in that order; and that there is a gradual improvement in performance with age which may level off in later childhood.

Serafine, Crowder and Repp (1984) have recently proposed an 'integration' hypothesis of memory for songs according to which melody and text are seen as integrated rather than as independent components of the song's representation in memory. Their undergraduate subjects were played excerpts from unfamiliar folk songs, followed by recognition and performance tests using five combinations of the same and different tunes and sets of words. The results supported the hypothesis: memory for and performance of exact songs heard in the presentation was better than for all other items. The authors were not primarily concerned with the developmental implications of their hypothesis in this study, and this aspect seems ripe for future exploration.

Davidson *et al.*'s use of the term 'first draft' song can best be understood in

Char - lie   o-ver the   o - cean,   Char - lie   o-ver the   sea,   Char-lie caught a black-bird, Might have been me!

Fig. 3.11 *The 'Charlie Song' (from Davidson, McKernon and Gardner (1981),* © *1981 by Music Educators National Conference. Reprinted by permission from* Documentary Report of the Ann Arbor Symposium)

the developmental perspective. By the age of five or so, children are clearly trying to 'fill in' the detail of the song outlines, or frames, of the previous stage; their attempts are very recognisable models of the songs of the culture. They are still far from completely accurate, however; and the term 'first draft' signifies this. The Boston researchers undertook a detailed observational study of development in this period by teaching a folk song, which they call the 'Charlie Song', to a group of five 4–5-year-olds over a period of a year: a comparison group of college music students also learnt it over a much shorter period. The song was played to the children on tape as well as sung to them by an instructor on various occasions during the course of the year. They were taught to 'echo' the different phrases on each occasion, and to play it on drums and xylophones. The 'Charlie Song' (see Fig. 3.11) was chosen for two reasons. Because it is little-known, none of the children would have been likely to have heard it before; the results would thus be unbiased by any effects of familiarity. At the same time, it is a song which follows the general canons of Western folk tunes: the children should have been familiar with the basic style, or type, of the melody.

Davidson *et al.* were interested in analysing three distinct aspects of the children's learning of the song. The *text* was of interest because the song falls naturally into two clear halves, with the first half containing two very similar lines. The *rhythm* was studied because the pattern of the first two phrases is essentially repeated in the second two; and the *contour* was of interest because the first and third phrases (rising) contrast with the second (falling), and the fourth (flat) phrases. The idea was that these three features could be regarded as different frameworks around which children might organise their production of the song; and thus that it might be possible to identify different methods of organisation at different developmental levels.

The findings of this research are summarised in Table 3.2. Davidson *et al.* were able to identify four main phases of song acquisition in 5-year-olds, and these accord with the findings of the longitudinal studies that were described earlier. The initial grasp of the song is *topological*; as described above, the emphasis is on its global 'outline' properties rather than upon its details, although the beginnings of a grasp of contour, rhythm, and pitch are already evident. The acquisition of the underlying pulse from the surface rhythm of the song is the first major advance that occurs, which is shown as the second phase in the table. When asked to play the song, children used the underlying dotted rhythm rather than that of the words. The second major advance that

Table 3.2 *Phases of song acquisition in five year olds*

Phase	Achievements
One: Topology	• Words of whole song, or most distinctive phrases. • Phrases, phrase boundaries, lengths, number and order of phrases all present. These are supported largely by the framework of the words. • Underlying pulse present in children's singing. • Pace of delivery established.
Two: Rhythmic Surface	• Child can extract the surface rhythm of the song (i.e., can play it note-for-note on a drum) synchronized with the underlying pulse. • Child sings an approximation of the pitch contours of the most distinctive phrases, but maintains no key stability across phrases, and sings varied intervals from one rendition to another.
Three: Pitch Contour	• Child attempts to match pitch contour for each phrase, but cross-phrase key stability is still absent, and intervals still vary across renditions.
Four: Key Stability	• Stages 1–3 stabilized. • Clear projection of key center across all phrases, though intervals not always correct. • Child can extract underlying pulse from surface rhythms. • New ability to perform expressive transformations (e.g., slower pace for sad version).

Reprinted by permission from Documentary Report of the Ann Arbor Symposium *(from Davidson, McKernon and Gardner (1981), © 1981 by Music Educators National Conference)*

occurs in the fifth year is the acquisition of key stability, which is summarised in the third and fourth phases of the table. The pitch contours of the song are fully mastered in phase three – each phrase is accurately reproduced – but there is still no key stability across the different phrases. This stability is only finally achieved in the fourth phase. By the end of the fifth year, all the phrases are organised into a common, stable key – and this brings with it increasing accuracy in the reproduction of contours and interval sizes.

As we saw earlier, the Boston group summarise these acquisitions in very general terms by proposing that the songs exhibit the properties of 'digital' as distinct from 'topological' mapping. By this they mean that quantitative values of pitch, intervals, note lengths, and so on are recognisable, if not yet fully developed, in children's singing. I shall follow up the question of key stability when looking at the development of tonality in later childhood, in Chapter 4.

Cognitive schemes and the development of song
The studies of singing that have been outlined in this chapter are very recent, tentative, and incomplete. What makes them exciting, however, is that they bring the study of musical development right into line with parallel developments in developmental psycholinguistics and in cognitive psychology; there can be no doubt that this approach will assume increasing importance in the psychology of music. I pointed out earlier that Dowling (1984) and Davidson (1983), two of the leading researchers in the field, have adopted very similar methodologies and explanatory constructs. They are also in close agreement in their developmental descriptions of singing. In summary, there seems to be agreement that early songs are not structureless or random, and that they form the basis for later songs. There is agreement that pitch control gradually develops from early 'floating' to accurate reproduction of tonal scales via an intermediate, 'outline' stage; and that intervals gradually expand, and become filled with intermediate notes, with age.

Perhaps the most important common theoretical construct that these researchers adopt is that of the *scheme*, or *schema*, which we have already encountered in Chapters 1 and 2. Dowling's conception of 'schemata' seems to be influenced primarily by psycholinguistics, whereas Davidson's approach is clearly Piagetian. We saw in Chapter 2 that Piaget's theory of cognitive development is based on the notion that a framework of schemes develops primarily through its interaction with the environment, and that this interactive model enables Piaget to account for the way in which children's thinking steers a path between *rationalism* – the acquisition of formal, adult ways of thinking – and *empiricism* – the child's own idiosyncratic construction of his experiences. Now this is an extremely useful distinction as far as music is concerned. We have been concerned throughout this section with the ways in which the child's spontaneous vocalisations gradually move with age towards adult rules of tonality, rhythmic organisation, and so on. These could be regarded as representing the *empirical* and the *rational* aspects of the child's musical development respectively, and this corresponds with Bamberger's (1978) distinction between *intuitive* and *formal* musical knowledge, which will be taken up in Chapter 4.

Krumhansl and Castellano (1983) have proposed that musical schemata are cognitive structures based on listeners' abstract knowledge about musical structure, which is acquired by observing and extracting regularities from different pieces. They exist in dynamic interaction with incoming sensory and perceptual information: 'The musical schema is the subset of abstract musical knowledge that is engaged during listening; the schema is assumed to be modified by the musical event in ways that are specific to it' (p. 325). Dowling (1984) has pointed out that this is primarily a theory of music *perception*, concentrating on stimulus structure: his own emphasis is on the plans that govern song *production*, that is, on 'production schemata'. These two emphases are quite compatible, and Dowling speculates that it may eventually be possible to identify common schemata underlying music perception *and* production. His research aims to describe 'the knowledge the singer and listener has of the stimulus structure', as well as 'the actual process by which that knowledge of the stimulus structure is applied' (p. 148).

Davidson (1983) has formulated the more specific term *contour scheme* to refer to the characteristic tonal structures sung by children. His use of this term is worth exploring in some detail, since it emerges from a consideration of alternative theoretical models of melodic development. Davidson contrasts the *contour-copying* model (e.g. Teplov, 1966) with the *interval-matching* model (e.g. Drexler, 1938). According to the former, children first approximate to the overall shape of the melody they hear, and then gradually sharpen the focus to incorporate pitches, intervals, and so on. The child's repertoire of contours should thus form the basis for early songs, and singing errors ought to reflect inadequacies in this repertoire. According to the latter model, children proceed by constructing their own 'reference pitch' to match a salient pitch in a melody; and the remaining notes are then added according to their interval relationships with the standard. Thus the smaller intervals are added first, and one would expect early singing errors to occur in the reproduction of larger intervals.

Referring back to my previous distinction, we could say that the contour-copying model is essentially *empirical*, and that the interval-matching model is correspondingly *rationalistic*. The value of Piaget's account of development resides in its ability to steer a course in between these two extremes; and Davidson suggests that a realistic model of melodic development should be able to do the same. To focus exclusively on either contour or interval leaves out their complementarity in describing what children actually sing, as well as the fact that some vocalisations may not adequately be described in terms of either. Davidson thus proposes the *contour scheme* as a construct that can incorporate both of these features.

Contour schemes have three important constituents: a *tonal frame*, a *level of pitch organisation*, and a *range of melodic motions*. The tonal frame is the size of the interval within which the notes of a song are sung. The boundary pitches that it defines can either be connected by what Davidson calls *leaps*, in which the intervening spaces are not filled by notes, or by *steps*, in which they are. The level of pitch organisation is self-explanatory; I described earlier how 'floating' pitch in early songs gradually becomes organised into a tonal scale, and contour schemes can be so organised in varying degrees. The range of melodic motions refers to the pattern of rising and falling notes within a given contour. Using the data from the longitudinal study of nine children that was discussed earlier, Davidson devised a coding procedure in which four different levels of contour scheme were identified, that is, of a third, a fourth, a fifth, and a sixth. This procedure combines aspects of tonal frame and pitch organisation; leaps and steps are dealt with within each level.

Some of the developmental findings described earlier, concerning the expansion of tonal frames, the filling of intervals, and the organisation of pitch, were the result of this kind of analysis. Davidson also made some suggestions about the ways in which contour schemes develop in standard and spontaneous songs. In general terms, his empirical results confirmed the sequence of the ordinal scales of the coding procedure. Contour schemes of a third were followed by those of a fourth, fifth, and sixth respectively; and leaps preceded steps developmentally. The results suggest that contour schemes tend to be more stable in standard than in invented songs: and Davidson also tentatively suggests three different patterns according to which development might proceed. In the *cross pattern*, leap scales are used for the development of invented songs and step scales for the development of standard songs (or vice versa). In the *parallel pattern*, the same schemes occur in both song types; and in the *zig-zag pattern*, they shift from one type to the other.

Descriptions such as this are tentative and exploratory, and clearly deserve further development and empirical testing. The empirical work of Dowling and Davidson is based on very small, and possibly unrepresentative subject-samples (e.g. in comparison to Moog's research); and it is all essentially based on the subjective interpretation of finished song *productions* rather than on the empirical manipulation of their *process*, for example by completion or structured improvisation tasks. Nevertheless, these descriptions represent important first steps in our understanding of children's internal organisation of their singing.

Development of rhythmic skills

We saw earlier in this chapter that rhythmic skills are probably the first to emerge, and develop, in the infant's response to music; they are manifested in the earliest stages by different types of physical movement, such as rocking, nodding, seesawing, and so on. Moog's (1976) investigation of babies' responses to songs sung to them showed that approximately one-tenth of his 18–24-month-old subjects could match their movements to the rhythm of the music for brief periods of time. These periods became longer with increasing age, although Moog found a plateau in which there seemed to be no noticeable improvement in co-ordination between music and movement between the third and fourth years. It seems quite likely that other developments, particularly those involving imaginative as distinct from imitative play, become more salient at this age.

Moog's results suggest that these early rhythmic imitations tend to occur before any equivalent imitations of pitch or contour, and this could be explained in terms of the 'primitive' characteristics of rhythm suggested earlier. Shuter-Dyson and Gabriel (1981) point out, however, that opinions differ as to whether or not rhythmic skills develop before melodic skills. Whereas Bentley (1966) found that the shared features of young children's group singing tended to be rhythmic patterns rather than unison in pitch, for example, Revesz (1953) considered that music and movement should be considered together, rather than separately, in the preschool years. The reason for this divergence of opinion is probably that different authors have worked on different levels of analysis. Findings about the relationship between rhythm and pitch within early songs, for example, may not necessarily have any bearing on that between physical movement and the melodic aspects of singing games.

Most studies of rhythmic development have investigated children's ability to produce regular patterns by tapping or clapping. Moorhead and Pond (1978) observed that the patterns that young children spontaneously produce tend at first to be regular, monotonous and unaccented. Some time after this irregular accents are introduced, but these are still clearly based on the underlying regular pulse. Empirical research in this field has concentrated on the development of children's ability to tap in time to given steady rhythms, and to reproduce short given patterns.

Most studies of the first type have indicated that younger preschoolers have difficulty in keeping in time for any more than brief periods. Williams, Sievers and Hattwick (1933), for example, found that only one-quarter of their 3-year-old subjects were able to tap in time to clicks produced on a Seashore rhythm machine, that occurred every half a second. This proportion rose to about three-quarters for their 5-year-olds, and only 4 per cent of their 6-year-olds were unable to succeed on the task. The studies of Petzold (1966) and Thackray (1972) have found similar developmental improvements in this ability in older children, using more complex tasks and more rigorous scoring standards. Rainbow's longitudinal study of the same ability (Rainbow, 1977; Rainbow and Owen, 1979) found that performance varies according to the nature of the task. Three-year-olds performed best when duplicating speech rhythms, for example; and they were better at tapping a regular rhythm with sticks than they were at clapping.

Studies of the second type, in which children are required to duplicate short rhythmic patterns, have revealed a similar developmental progression. Zenatti (1976a), for example, asked 4- and 5-year-olds to tap back 2-, 3-, or 4-note rhythms on two trials. She found a marked improvement at the age of 4.8. Children up to this age who failed on their first trial showed significant improvement after observing the experimenter tap the rhythm a second time. By the age of 4.9, however, 70 per cent of the first attempts were successful. Zenatti also found that performance varied according to the mode of presentation of the patterns. Children up to the age of 4.8 performed better if the rhythms were played on a piano, but there was no difference between this form of presentation and non-melodic taps between the ages of 4.9 and 5.2. Above this age, a reversal occurred in that performance was better with the taps than with the piano presentations: the latter might by this stage have become distracting.

Other studies have revealed a clear, steady development in this ability between the ages of six to eleven or so. Stambak (1960) played from three to eight taps to children aged between six and twelve, and recorded the number of errors made in their reproductions. Six-year-olds averaged 9 errors in twenty-one trials; most of them were able to reproduce 3 to 4 taps accurately. The equivalent figures for 8-year-olds and 12-year-olds were 5.5 and 3 errors: they could accurately reproduce 5 and 7/8 taps respectively. Gardner (1971) carried out a replication of Stambak's study, and essentially confirmed the original results. He also found, interestingly, that some children significantly improved their ability to perform the task over the experimental session itself, which only lasted half an hour or so. This serves as a useful practical hint for music educators, as well as a cautionary note for administrators of psychometric tests of rhythmic ability!

These findings take us beyond the preschool period, and I shall return to some related issues in the next chapter. Shuter-Dyson and Gabriel (1981) provide a valuable, characteristically detailed review of research on the 'Further development of rhythmic abilities', which draws to a considerable extent on studies of conservation of metre: I shall not attempt to duplicate this coverage. Instead, as far as rhythm is concerned, I will concentrate on some interesting research that is currently being carried out on children's representations of melodic and rhythmic patterns in other media, notably in drawing. This kind of cross-modal research enables us to take a broader view of some of the rather narrow and specialised abilities that have been reviewed in this chapter. It also encourages us, once again, to focus on the cognitive structures underlying developments in musical and other symbol systems.

4

Musical development in the schoolchild

The previous chapter led to the clear conclusion that by the age of six or seven, children possess many of the fundamental skills required for full-scale musical perception and performance. Gardner (1973a) has made this point very forcibly, and has drawn from it the clear implication that Piagetian concrete operational thought is not essential for what he calls 'participation in the artistic process'. This point was discussed in Chapter 2, in the context of Gardner's general view of artistic development. As far as music in particular is concerned, Gardner suggests that 'a reasonably competent 7-year-old should understand the basic metrical properties of his musical system and the appropriate scales, harmonies, cadences, and groupings, even as he should be able, given some motifs, to combine them into a musical unit that is appropriate to his culture, but is not a complete copy of a work previously known. What is lacking is fluency in motor skills, which will allow accurate performance, experience with the code, tradition and style of that culture, and a range of feeling life' (1973a, p. 197).

The studies of the development of song that were reviewed in the previous chapter bear out Gardner's conclusion, as does Dowling's (1982) overall view of the development of melodic information processing. The 'first drafts' of musical perceptions and performances can clearly be identified in pre-schoolers, and these drafts are refined and polished in later childhood. The experience of schooling itself exerts a significant influence on musical development, of course, particularly as far as exposure to the common songs and musical forms of the culture are concerned. This begins between the ages of five and seven for most children in Western society, although a significant proportion will have encountered musical activities earlier than this, in preschool and nursery school play.

The distinction between musical *acculturation* (or enculturation) and *training* is a useful one here, and its details have been spelt out by Sloboda

(1985). In essence, acculturation refers to musical developments which take place spontaneously, that is, without any self-conscious effort or direction. Most children in a given culture have a similar sequence of developmental achievements as a joint result of their physical and cognitive maturation, and of their common socialisation experiences. Training, on the other hand, refers to the self-conscious, directed efforts that are made to improve specific musical skills.

The main body of this chapter will be devoted to the musical acculturation that takes place during the school years. It will look at the further development of melodic and harmonic skills, and at children's representations of music in other media, notably in drawings. The last part deals with specific environmental influences upon musical development, namely the effects of practice and training, and of the home and cultural environment.

Development of melodic skills

Pitch discrimination

There is general agreement amongst researchers that pitch discrimination improves in later childhood, but disagreement about the levels of discrimination that are attained at different ages (see review by Shuter-Dyson and Gabriel, 1981). Bentley (1966), for example, in developing his measures of musical ability, found that the majority of the 7-year-olds in his sample could discriminate a quarter-tone pitch difference (12 Hz) at 440 Hz, and that this gradually improved with age so the majority of his subjects could detect an eighth-tone difference by the age of twelve or so. He found a 30 per cent improvement in performance between the ages of seven and fourteen for the detection of pitch differences of 26, 12 and 6 Hz, and a corresponding 10 per cent improvement for 3 Hz differences.

Sergeant and Boyle (1980), however, suggest that considerably higher levels of discrimination than this can be attained if the task is presented differently; their study involved a comparison of the effects of five different 'task structures' on discriminative ability. Bentley and others have employed what Sergeant and Boyle call a 'two-step' task, in which subjects are asked to judge whether the second of two presented tones is higher, lower, or the same as the first. The first step involves the ability to discriminate whether or not the tones are identical; and the second, given a 'different' response, involves determining the direction of the pitch change. 'One-step' tasks, in contrast, involve only the first of these two abilities (i.e. making a 'same' or 'different' response only). Sergeant and Boyle predicted that pitch discrimination might reasonably be expected to be higher for the simpler, one-step tasks; and also that subjects' adoption of a guessing strategy would lead to higher scores in the latter case. The likelihood of producing a correct response by chance is 33 per cent when three alternatives are available, but 50 per cent when there are two. Furthermore, it has frequently been shown in the Piagetian literature that young children vary widely in their use and interpretation of terms like 'more' and 'less', and 'higher' and 'lower'; in fact this has become an interesting field of study in its own right (see e.g. Inhelder, Sinclair and Bovet, 1966; Durkin and Crowther, 1982).

Sergeant and Boyle's study was primarily designed to investigate this issue by comparing 11–12-year-old children's performances on two one-step tasks (the pitch discrimination task from the *Kwalwasser-Dykema music tests* (1930), and the *Sergeant pitch discrimination test* (1979)), and three two-step tasks (pitch tests from Bentley's *Measures of musical abilities* (1966), Colwell's *Music achievement tests* (1970), and the *Seashore measures of musical talents* (1919)). The researchers were also interested in two other parameters of the 'task structures' of these tests, namely variations in the intensity and complexity of the tones, and the order of difficulty level of the items. Their results showed clearly that task structure did influence the subjects' performance levels; in particular, scores were significantly higher on the one-step than on the two-step tasks. Overall levels of accuracy were approximately 95 per cent and 75 per cent respectively, which indicates that the different features of task structure can contribute a considerable amount of error variance to sets of pitch discrimination scores.

Hair (1977) also investigated the effects of task structure on a pitch discrimination task; she was concerned with 6-year-olds' ability to detect tonal direction. In the first of her three tasks, children were asked to respond 'yes', 'no', or '?', according to whether they perceived two pairs of tones as moving in the same direction. In the second task, they were required to match short tonal patterns by playing them on resonator bells; and the third task required them to verbalise the directions of the tonal patterns heard and played in the first two tasks. Hair found that performance levels were highest on the second, performance, task, and that scores on the third task were very low. Very few of her subjects were able to verbalise the concepts of 'up' and 'down'; this confirms the suggestion above. Once again, it is apparent that judgements about children's competence cannot be made directly from observations of their performance. This is a point which recurs in Piagetian studies of cognitive abilities, and it must be clearly borne in mind in assessments of the course of musical development.

Absolute pitch

'Absolute pitch' (AP), or 'perfect pitch', is the ability to correctly identify the musical name or frequency of a given tone, or to produce a specified tone 'out of the blue', that is, without reference to any other objective 'anchor' tone. Ward and Burns (1982), in a very comprehensive review, give an entertaining example of how this ability relates to the musical perception of the population at large:

Suppose we present to an individual the following sequence of frequencies: 260, 260, 290, 330, 260, 330, 290 Hz and ask 'What was that?' Individuals who are 'tone-deaf'

. . . are apt to answer with something no more specific than 'a bunch of tones'. The medium American nonmusician will probably answer 'Yankee Doodle' (identification of tune), although many may remember enough from grade school to add that it was 'do, do, re, mi, do, mi, re' (identification of solfeggio). The typical performing musician can do all of that and may add that 'the sequence of successive intervals was unison, ascending major second, another ascending major second, descending major third, ascending major third, and descending major second' (identification of intervals). But only the person with AP is able to answer 'Middle C, C, D, E, C, E, D' (identification of the musical designation of individual components)   (pp. 431–2).

Possession of this ability is commonly regarded among musicians as a valuable endowment. It is thought to bring the advantages of helping to start unaccompanied singing on the correct note, to play an instrument in tune, to sight-sing accurately, to 'hear' musical scores without playing them, and so on, although Ward and Burns conclude that there is little evidence for these claims. It may even confer certain disadvantages upon its possessor, such as decreased ability to perform certain relative-pitch tasks, and to process atonal music. Absolute pitch occurs much more frequently amongst professional musicians than in the general population, although it is not necessarily correlated with a high degree of musical talent (Shuter-Dyson and Gabriel, 1981).

Because of these apparently paradoxical features, absolute pitch has captured the attention of researchers for over a century, beginning with Stumpf (1883). Three main issues have been investigated, namely the relationship between absolute and relative pitch; the explanation of the genesis of absolute pitch, especially whether it is inherited and/or acquired; and the effects on absolute pitch of training and experience at different ages. Let us consider these issues with special reference to their developmental implications.

Most musicians and musically experienced people possess a good sense of relative pitch. They have developed an internally consistent scale of pitch which accurately represents the relationships between the 12 semitones of the Western tonal scale. A model of this internal scale is the 'pitch spiral', or 'helix', that is shown in Figure 4.1. The 'height' (subjective frequency) of a given tone is represented by its projection on the vertical axis of the helix; its 'chroma' (scale-note) by its projection on the horizontal plane, and its 'octave height' by the coil of the helix that it lies on. Such models are currently being modified and refined (e.g. Shepard, 1982; Krumhansl, 1983), but it is beyond our scope to go into these here. What distinguishes possessors of relative pitch from those of absolute pitch is that this helix is movable or 'free-floating' in the case of the former, but permanent or 'anchored' in the case of the latter. Thus when a person with good relative pitch is presented with a given tone and told its musical label, he mentally 'rotates' the helix to anchor it to this reference point. He is then able to produce, label, and internally represent any other note by reference to this standard. This tendency to apply the internal relationships of the pitch helix is known as *categorical pitch perception* (see

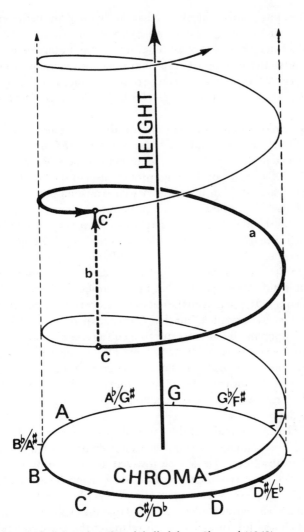

Fig. 4.1 *The simple helix of pitch (relabelled from Shepard (1965): reproduced by permission of Stanford University Press)*

e.g. Siegel and Siegel, 1977). Under certain circumstances, this can actually reduce discriminative accuracy; if a given tone is presented slightly out of tune, there is a tendency for trained musicians to hear it as though it were in tune.

Some musicians possess what has been called 'quasi-absolute pitch' (Bachem, 1937); this is something like absolute pitch for a single tone. Some oboists who regularly play A-440 as a standard for orchestral tuning, and violinists who frequently play this note on the open string, for example, can auralise and sing this note at will; and they can then produce any other note by using relative pitch skills. This shows that the dividing line between absolute and relative pitch is by no means a clear one, and Costall (1982) indeed suggests that many absolute pitch judgements may in fact be relative. His review of the strategies adopted in absolute pitch identification tasks suggests that most people 'bend' these into those of relative judgement, and that even possessors of absolute pitch may in fact be using relative judgments in certain respects.

Perhaps the most interesting question from the developmental point of view is the extent to which absolute pitch can be learnt; and the nature/nurture debate has taken place in this area, as in many others. Revesz (1913) and Bachem (1937) were two of the main protagonists of the hereditarian view, according to which absolute pitch was viewed as an innate endowment which manifested itself regardless of early training. There are three different environmental theories of absolute pitch, which are reviewed by Ward and Burns (1982). Briefly, the extreme Skinnerian form of *learning theory* (e.g. Oakes, 1951) proposes that the acquisition of absolute pitch results entirely from an appropriate pattern of reinforcements derived from the environment – though it is difficult to specify what this might be. The *unlearning theory* (e.g. Abraham, 1901) is based on the notion that most people possess an innate propensity for absolute pitch, but that musical experience actually prevents this from developing. Because we are trained to recognise tunes in different keys and to label notes according to various different systems, absolute pitch recognition may be 'trained out'. Finally, the *imprinting theory* (e.g. Copp, 1916) is based on the idea that there may be something like a 'critical period' in childhood, during which certain learning experiences are crucial if absolute pitch is to develop.

Some evidence in support of this latter theory comes from studies of the effects of musical training and experience on pitch processing. Crozier (1980) showed that absolute pitch can be fostered at any age by training, and Sergeant (1969) produced some detailed evidence concerning the effect of the age at which music lessons are begun. His surveys of professional musicians, music teachers, and music students revealed that the likelihood of developing absolute pitch was directly and inversely related to the age of commencement of musical training. This could be interpreted as general support for the 'imprinting' theory, although there was no sign of a 'critical period' in Sergeant's data. Sergeant and Roche (1973) looked at this question in more detail by training children between the ages of three and six to sing three 8–16-bar tunes, in six training sessions, over a three-week period. One week after the last session, all the children were asked to sing back the tunes, and their reproductions were scored for pitching, melodic shape, intervals, and tonality. Whilst the 5- and 6-year-olds performed better on the latter two measures, it was the youngest subjects (3–4-year-olds) whose pitching was most accurate. It thus appears that pitch representations may be strongest in the very young; and this may help to explain the results described above. With increasing age, the salience of this ability gives way to the ability to process and store the overall shape and tonality of a tune; this development is traced in the next section.

Acquisition of tonality

We have seen already that the mastery of pitch and contour is largely accomplished by the end of the preschool period, and that the main features of melodic development in later childhood are those concerned with the accurate representation of pitch–interval relationships, that is, with the formal characteristics of the tonal system. Some clues about this were gained from the research on the 'conservation' of melodic properties that was discussed in Chapter 2. Some of our own research (Hargreaves, Castell and Crowther, in press), for example, showed that school-age children were able to 'conserve' familiar, tonal melodies much more easily than unfamiliar, atonal 'statistical approximations to music'. This result was interpreted as suggesting that the familiarity and tonality of melodies jointly affect the extent to which they are processed in terms of contour or pitch-interval relationships. Meaningful (familiar, tonal) melodies seem likely to promote the latter, whereas less meaningful (unfamiliar, atonal) melodies are likely to promote the former.

This issue was investigated in a specifically developmental context by Bartlett and Dowling (1980). They played the first part of a familiar melody ('Twinkle Twinkle Little Star') to subjects of different ages, in the key of C, followed by one of two transformations of it. These were *pitch transpositions* in which both contour and interval relationships were retained, and *tonal imitations* in which the contour was preserved but the interval sizes were changed. An example of each of these appears in Figure 4.2. Each type of transformation was presented in either a nearly related (or the same) key as the standard, or in a distant (far) key. G major would be an example of the former, since it shares most of its notes with the original key of C: B major would be an example of the latter, since it does not. The subjects' task in each case was to say whether the two presentations of the melody were the same or different; one would intuitively predict that the transpositions should be perceived as the same, and the tonal imitations as different.

Non-musician adult subjects did indeed follow this pattern: over 90 per cent of them responded 'same' to the transpositions, and less than 10 per cent responded 'same' to the tonal imitations. In the case of the latter, the adults performed better – that is, they responded 'same' less – with far key than with near key imitations. This result indicates that adults can detect changes in interval size, as well as in key signature. Five-year-old subjects produced a quite different pattern of results. For both of the near key tasks (transpositions and imitations), they were unable to distinguish between the standard and transformed melodies; but for both of the far key tasks, they were able to do so, that is, they tended to avoid the 'same' response. Bartlett and Dowling called this the *key-distance* effect. It indicates that 5-year-olds possess the

Fig. 4.2 *Experimental transformations of a familiar melody (reproduced from Dowling (1982) by permission of W.J. Dowling and Academic Press, Inc.)*

ability to detect changes in key signature, in common with adults, but not those in interval size. The performances of older children showed a general shift towards the adult pattern; 8-year-olds responded 'same' to near key imitations less often than they did to far key transpositions. Thus 8-year-olds are able to use both key changes and interval changes to compare two melodies.

There are other sources of evidence which suggest that tonality emerges around the age of six or so. Imberty (1969) carried out a series of experiments on different aspects of this topic. In some studies of cadences, children of different ages were played fragments of Bach chorales, and asked to judge whether they were 'completed' or 'not completed', or to respond 'don't know'. Imberty found that most 6-year-olds rated the fragments as 'completed' regardless of where they ended, indicating that they had little conception of the place of cadences in tonal structures. There was a significant improvement by the age of eight, however; Imberty's subjects perceived a phrase without a cadence as 'incomplete'. They also seemed to recognise the difference between the tonic and dominant at this stage, and to grasp the function of the perfect cadence (V to I). By the age of ten the half-cadence had also been grasped. In some further studies of children's perception of modulations, Imberty played familiar tunes to his subjects, followed by versions of them into which different key and mode changes had been introduced. He found that his 7-year-old subjects could reliably detect key changes in the middle of familiar tunes, and that his 8-year-olds could detect changes from major to minor modes.

Imberty's findings concerning children's perceptions of the 'correctness' of endings of tunes with respect to tonality are corroborated by other research. Brehmer (1925) demonstrated that 6-year-olds could perceive the 'goodness' of the tonic triad as an ending by showing that they could detect changes in such endings more easily than changes which did not affect the tonic triad. Reimers (1927) showed that 9-year-olds could select the tonic as the most appropriate final note for a melody by asking them which of a range of tunes had the best ending. Teplov (1966) found that 8-year-olds could distinguish between completed melodies, and those that did not possess a stable final note such as the tonic. There is fairly close agreement between the results of these studies, and the variations in the precise age at which sensitivity to the 'correctness' of endings emerges can probably be accounted for in terms of differences between the difficulty levels of the different tasks employed.

Zenatti (e.g. 1969; 1983) emphasises the importance of acculturation in her studies of the acquisition of tonality. Her view is that children's performances on tests of melodic perception and memory are likely to be much better when the test stimuli are musically meaningful; this confirms the point that I made at the beginning of this section. Zenatti investigated this question by comparing children's 'perceptual-discriminative ability' at different age levels on tasks with tonal and atonal melodies. In one typical task, for example, children were asked to say which one of three notes in a sequence had been altered in pitch on a second presentation. Zenatti found that 5-year-olds performed at chance level on such tasks with both tonal and atonal sequences, and that superior performance on the tonal sequences began to emerge in the sixth and seventh years. Performance on the tonal sequences continued to improve up to the age of thirteen; and in the case of equivalent four- and six-tone sequences, up to the age of sixteen. One interesting aspect of Zenatti's results was a sex difference, in which boys at some age levels appeared to show less evidence of acculturation than girls. She suggests that this may result from boys' greater interest in contemporary atonal music, or from their general lack of interest in music relative to other interests.

Zenatti's subsequent research has investigated many aspects of harmony and rhythm, as well as melody. She has found some evidence of 'tonal acculturation' in groups of subnormal children (Zenatti, 1975), and some of her recent work (Zenatti, 1984) has looked at the effects of the 'concretisation' of musical memory tasks (i.e. of using concrete representations, such as on cardboard strips, of the tone sequences employed). The results provide general support for her view that children's processing ability is greatest for items that approximate to tonality and consonance, and for rhythmic structures that are based on tonal rather than on atonal patterns.

This evidence of acculturation, or 'musical socialisation', is of course based on the diatonic system of Western music; no evidence is available about the acquisition of other tonal systems in non-Western cultures. Winner (1982) speculates that there is probably nothing special about Western scales, in the sense that children growing up in other societies are likely to acquire their own scales in a similar manner. The acquisition of tonality is thus comparable with language acquisition, in that the general capacity to master a language is a maturational one that is independent of exposure to and training in the particular language acquired.

Development of harmonic skills

The view of children's acculturation to tonality outlined above is equally applicable to their acquisition of harmonic skills. Although these have not generally received a great deal of research attention, two topics that have been investigated are the perception of melodies in counterpoint, and the development of concepts of consonance and dissonance. Zenatti (1969) studied the former by playing children two-part, three-part and four-part fugues based on a tune that was well known to them ('Marlbrough s'en va-t-en guerre'). They were asked to indicate when they spotted this theme, which was described as 'playing hide-and-seek' behind some other notes. Zenatti found a steady improvement in the ability to do this between the ages of eight and ten, but even twelve-year-olds had difficulty with it under certain conditions. Shuter-Dyson and Gabriel (1981) comment that this result is in general accordance with norms of scores on tonal harmony tests such as that in Gordon's (1965) battery. These show a developmental rise that continues until the age of seventeen or so.

Although the concepts of consonance and dissonance have received a good deal of theoretical and empirical attention in the literature, the question of their development in children has been something of a side-issue. Several good discussions of the definition and explanation of these concepts are available elsewhere (e.g. Lundin, 1967; Davies, 1978; Rasch and Plomp, 1982), so I will do no more here than summarise the implications for developmental studies. As far as definitions are concerned, it is important to distinguish between *tonal*, or *sensory* consonance, on the one hand, and *musical* consonance on the other (Plomp and Levelt, 1965; Terhardt, 1976). The former is essentially a perceptual definition: the consonance of an interval consisting of two tones is defined in terms of the relationship between their frequencies (and there are differing views as to how this should be done). The latter form of definition takes into account the rules and conventions of the music of the culture; it is essentially *context-bound*.

Most experiments in this field have obtained subjective judgements of consonance and dissonance; in particular, several studies have been made of people's subjective rankings of the consonance of different intervals. Subjects have been asked to judge the extent to which they are 'pleasant', 'beautiful', 'euphonious', and so on, as well as the extent to which they display 'blending', 'purity', or 'fusion'; there is fairly good agreement between the findings of various studies (see review by Davies, 1978). Davies comments that there is general agreement that the octave and the fifth are consonant, and that seconds and sevenths are dissonant; and that opinions vary as to the intermediate intervals.

The theories that have been proposed to account for these phenomena fall very clearly into two types, which Lundin (1967) has termed 'natural law' and 'cultural' theories. The former type are based on the physical characteristics of intervals, and some well-known early versions include Helmholtz's (1862) view that consonant intervals are those whose overtones and/or fundamentals are free from the 'roughness' caused by beats; Stumpf's (1898) formulation of the laws according to which two tones can 'fuse' into a single sensation, thereby producing consonance; and Lipps' (1885) view, which goes back to those of Pythagoras and Euler, that consonant intervals are those with simple rather than complex frequency ratios. Plomp and Levelt's (1965) *critical bandwidth* theory, according to which consonance depends on the frequency difference between two tones rather than upon their ratio (the interval), follows in the same tradition as these earlier theories.

The 'cultural' theories start from the view that consonance and dissonance are learnt phenomena that develop over time in a given culture. They include the *adaptation* theories of Moore (1914) and Ogden (1924), according to which consonance depends on the amount of exposure the listener and his ancestors have had to different intervals; these theories are largely discounted today because they are based on the inheritance of acquired characteristics. Lundin's (1967) view is that the tendency to judge an interval as consonant or dissonant depends on the current conventions of the musical culture. It also depends on the specific context of a given musical passage: Gardner and Pickford (1944) showed that subjects' judgements of the dissonance of a chord (the seventh on the subdominant) were strongly influenced by the 'musical effect, import or intention of the passage as a whole', as well as by its physical composition, and by the listener's musical experience.

These two types of theory are complementary rather than contradictory in terms of the two definitions of consonance that were distinguished earlier. The 'natural law' theories refer mainly to sensory consonance, and the 'cultural' theories to musical consonance. There is nevertheless a hazy middle ground in which it is difficult to pin down exactly which frame of reference is salient. As far as developmental studies are concerned, the main interest lies in the latter; our focus is on acculturation to conventions of *musical* consonance.

Valentine (1962) carried out some studies in 1910 on the development of preferences for intervals in 6–14-year-olds. His main sample consisted of 200 'elementary school' (i.e. unselected) children who made either 'like', 'dislike', or 'don't know' judgements about piano presentations of the twelve intervals. Valentine refers to the major second, minor seventh, major seventh, and minor second as 'discords', and to the other eight intervals as 'concords'. He found no preference for 'concords' over 'discords' until the age of nine, when a marked 'advance' took place in this respect. By the age of eleven, children not only preferred the 'concords', but also showed a dislike for the 'discords' in terms of the relative frequencies of their 'dislike' and 'don't know' judgements. By the ages of twelve and thirteen, Valentine found that these preferences had developed such that they resembled the typical adult pattern described above. In a separate study, Valentine carried out equivalent tests on 76 pupils in a girls' preparatory school. These children were generally much more musically experienced than the elementary school pupils, nearly every one learning a musical instrument. Valentine found, in general, that their preferences approximated to the adult pattern much more quickly: the adult order of preferences for intervals was reached by the age of nine, as compared with twelve to thirteen in the elementary school group. Even the 6–7-year-olds showed a definite dislike of the 'discords'. This is completely consistent with an explanation in terms of musical acculturation, which appears to have been accelerated in the preparatory school group. There is no present-day equivalent to the distinction between elementary and preparatory schools that existed in 1910, and the massive increase in children's exposure to music through the mass media would tend to blur any such distinction in any case.

Most of the discussion of consonance and dissonance so far has been confined to studies of two-tone intervals; Zenatti (1974) went further by investigating children's reactions 'in context', using chords and musical passages. Zenatti asked her subjects to compare pairs of chords in which one member was consonant and one dissonant, and pairs of musical extracts which were rhythmically and melodically identical, but which had either consonant or dissonant harmonisation. The first task was presented to her entire sample of 422 children aged between four and ten, and the second task to the subsample of 201 children aged six or over. She found that most of her subjects made consistent judgements across different presentations of the two tasks, on the basis of consonance or dissonance, by the age of seven or so. Amongst the children who made consistent judgements, preference for consonance emerged earlier for the chords than for the musical passages (i.e. by the ages of five and seven respectively).

Further studies along these lines, investigating the development of children's preference for consonant as distinct from dissonant harmonis-ations of musical passages, have been carried out by Bridges (1965), Imberty (1969), and Sloboda (1985): these are reviewed by Shuter-Dyson and Gabriel (1981). They all find a gradual increase in preference between the ages of approximately five and eleven years, that is (in the U.K. at least) over the primary school period. The implicit assumption in this conclusion is that an increase in *liking* for consonance is probably evidence of musical accultura-tion. Whilst this may be quite reasonable in the description of children's musical development, it is not necessarily true at higher levels. Some adults presumably possess a full understanding and appreciation of tonal harmony without necessarily liking it. This kind of question about extra-musical influences on musical behaviour will surface again in Chapter 7.

Children's representation of music

Children's drawings have cropped up at various points of the discussion so far, because they form a parallel symbol system whose explanation can shed light on musical development. This was most clearly apparent in the descriptions of the development of song that were discussed in Chapter 3; some aspects of 'outline' and 'first draft' songs are directly analogous to features of drawings. In this section I shall review some research in which the two symbol systems interact directly. Experiments have been conducted in which children of different ages have attempted to represent musical stimuli by drawing, and (conversely) to produce musical representations of graphically presented stimuli.

Research of the latter type is relatively scarce: Stambak's (1951) study is probably the best-known example. Stambak asked children to tap out the musical equivalent of four sets of dots, which are shown in brackets as follows: (..) (. .) (.. ..)).. . ...). She found that only 2 per cent of her 6-year-old subjects understood that the time interval between taps should be shorter in the first than in the second set of dots; this had risen to 54 per cent by the age of eight, and to 96 per cent by age twelve. Even though the older subjects apparently understood the correspondence between spatial and temporal intervals, they still had difficulty in reproducing the longer, more complex sequences accurately.

Goodnow (1971) effectively reversed Stambak's task by presenting similar sequences of taps to children and asking them to write them down. She found that her youngest (kindergarten) subjects were unable to make any spatial representation of the time intervals; most simply drew one dot or one circle for each tap, or just an (uncounted) collection of dots or circles. Around the age of five, however, children began to produce what Goodnow (1977) calls 'action equivalents' of the sequences. This involved drawing the first group of dots; pausing; and then drawing the second group without any *spatial* interval. Two such representations are shown in Figure 4.3 (a) and (b). It is impossible to tell from these that any temporal grouping was involved in their production, and we can see that the number of dots produced is not necessarily correct at this stage. Between the ages of five and seven, children start to use *size*, *position*, and *gaps* in order to represent the time intervals. In Figure 4.3, (c) shows the use of a spatial gap alone; (d) shows the use of size alone; and (e) and (f) show the use of both spatial gap and position on the page. Goodnow comments that this latter use of two equivalents simultaneously could be regarded as a rather excessive 'flourish', and that it tends to drop out in favour of the use of a single (spatial gap) equivalent around the age of six.

I informally tried Stambak's and Goodnow's tasks on my own elder son at the age of 6.4, and his responses revealed some interesting and suggestive features. His first three attempts to clap one of Stambak's dot patterns were unsuccessful, but my verbal explanation of his errors produced a dramatic improvement; he accurately reproduced the three other patterns without any further prompting. Similarly, his first three attempts to draw some tapped sequences similar to those of Goodnow produced 'action equivalents' like those shown in Figure 4.3 (a) and (b), without any spatial interval. My direction that he should 'remember to leave a space' prompted him to invent

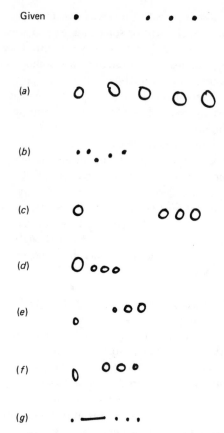

Fig. 4.3 *Children's graphic representations of tapped sequences ((a)–(f) adapted from Goodnow (1971) by permission of the Society for Research in Child Development, Inc.)*

his own convention, which is shown in Figure 4.3 (g): he used a continuous 'space bar' line to represent intervals between groups of taps rather than a spatial gap. Having adopted this convention, he adhered to it over seven subsequent trials even when (on the last two) I prompted him *not* to use it. Although this evidence is anecdotal, it confirms the general finding of social cognition research (cf. Chapter 2) that children's strategies are very sensitive to subtle situational (in this case instructional) influences. Children seem to be resourceful, flexible, and adaptable to the immediate task demands in inventing different notational systems, and this might be given more research attention. It might also be profitable to investigate responses to Stambak- and Goodnow-type tasks within the same experimental design.

Bamberger (e.g. 1975, 1978, 1980, 1982), working in conjunction with the Boston Project Zero group, has developed a more sophisticated and musically oriented developmental description of the representational strategies children employ in Goodnow-type tasks. One of her motives was the feeling that traditional schooling tends to favour certain modes of representation at the expense of others, such that some forms of creative expression may effectively be stifled. This view stems from her distinction between *formal* and *intuitive* types of musical knowledge. The former is that which provides the basis of most traditional music education; and the latter is the unschooled, 'natural' response to music that might manifest itself in unorthodox forms of musical representation.

Bamberger (1982) summarises and re-evaluates the results of three studies (of 8–9-year-olds, 4–12-year-olds, and adults respectively), all of which were based on experimental tasks very similar to those of Goodnow. Subjects were asked to listen to a clapped rhythm (invented by themselves in some cases), and to write it down so that they could remember it later or so that someone else could clap it. Analysis of the drawings produced in the first study led to a tentative typology of drawing strategies, which was based on the central distinction between *figural* and *metric* modes of representation. Figural drawings focus on the function of claps within a figure. They represent the way in which the individual subjectively 'chunks' the rhythm, such that the immediate context of an event affects the way in which it is heard. This is not true in metric drawings; beats are perceived in a context-independent fashion, since attention is paid to the exact duration of the claps.

The initial typology was subsequently extended and refined to include the drawings made by the younger children in the second study: it is summarised in Figure 4.4. This shows the conventional notation of the tapped rhythm (which Bamberger called the 'class piece': it is something like the second and third lines of the nursery rhyme 'One, two, buckle my shoe'), as well as a typical example of each of the six drawing types which were finally identified. The typology has two basic dimensions: there are three qualitatively different drawing strategies (O, F and M) which interact with three broad developmental levels (1, 2 and 3). This *interactive* aspect is an important part of Bamberger's model; she views figural and metric modes as complementary and 'transactional', each contributing to the other, rather than as independent.

Type O, 'rhythmic scribbles', are essentially pre-representational. The child 'plays' the rhythm with her pencil on the paper, and there may be some representation of the continuous pulse of the clapping, but as yet there is no differentiation of the *clap* (sound) from the *clapping* (actions): the drawing is ungrouped and unvaried. Types F1 and M1 are the earliest versions of figural and metric drawings respectively. Both show the correct number of events, and the regulation of movements. Type F1 drawings are rather like Goodnow's 'action equivalents'. The child 'plays' the rhythm with her pencil on the paper in a continuous zig-zag line, and this leaves a record of each event which bears no relation to the temporal pattern of the sequence. Type M1

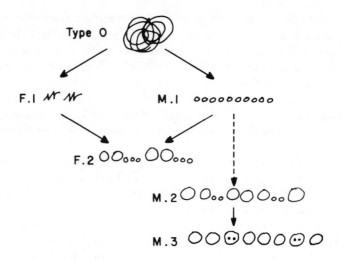

CLASS PIECE: 𝅘𝅥𝅘𝅥𝅘𝅥𝅮𝅘𝅥𝅮𝅘𝅥𝅘𝅥𝅘𝅥𝅘𝅥𝅮𝅘𝅥𝅮𝅘𝅥

SOUNDS LIKE: 𝅘𝅥   𝅘𝅥   𝅘𝅥𝅮𝅘𝅥𝅮𝅘𝅥   𝅘𝅥   𝅘𝅥   𝅘𝅥   𝅘𝅥𝅮𝅘𝅥𝅮𝅘𝅥   𝅘𝅥
Three, four shut the door ; five, six pick up sticks

Fig. 4.4 *Bamberger's typology of children's drawings of rhythmic patterns (reproduced from Bamberger (1982) by permission of J. Bamberger and Academic Press, Inc.)*

drawings are not action-based; instead, they show the child's effort to capture each separate clap on the paper. The result is what Bamberger calls a 'count-up' of undifferentiated metric *units*, which still as yet bear no relation to the pace of the sequence.

Type F2, 'fully developed figural drawings', possess the characteristics of both F1 and M1: the broad two-part pattern of the sequence is represented (cf. F1), and each event appears as a separate unit (cf. M1). The size of each unit is also varied to indicate relative duration: large and small shapes stand for slow and fast actions respectively. However, this convention is not fully developed in that the representation of claps 5 and 10 is essentially 'wrong': these ought, by musical criteria, to be large shapes. This 'error' conveys the essence of the F2 strategy. Bamberger accounts for it by suggesting that claps 5 and 10 are coded as parts of the sub-sequences 3–4–5 and 8–9–10 respectively: they are drawn in the same way as their two immediate precedents rather than in metrical equivalents, because they act as the 'end boundaries' of these two sub-sequences. In other words, claps 5 and 10 are effectively perceived by the children as (equivalent) parts of two 'felt paths', rather than as separate units, and this is essentially a *figural* strategy.

Type M2 drawings overcome this limitation; all units are now 'correct' with respect to relative duration, irrespective of their group membership. Bamberger suggests that whereas the first five units in the F2 drawing could be thought of as a *figure*, in the M2 drawing they become a *class*, that is, they possess the formal durational properties of group membership. This membership is still relative to the other events in the sequence, however, and it is only finally in type M3 drawings that units are anchored to a fixed, underlying pulse, or absolute 'reference metric'. This pulse is shown in the drawing in Figure 4.4 by the eight regular circles, and each clap's precise relationship to it is made explicit.

Over all three of her studies, Bamberger found that most of the youngest children (6–7-year-olds) produced either F1, M1, or F2 drawings, and that most of the older children (11–12-year-olds) produced either F2 or M2 drawings. Very few of her subjects made M3 drawings. In general terms, Bamberger suggests that musically untrained adults and children over the ages of eight/nine tend spontaneously to produce fully developed figural drawings, whereas only those trained in standard music notation are likely to produce fully developed metric drawings.

This general pattern of developmental progression is by now a familiar one, which has cropped up in various different contexts. The shift from figural to metric representation is very clearly paralleled in the progression from 'outline' to 'first draft' songs (Chapter 3), as well as in that from pitch contours to tonal scale intervals in melodic processing (this chapter). There are also direct parallels with the shift from preschematic to schematic organisation in studies of other aspects of children's drawing (Chapter 2). All these descriptions reflect Gardner's view of the transition between 'topological' and 'digital mapping', which is very much in line with Piaget's general view of the transition between pre-operational and concrete operational thought. The acquisition of fully developed metric strategies in the present context, in which the surface rhythm of a sequence is perceived and represented in relation to an invariant dimension (the underlying metre), may well be susceptible to precise explanation by the logic of concrete operations.

Bamberger has looked in some detail at transitional or intermediate strategies which incorporate both figural and metric features: she insists that these are interdependent, and that both are essential for fully-fledged musical cognition. She consequently argues against the commonly held view that metric drawings, which approximate to orthodox notation, represent a more advanced level of musical thinking than figural drawings, and that the latter might in some ways be regarded as 'wrong' or immature. Although metric notation conveys the precise duration of the musical elements, it leaves out any guidance as to overall interpretation, in particular *phrasing*. The phrase markings that appear in some scores, interestingly, are effectively guidelines to *figural* groupings. In other words, figural expression comes nearer to capturing the intuitive, 'musical sense' of a piece. The distinction is very clearly observable in the case of written transcriptions of jazz solos. The split-second variations in timing, accentuation, pitch, and timbre that make great jazz soloists instantly recognisable, and that make most jazz players readily identifiable as such, are very difficult to capture in conventional notation. This is why literal interpretations of jazz scores by 'straight' (non-jazz) musicians usually sound wooden or plodding; they lack 'swing'.

In the wider context, this is what Bamberger means by her claims that school music promotes formal, at the expense of intuitive, understanding. She observes that as the children in her study gained facility in reading and writing standard notation, they simultaneously appeared to be losing their sensitivity to the figural, 'musical sense' of the rhythm. She refers to this (rather inelegantly, in my (British) opinion!) as the *wipe-out* phenomenon. Intuitive understanding is therefore an important part of musical cognition that teachers should take care not to stifle with training in more formal skills.

Bamberger's research is like the Project Zero research on the development of song in many respects. It represents a detailed, elaborate, and essentially speculative theoretical edifice which has a relatively slender empirical foundation. It is primarily based on the subjective interpretation of children's finished products, and consequently pays little attention to the experimental control of potential confounding variables. Future research along the same lines will undoubtedly use alternative methodological approaches, and add rigour and detail to the important findings that have already emerged; the effort will undoubtedly be worthwhile.

Environmental influences on musical development

Effects of practice and training

It is fairly well established that pitch discrimination can be improved by training, and we saw earlier in this chapter that the age at which musical training begins could well have a crucial bearing on the development of absolute pitch. This may be an important factor in the development of singing ability, since several studies (e.g. Bentley, 1968) have found that poor singers and 'monotones' tend to obtain low scores on pitch discrimination tests. This association does not necessarily tell us anything about the direction of causality; but the present climate of opinion seems to be that poor pitch discrimination is likely to be the result, rather than the cause, of poor pitch control in singing (see Welch, 1979). Various attempts have been made to improve children's ability to sing in tune, using pitch matching of single notes, behavioural modification techniques, vertical keyboard instruments, bone conduction to bypass the ear, and so on (see review by Shuter-Dyson and Gabriel, 1981). Many of these attempts have met with some degree of success, and they may even have beneficial non-musical side-effects in terms of general developmental acceleration (e.g. Boardman, 1964).

Dowling and Goedecke (in press) were specifically interested in the effects of instrumental training on the ability to process pitch and contour information in melodies. They presented brief, novel tonal melodies to their 6- and 8-year-old subjects, along with transformed versions of them, in two short-term recognition memory tasks. In the first task the contours and pitches were changed, and in the second, the same pitches were presented in a different order, which resulted in a corresponding contour change. Dowling and Goedecke found that training improved the performance of the younger children on the first task much more significantly than on the second; 6-year-olds' readiness to learn contour discrimination seemed to be greater than their readiness to conserve the temporal order of a series of events (a much more difficult task). The 8-year-olds performed well on the first task both with and without training; and at about the same level as the 6-year-olds without training on the second task. With training, however, performance improved dramatically on this second task. It appears that the 'developmental readiness' to benefit from training and practice occurs at different stages for different musical skills. The result on Dowling and Goedecke's second task is quite likely to parallel those from studies of the effects of training on 'music conservation' abilities. Botvin (1974) and Foley (1975), for example, the former using operant shaping techniques, were both able to demonstrate improvements in performance on 'musical conservation' tasks such as those discussed in Chapter 2: and Ramsey's (1981) study also provided evidence that instrumental and non-instrumental training improved various aspects of preschoolers' melodic perception.

Shuter-Dyson and Gabriel (1981) have carried out a detailed and comprehensive review of research on the effects of specific practice and music lessons on musical development. Most of this is explicitly geared towards improving, or accelerating, musical development; and this is typically assessed in terms of scores on standardised ability tests. The reviewers conclude that specific coaching can indeed improve specific skills in many cases, but that the long-term stability of these improvements is less well established. Rhythmic tests, for some reason, seem to be more resistant to the effects of music lessons than most others.

Investigations have also been made of the effects of training on musical taste, or preference; we can distinguish between those studies concerned with *long-term* effects (e.g. comparisons between musicians and non-musicians) and those which have investigated the effects of *short-term* training programmes, often within experimental designs. Amongst the former type are the studies of Duerksen (1968) and Hargreaves, Messerschmidt and Rubert (1980). Both of these found that musically experienced subjects expressed greater overall liking for all types of music investigated (including classical and popular, in both studies) than did inexperienced subjects. Another typical finding (e.g. Birch, 1963) is that musically experienced listeners are more likely to express greater liking for 'serious' forms of music than inexperienced listeners.

Short-term training programmes have generally been found to exert a significant influence upon musical taste, although it is difficult to know, without follow-up data, whether or not these effects are transitory. Archibeque (1966) found that seventh-grade students who had studied 'contemporary music' expressed a greater preference for it than those who had not, but there was no evidence that previous (i.e. long-term) musical training had any effect on this. Standifer (1970) found that instruction in perceiving musical elements improved some subjects' scores on a test of aesthetic sensitivity, and Bradley (1972) demonstrated that special analytical training increased seventh graders' preferences for 'contemporary art music'. Williams (1972) found that music appreciation instruction over a two-month period increased liking for serious music, and decreased that for popular pieces.

There seems to be little doubt that long-term and short-term training do affect musical taste, but it is difficult to make generalisations about the results of these studies because of the wide variation in their aims and methods, and in the types of training investigated.

The home and cultural environment
Numerous studies have been carried out to investigate the relationships between different aspects of the home environment and children's musical ability. The most direct studies are those of the 'musical background' provided by the home, which is presumably shaped by the broader social and cultural environment. Socioeconomic status is particularly likely to exert a powerful effect, and this, in turn, must be viewed in the broader cross-cultural perspective. Let us look very briefly at the nature of research in each of these three areas.

There is plenty of evidence that children with musically stimulating home environments generally perform well on various measures of musical development and ability. Those aspects of the home environment that have been investigated empirically include parental singing and instrumental playing, both to and with children; number of instruments in the home; availability and playing of recorded music in the home; parental attitudes towards and participation in music; extent of participation in music by siblings; and so on. These different features are very likely to be interrelated, of course; parents who encourage and participate in their children's music-making are likely to provide the appropriate hardware and facilities. Shuter-Dyson and Gabriel's (1981) review of this research shows that these features are positively correlated with the children's scores on a variety of standard musical ability tests, as well as on other measures of pitch and melodic discrimination, rhythmic ability, singing ability, and musical acculturation.

Assessing the effects of socioeconomic status on musical development is fraught with potential problems, especially when viewed in the context of comparable research on cognitive abilities in general. Apart from the inherent difficulties of establishing adequate indices of social class and of the abilities themselves, the whole area has been thrown into even greater confusion by the reverberations of the Cyril Burt affair (see Beloff, 1981). The rejection of Burt's central evidence from his studies of twins, which may have implications for his work on social class (e.g. Burt, 1961) is an important matter because Burt's thinking shaped a good deal of the research in this field, especially that carried out in the U.K. Although the area of musical development is more circumscribed, and though its empirical data is based on American and other non-European samples, research on social class effects is nevertheless extremely complex and hazardous.

Valentine's (1962) study, which was discussed earlier, showed that 'preparatory school' children showed greater evidence of musical acculturation than their 'elementary school' counterparts; this result is almost certainly mediated by social class. Zenatti (1976b) obtained a similar, though rather weaker, relationship in her extensive studies of French schoolchildren: musical acculturation was associated with father's occupation as well as with other aspects of the home environment. Shuter (1964) found a positive association between father's occupation and scores on the Wing test among junior members of the Royal Marine School of Music, though this was not statistically significant. Sergeant and Thatcher (1974) found a significant positive association between socioeconomic status and scores on melodic and rhythmic perception tests; socioeconomic status was also positively associated with general intelligence test scores, and with home musical background.

Similar results have emerged from studies carried out in the U.S.A. Gilbert (1942) found a positive association between the socioeconomic status of the colleges attended by his sample of students and their scores on the Kwalwasser-Dykema tests, for example, though this result is confounded by the fact that a greater proportion of the students in the higher socioeconomic status colleges had received music lessons. Rainbow (1965) found that socioeconomic status (assessed in terms of education and occupation of the head of the household) was a significant predictor of musical aptitude.

We should be very cautious in drawing general conclusions about the relationship between social class and musical development. Some of the evidence reviewed above is equivocal and/or confounded, and it is always difficult to establish causal relationships in a complex social field such as this. The distinction between middle- and working-class families is narrowing and becoming more blurred, in educational and attitudinal as well as financial terms; this may be even more true in the U.S.A. than in Europe and the U.K. Such studies of musical development, moreover, may well suffer from cultural bias. Testers are usually middle class, and test material usually derives from 'serious' music: this could well depress working-class subjects' scores for reasons which are quite unrelated to their musical abilities.

If the investigation of social class differences in ability *within* a given society is fraught with problems, then the exploration of racial and cultural differences *between* societies is a veritable minefield. A good deal of effort and emotion has been expended over recent decades on the vexed issue of explaining racial differences in intelligence test scores, particularly those from black–white comparisons in the U.S.A.; and the research on ethnic differences in musical abilities is similarly confused and confusing (see reviews by Vernon (1979) and Shuter-Dyson and Gabriel (1981) respectively). Some of the musical studies have focussed on rhythm as a salient dimension (e.g. Van Alstyne and Osborne, 1937; Igaga and Versey, 1977, 1978), but their results are generally inconsistent, and it is virtually impossible to disentangle the effects of the racial/ethnic difference from those of social class, and other confounding variables. It is almost certain that the implicit values and assumptions of the tester affect any results that are obtained, as do the assessment procedures that are used. It probably therefore makes more sense to regard the results of these studies as demonstrations of relative degrees of acculturation to Western music, rather than as objective group comparisons of musical ability.

5

Development of responses to music

Many people hear music every day of their lives. Most households in twentieth-century Western society possess a radio, television, and record- or tape-playing equipment, and music is ever-present in shops, railway stations, cafes, waiting-rooms, and so on. Music, live as well as recorded, is ubiquitous, and it follows that the potential range and diversity of the musical experience of any individual is vast. People do not listen in a vacuum; they choose different types of music to suit different activities and environments, and actively or passively 'listen' with varying degrees of attentiveness. In other words, 'musical response' covers a very wide range of human experience.

It is hardly surprising, given this diversity, that the study of responses to music is scattered throughout various areas of psychology, music, and education. Konečni (1982), in reviewing the literature, makes what would seem to be the fairly obvious point that psychological explanations should deal with the range of musical experience in its entirety. In other words, we should consider music in all its diverse contemporary forms, and we should take account of all the psychological factors that might affect people's responses to it: '. . . a thorough understanding of aesthetic behavior cannot be achieved without examining how it changes as a function of its immediate social and nonsocial antecedents, concurrent cognitive activity, and resultant emotional states' (Konečni, 1982, p. 498). In fact, as we shall see in this chapter, most psychological studies of responses to music have adopted a microscopic, laboratory based approach to specific musical or quasi-musical stimul rather than attempting to fulfil Konečni's 'ecological' requirements.

Different terminologies and definitions abound; this chapter will therefore start with an outline of the scope of the field, and attempt to clarify some of its main definitions and terms. The question of methodology will next be considered; I look at the relative advantages and disadvantages of what might be called 'naturalistic' and 'experimental' approaches, and consider the experimental measurement techniques that are most appropriate to different types of musical response.

Six areas of research on responses to music, which employ differing methodological approaches, form the basis of the rest of the chapter. Experimental aesthetics has a great deal of explanatory potential in relation to music, so I present some of the theoretical and empirical work of myself and my colleagues in the Leicester Aesthetics Research Group, and set this in the context of the field as a whole. The second research area is concerned with the establishment of the broad dimensions of listeners' reactions to different musical styles, and employs sophisticated statistical scaling analyses of responses to real-life music. The third area is also based on responses to complex, real-life music, though it adopts what might be called an archival/historical approach rather than contemporaneous analyses of expressed responses. The fourth area consists of studies that have been carried out from the behavioural point of view – most of these are explicitly based on the environmental determinants of musical response. Finally, I consider some research that has been carried out within the psychometric tradition and, in particular, the attempts that have been made to devise tests of musical preference, and to assess individual differences in responses to music (especially those in age, ability/training, and personality).

Scope of the field: definitions

One straightforward way of classifying this diverse literature is that of Wapnick (1976), who points out that studies tend to emphasise either the *music*, the *listening situation*, or the *listener*. Studies in the first category, such as many in the field of experimental aesthetics, focus on the structure and other content characteristics of the musical stimuli. Those in the second (which are considered in Chapter 7), are concerned with the social *context* of particular listening situations as compared with others; and studies in the third category include investigations of the effects of subject variables such as age, sex, I.Q., social class, and so on.

LeBlanc (1980) has proposed a model of sources of variation in musical taste that should be mentioned here. This is a comprehensive model which is hierarchically arranged on eight levels (see Fig. 5.1). At the bottom of the hierarchy, on level 8, are what LeBlanc calls 'two classes of variables for input into the decision making system' (p. 29). These are essentially what were referred to above as aspects of the *music* and the *listening situation*, respectively. Levels 5–7 represent what LeBlanc calls 'enabling conditions', which describe the current physiological, attentional, and affective state of the subject. Level 4 covers the comparatively stable characteristics of the subject, which are normally thought of as 'individual differences', and levels 1–3 deal with 'respondent action variables', that is, with the individual's patterns of

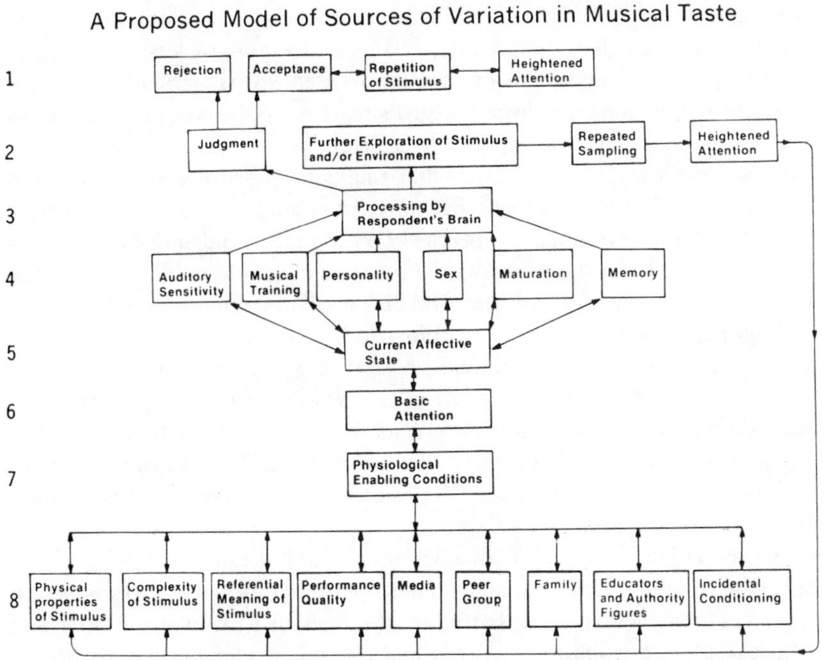

A Proposed Model of Sources of Variation in Musical Taste

Fig. 5.1 *LeBlanc's model of sources of variation in musical taste (from LeBlanc (1980), © 1981 by Music Educators National Conference. Reprinted by permission from* Journal of Research in Music Education)

response to a given musical stimulus. The model is almost certainly far too complex and detailed to be subjected to any kind of adequate empirical test, but at the very least it serves the interim purpose of systematically mapping out the wide range of variables influencing musical response, and may encourage others to develop and refine it.

The terms 'aesthetic response' and 'affective response' are sometimes used interchangeably in the literature, and sometimes not (Abeles, 1980). Abeles suggests that those authors who *do* make the distinction tend to see an 'aesthetic experience' as intense, subjective, and personal; as an experience which might provide 'insight into the nature of human life' (p. 105). 'Affective responses', on the other hand, are those which involve some emotional component, and are generally regarded as being more superficial. The term 'appreciation' can be thought of as an 'umbrella' for both of these terms; as a general description of the response to music which includes both 'aesthetic' and 'affective' components.

My own approach, like that of some other researchers, is to side-step these fine distinctions by using the terms in a much broader, operational sense. My own view of an 'aesthetic experience' is not restricted to the high-level, abstract, and almost mystical events that might occur when a sophisticated connoisseur experiences a sublime work of art. My use of the term is much more down-to-earth and mundane, and refers to more or less any reaction that any person might have to any work of art, defined in the broadest possible terms. This encompasses the schoolgirl's reaction to the latest pop record as well as the music critic's response to a Beethoven symphony; the principal interest lies in trying to explain what might be called *everyday* likes and dislikes in music. One argument that runs throughout this book, in agreement with the views expressed by Konečni (1982), is that any adequate psychology of music must be based on the widest possible range of people, as well as of musical forms. The everyday likes and dislikes of non-expert listeners are just as important phenomena for psychological investigation as are the sophisti- cated experiences of the connoisseur; and they undoubtedly occur more frequently in the listening population as a whole. The term 'preference' is accordingly used in a neutral sense to refer to a person's liking for one piece of music as compared with another; and 'musical taste' is used to refer to the overall patterning of an individual's preferences in whatever field they might be.

Abeles (1980) has provided a thorough and detailed account of the sprawling empirical literature on what he neutrally refers to as 'Responses to music'. His review is organised along the lines of Krathwohl, Bloom and Masia's (1964) *Taxonomy of educational objectives*, referring in particular to their analysis of the 'affective domain'. On this basis, Abeles suggests that there are three distinct *levels* of responses to music that can be identified, and these vary in the extent to which they are internalised by the listener. *Mood/emotional* responses are those which are least internalised, in the sense that listeners exert relatively little control over them. *Taste* responses, on the other hand, are under a high degree of conscious control; these reflect long- term predilections, and are reflected in activities such as concert-going and record-buying. Intermediate between the two are *preference* responses, which are seen as representing more than a simple reaction to music, but less than a long-term commitment. Kuhn (1981) uses the terms 'preference' and 'taste' in the same way as Abeles, and adds three further types of response: 'attitudes', 'opinions', and 'behavioral intentions'. Attitudes are psychological predispo- sitions to respond in a favourable or an unfavourable way to classes of objects, such as musical stimuli, and opinions are the verbal expressions of these predispositions. Behavioral intentions refer to the 'opinions expressed in the absence of a stimulus object but with contextual referents given. For instance, what recording would a subject purchase for ten dollars?' (p. 6). These are fairly subtle distinctions, and there is very likely to be a good deal of overlap, in practice, between the use of Kuhn's five terms.

Methodological approaches

The most important distinction between different methodological ap- proaches to research on responses to music is that between what might be called 'experimental' and 'naturalistic' approaches (Sluckin, Hargreaves and Colman, 1982). This has clear parallels with Berlyne's (1974) distinction between 'synthetic' and 'analytic' approaches in experimental aesthetics, as well as with that between musical ability tests that use 'real' music as test items and those that do not. The experimental approach uses stimuli such as electronically generated wave forms, intervals or tone sequences played to children under laboratory conditions; responses are assessed by means of standardised rating scales, questionnaires, and the like. The naturalistic approach, on the other hand, uses 'real' music which is played under conditions that are designed to be as lifelike as possible; children's reactions are typically assessed by more open-ended techniques, such as transcription or tape-recording of spoken statements. The former approach has the advantage of precise control and manipulation; it ought to be possible, for example, to systematically vary one aspect of the musical material while holding all the others constant, and to examine the effects of this variation on the listener's response. Its concomitant disadvantage, of course, is that the tasks could be seen as trivial, artificial, and far removed from real-life listening conditions.

The naturalistic approach is less concerned with the detailed elements of musical response, and more with the complex, overall patterns of feeling that a piece of music might evoke. What this approach gains in ecological validity it loses in precision, however. It is much more difficult to pin down precise cause-and-effect relationships between particular characteristics of the music and specific responses in the listener when many different features of the music are changing simultaneously.

The two approaches could perhaps be thought of as lying at opposite ends of a single scale; in practice, most studies use methods that are both naturalistic *and* experimental to some degree. Many could be described as 'naturalistic' in their choice of musical materials, and 'experimental' in their choice of measures of response. Heyduk (1975) went further in combining the two approaches by composing some short piano pieces that sounded natural, and which were at the same time precisely controlled for musical complexity.

The actual techniques of measurement that have been used in the assessment of responses to music are essentially the standard tools of psychometrics: these have been thoroughly reviewed by Wapnick (1976), Abeles (1980) and Kuhn (1981). I shall not attempt to duplicate their reviews here, but shall simply mention the techniques that they describe. Abeles describes four techniques that have been commonly employed in the assessment of musical *preferences* and *taste*: attitude scales, paired-comparisons, rating scales, and behavioural measures. The first three of these could be described as self-report measures, and to these Kuhn (1981) adds open-ended questions, multiple choice scales, pictographic scales, summated rating scales, and semantic differential scales. Kuhn also describes a variety of different behavioural measures, including observational measures, single stimulus listening time, reward value, multiple stimulus listening time and manipulative response measures. I shall describe and discuss the behavioural approach in a later section of this chapter.

Abeles suggests that the two main methods of assessing *mood/emotional* responses to music are by verbal reports and physiological measures. Heart rate, respiration rate, and skin response are most common amongst the latter, though electroencephalograms, galvanic skin responses, and blood pressure have also been employed. Adjective check lists, semantic differential techniques, and rating scales are the main techniques of the former type; adjective check lists were used extensively in a body of research that was carried out some decades ago on the effects of music on affective or emotional mood.

Schoen and Gatewood (1927), for example, carried out a mammoth study of the responses of some 20,000 listeners to a variety of compositions. The results revealed a surprisingly high degree of similarity amongst the reported mood effects of different pieces and groups of pieces, given the diverse nature of the subject-sample. Hevner (1935) devised an 'adjective circle' for the characterisation of mood/emotional responses to music which has influenced a good deal of the subsequent research in this area. This is shown in Figure 5.2(a): the circle consists of eight groups of adjectives numbering 67 in all, which are arranged in a manner that implies the existence of four bipolar scales. Hevner studied affective responses to a large number of musical compositions using this technique, with a focus on the effects of different elements of music, such as modality, rhythm, and tempo, on mood response. Like Schoen and Gatewood, she found general agreement between experimental subjects in terms of the adjectives that were used to describe given pieces. Farnsworth (1954) subsequently revised Hevner's list, and produced a group of ten adjective clusters that are reported to possess more mood consistency: these are shown in Figure 5.2(b). Although these techniques seem fairly valid and reliable, they have not given rise to a great deal of subsequent research on mood and music.

Experimental aesthetics and responses to music

The historical background to the field of experimental aesthetics was outlined in Chapter 1. There can be no doubt that it has great potential for the systematic investigation of responses to music, though relatively little research has been done on auditory as compared with visual stimuli. Most investigations have focussed on the relationships between what Berlyne (1971) termed the 'collative variables' of stimuli, such as complexity, novelty/familiarity, redundancy/uncertainty, and orderliness, and various measures of 'aesthetic' response including liking, interestingness, and subjective familiarity and complexity. These are effectively treated as independent and dependent variables, respectively, in most of the experimental research.

My attempt to present a coherent account of this literature here will use the work of the Leicester Aesthetics Research Group as its organising theme. Our research focusses on *stimulus familiarity* as a key explanatory variable (see reviews by Sluckin, Hargreaves and Colman, 1982, 1983): this is one of the most important of the collative variables that were mentioned above. The history of music abounds with examples of acknowledged masterpieces that met with incomprehension and derision when they were first heard by the public. Beethoven's *Eroica* symphony, Stravinsky's *Rite of Spring*, and Debussy's *La Mer* are well-known examples from symphonic music, and some of the major innovators in jazz, such as Charlie Parker, John Coltrane, and Ornette Coleman, have encountered similar reactions to their work. It seems clear that novelty, or unfamiliarity, is an important potential source of musical dislikes, and experimental aesthetics ought to be able to account for this, as well as for the changes in likes and dislikes that occur over time.

Our general review of the literature on novelty, familiarity, and liking (Sluckin, Hargreaves and Colman, 1983) described two contradictory views about their interrelationships. The first is Zajonc's (1968) well-known 'mere exposure' hypothesis, that 'mere repeated exposure of the individual to a stimulus is a sufficient condition for the enhancement of his attitude toward it' (p. 1). Zajonc presented a variety of experimental evidence to demonstrate that liking for experimental stimuli increases as they become familiar. The opposing view is that liking for stimuli *decreases* as they become more familiar; for example, Berlyne (1970) found such an effect in some studies using simple representational and abstract works of art, as did Cantor (1968), Cantor and Kubose (1969), and Faw and Pien (1971) in research on children's and adults' ratings of different visual stimuli.

Our own suggestion is that these apparently contradictory findings can be reconciled by proposing an *inverted-U function* relating familiarity to liking. Different forms of this function were originally suggested by Wundt, and later adapted by Berlyne (1971) and others. Figure 5.3 (a) shows some of these earlier formulations: the pleasantness (Wundt) or hedonic value (Berlyne) of stimuli was seen to be zero for stimuli at low levels of stimulus intensity (Wundt), arousal (Berlyne), or novelty (Berlyne); and then to rise to a peak and subsequently decline with further increases in these variables. Our own adaptation of the curve is shown in Figure 5.3 (b). This incorporates a reversal of the abscissa; it intuitively seems to make more sense to think in terms of zero familiarity, that is, of nil exposure to a stimulus, than of zero novelty, which implies 'complete familiarity' with the stimulus – this latter concept is awkward to conceive and define. Our own curve also implies that liking for completely novel stimuli is initially negative: people initially *dislike* novel objects. As the objects become more familiar, liking becomes increasingly positive, reaching a peak at some optimum familiarity level, and further increases in familiarity give rise to a decline in liking, which eventually becomes negative at very high levels of familiarity.

Our suggestion is that this inverted-U function represents the universal relationship between familiarity and liking, and that its presence or absence in

(a)

6
bright
cheerful
gay
happy
joyous
merry

7
agitated
dramatic
exciting
exhilarated
impetuous
passionate
restless
sensational
soaring
triumphant

5
delicate
fanciful
graceful
humorous
light
playful
quaint
sprightly
whimsical

8
emphatic
exalting
majestic
martial
ponderous
robust
vigorous

4
calm
leisurely
lyrical
quiet
satisfying
serene
soothing
tranquil

1
awe-inspiring
dignified
lofty
sacred
serious
sober
solemn
spiritual

3
dreamy
longing
plaintive
pleading
sentimental
tender
yearning
yielding

2
dark
depressing
doleful
frustrated
gloomy
heavy
melancholy
mournful
pathetic
sad
tragic

(b)

A	B	C	D	E
cheerful	fanciful	delicate	dreamy	longing
gay	light	graceful	leisurely	pathetic
happy	quaint	lyrical	sentimental	plaintive
joyous	whimsical		serene	pleading
bright			soothing	yearning
merry			tender	
playful			tranquil	
sprightly			quiet	

F	G	H	I	J
dark	sacred	dramatic	agitated	frustrated
depressing	spiritual	emphatic	exalting	
doleful		majestic	exciting	
gloomy		triumphant	exhilarated	
melancholic			impetuous	
mournful			vigorous	
pathetic				
sad				
serious				
sober				
solemn				
tragic				

Fig. 5.2 *(a) Hevner's adjective circle, and (b) Farnsworth's revision (reproduced from Farnsworth (1969) by permission of Iowa State University Press)*

a given set of experimental results is partly dependent on the range of the familiarity variable that is sampled in the experimental stimuli. Studies in which the experimental stimuli are relatively unfamiliar to the subjects might only sample from the rising part of the curve, which could give rise to an apparent 'mere exposure' effect in the results; those using relatively very familiar stimuli might sample from the falling part, producing an apparent Cantor-type 'boredom' effect. Our model thus subsumes both positive and negative monotonic familiarity/liking relationships, and either or both of these should emerge in experimental data according to the range of sampling of the familiarity variable. The questions of methodology that are raised here, including the use of subjective as distinct from objective measures of familiarity, of between-subjects and within-subjects designs, and the advantages and disadvantages of 'repeated exposure' techniques are discussed by Sluckin, Hargreaves and Colman (1982).

The presence or absence of the inverted-U function in a given set of experimental data is also dependent on other properties of the experimental stimuli, that is, on the collative variables mentioned above. These properties also affect the parameters of the curve. We might expect its peak to occur at higher levels of familiarity for complex than for simple stimuli, for example, and some stimuli may be so complex that the peak is never reached for some subjects. Our own research is exploring these questions, using a variety of

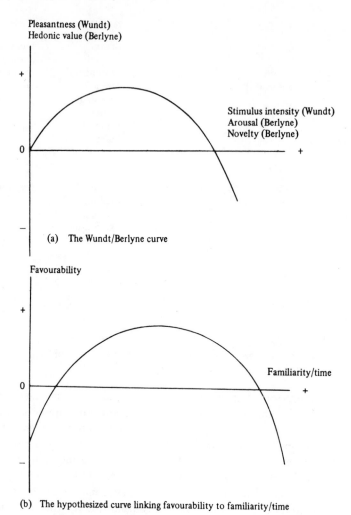

Pleasantness (Wundt)
Hedonic value (Berlyne)

Stimulus intensity (Wundt)
Arousal (Berlyne)
Novelty (Berlyne)

(a)   The Wundt/Berlyne curve

Favourability

Familiarity/time

(b)   The hypothesized curve linking favourability to familiarity/time

Fig. 5.3 Inverted-U curves (reproduced from Sluckin, Colman and Hargreaves (1980) by permission of the British Psychological Society)

'naturalistic' and 'experimental' stimuli including nonsense syllables, letters and words, names, faces, fashions in dress, and other consumer products. Some of the work on names led us to propose a 'preference-feedback' theory of cyclical vogues and fashions which has implications for social phenomena well beyond the bounds of experimental aesthetics. I focus in this chapter on our empirical research on familiarity and liking for music, and return to the preference-feedback theory in considering musical fashions in Chapter 7.

Application of the inverted-U theory to music raises a variety of new theoretical issues, since musical events are ordered in the dimension of time. This consideration has led us to develop two separate applications, which differ primarily in their approach to the familiarity variable. The first application deals with likes and dislikes for different musical pieces at a given point in time, and the second with the changes in liking that occur over time when listeners are repeatedly exposed to the same piece. The empirical evidence for these two applications will be reviewed in the following sections on 'Subjective complexity and liking' and 'Repetition and liking' respectively.

It may be helpful to think of the different experimental operationalisations of the familiarity variable as being either *stimulus-based* or *subject-based*. The main stimulus-based approach is to compare listeners' responses to pieces whose objective fame, or frequency of exposure, can be established by external criteria; very well-known and very little-known pieces might be compared, for example. The most common subject-based approach has been to compare the responses to given pieces of experienced, trained musicians with those of musically naive listeners. A second subject-based approach is to operationalise familiarity in terms of *age*. Some of our work on children's liking for melodies (Hargreaves and Castell, 1986) is based on the developmental assumption that older children will have had more exposure to well-known music than will younger children, as a simple result of enculturation. The research on the effects of experimental repetition on liking could also be thought of as primarily subject-based; subjects' repeated exposure to the same pieces presumably results in increasing familiarity with them. Some of these repetition studies also incorporate stimulus-based variation of familiarity by comparing the effects of repetition of common and uncommon pieces. Finally, a third conceptualisation of familiarity that is in a sense both stimulus- *and* subject-based is that which is adopted in what I have called the archival/historical approaches, which are discussed later in this chapter. These are concerned with long-term changes in musical taste over time, and implicitly conceive of familiarity in terms of the particular works and pieces that become most popular.

It is impossible to study familiarity in isolation from the other independent and dependent variables in a given listening situation; in particular, its relationship with stimulus complexity forms an integral part of the application of the inverted-U theory. McMullen (1980) has proposed that all of the main *independent* variables, that is, the collative variables of musical stimuli, could be subsumed under two dimensions which he calls 'energy' and 'structure'. The 'energy' dimension includes variables such as 'excitement', 'intensity', and 'stimulation', and 'structure' incorporates both 'order' and 'complexity'.

There are also considerable overlaps and interactions amongst the different *dependent* variables that have been employed. Russell (1982), for example, found that undergraduates' pleasingness and interestingness ratings of one-minute samples of modern jazz were positively correlated, and that both were decreasing linear functions of complexity ratings, though the correlation between interestingness and complexity was low and only marginally significant. He suggests that pleasingness acts as a suppressor on the interestingness/complexity correlation. Hargreaves, Messerschmidt and Rubert (1980) found strong positive correlations between undergraduates' affective ('liking') and evaluative ('quality') ratings of classical and popular music excerpts, and that these correlations were higher for trained than for untrained subjects, and for popular than for classical excerpts. They suggested that non-musician subjects were more likely to fragment the cognitive and affective components of their attitudes to music than were the musicians, and that this seemed to be more likely when the music was regarded as being of high quality. Such interrelationships between different response variables need a good deal of further systematic exploration; in the meantime, we shall concentrate on liking as the main dependent variable.

Subjective complexity and liking

The first application of the inverted-U theory deals with likes and dislikes for different pieces at a given point in time, and derives from the work of Berlyne (1971), Heyduk (1975), and Davies (1978). One foundation of Berlyne's theory is that people prefer moderate, rather than extreme levels of arousal (see Figure 5.3(a)), and that this is related to the amount of *information* that they receive from different stimuli. The basis of Davies's argument is that people prefer music that provides them with information, that is, which reduces their uncertainty about subsequent events. Extremely unfamiliar music does not reduce uncertainty, since the events within it are totally unpredictable to the listener; and very familiar music does not do so because it contains very little new information. The hypothesis therefore predicts that people will prefer music that is moderately familiar, that is, that which contains an optimum amount of information *for them.*

Since Berlyne, Ogilvie and Parham (1968) have demonstrated that the amount of information conveyed by a stimulus is a function of its subjective complexity, we are led to predict an inverted-U curve with liking as the ordinate, and subjective complexity as the abscissa. In general terms, people should dislike pieces of music that they perceive as being very simple or very complex, and they should like those which they perceive as being of intermediate complexity. Now the subjective complexity of a given piece is a function both of its objective complexity, and of the familiarity of the listener with respect to that piece. We would expect it to be very low in the case of a sophisticated musician listening to a simple piece, and very high in the case of a non-musician listening to a very complex work. Subjective complexity level summarises the effects of both interacting variables, reflecting the effects of objective stimulus complexity as well as familiarity.

There is a growing amount of empirical evidence in the literature in favour of different versions of this basic model; one approach has been to manipulate the objective complexity levels of the musical stimuli in terms of their information content, or redundancy. Vitz (1966) found an inverted-U relationship between the information content of tone sequences, and subjects' ratings of their pleasantness; Crozier (1974), and Simon and Wohlwill (1968) followed similar lines of investigation. McMullen (1974) found that his school-age subjects preferred melodies of intermediate complexity, defined in terms of their informational redundancy and of the number of pitches from which they were constructed, to those of high or low complexity. McMullen and Arnold (1976) found that preference for rhythmic sequences was an inverted-U function of their redundancy, though his undergraduate music major subjects' interest in the sequences was a positive monotonic function of redundancy.

Walker (1980) refers to his own inverted-U theory of the relationship between preference and psychological complexity as a 'hedgehog theory', because it is based on one central idea which is applicable in a wide range of situations. (The hedgehog's one and only response to problems is to roll up into a ball. In any situation it either does this, or nothing at all.) Walker has adduced empirical support for the model in various areas of learning and motivation, and Radocy (1982) has also produced some empirical support. Heyduk's (1975) 'optimal complexity' model, which receives support from his own results from subjects' preference ratings of four piano compositions that were specially constructed to represent different levels of objective complexity, is very similar to Walker's 'hedgehog'. Steck and Machotka's (1975) results also support the optimal complexity model, as well as suggesting that complexity preferences are relative, not absolute. They found that the shapes of the preference curves for sounds of varying complexities were determined by the overall stimulus range, that is, by the *context*, rather than by the absolute complexity levels of the stimuli.

An innovative approach to the manipulation of familiarity was taken by Colman, Walley and Sluckin (1975). They compared the preferences of groups of subjects at different age levels for stimuli which, because of enculturation, are normally increasingly familiar with age (i.e. common words as compared with uncommon words and non-words). The same approach was applied to musical stimuli by Hargreaves and Castell (1986). Groups of subjects in six age groups (4–5 years, 6–7 years, 7–8 years, 10–11 years, 13–14 years, and 18 + years) rated their liking for four types of melodic sequence, which were selected so as to vary widely in their likely familiarity to the subjects. These were 'near' and 'far' statistical approximations to music (see Davies, 1969) and very familiar or very unfamiliar real-life melodies (nursery rhymes and carols, and little-known English folk song melodies respectively). The results are shown in Figure 5.4. The ratings of the familiar melodies reveal an inverted-U relationship with increasing age; those of the unfamiliar melodies reveal a similar relationship, with a later peak; and those of both types of statistical approximation to music decline with age. These results support the optimum complexity model, and also corroborate Colman *et al.*'s earlier result with non-musical stimuli.

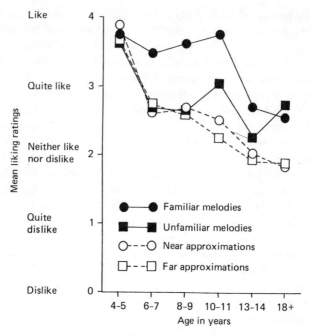

Fig. 5.4 *Development of liking for familiar and unfamiliar melodies (reproduced from Hargreaves and Castell, 1986)*

Repetition and liking

The second application of the inverted-U theory deals with the changes in familiarity that take place over time when listeners are repeatedly exposed to the same piece. In this case, the most general form of the theory predicts that liking for novel, initially unfamiliar pieces should be low; that it should rise to a peak with increasing exposure and familiarity; and then decline with further exposure. This is the typical pattern that is described by the position of a pop song in the 'charts' (see Figure 7.3). The preceding discussion implies that the shape of such a curve for any given piece of music should depend upon its associated collative stimulus properties, and upon its level of subjective complexity before any repetition occurs.

The 'repeated exposure' paradigm has frequently been employed in research deriving from Zajonc's (1968) 'mere exposure' theory; and the results of experiments using this technique are of considerable practical as well as theoretical importance. Broadcasters and recording companies presumably have a keen commercial interest in the effects of 'plugging' of pop songs and of advertising jingles on audience reaction. Although some research was carried out along these lines under the auspices of the Office of Radio Research at Columbia University, New York (Lazarsfeld and Stanton, 1944), Wiebe's (1940) study is the only 'real-life' investigation of the effects of radio plugging to incorporate any degree of the experimental control that is characteristic of the laboratory studies. Wiebe found that plugging did not affect students' liking ratings of initially well-liked popular songs, but that it did affect the ratings of songs that were initially less well-liked. There is a pressing need for more field studies along these lines, since most of the audience research carried out by broadcasters themselves is characterised by *ad hoc* description rather than by experimental hypothesis testing.

I suggested earlier that subjective complexity is a function of objective complexity as well as of familiarity; it is helpful to make a similar distinction between subjective and objective familiarity in predicting the likely effects of repetition (cf. Hargreaves, 1984). Objective familiarity is presumably a direct function of repetition, and repetition could reasonably be expected to produce a corresponding increase in measures of subjective familiarity. There may well be a similar correspondence between objective and subjective measures of complexity, but the most important link is that the increases in subjective familiarity that occur with repetition are accompanied by decreases in subjective complexity. Heyduk (1975) has provided a thorough conceptual analysis of the relationships between familiarity, complexity, and preference, which leads him to the conclusion that 'the expected functions relating experience to preference may be derived from the functions relating complexity to preference' (p. 85).

This means that direct predictions about the effects of repetition on liking can be made from the inverted-U theory. If the initial level of subjective complexity of a piece of music is below a listener's optimum level (e.g. in the case of an experienced musician listening to a common nursery rhyme), repetition would have the effect of shifting liking further down the descending part of the inverted-U curve, that is, it should decrease liking still further. If the initial subjective complexity level is higher than the optimum for the listener, however (e.g. in the case of a non-musician listening to a highly complex piece), repetition should serve to shift liking up the ascending part of the curve, that is, liking should show an increase.

The repetition studies that bear directly on this prediction are summarised in Table 5.1. We could draw the very broad conclusion from this summary that the results of approximately half of the studies seem to support the inverted-U hypothesis, whilst the other half show a positive monotonic 'mere exposure' relationship between familiarity and liking. Such a conclusion is almost certainly crude and oversimplified, however. I have been forced into various oversimplifications, and possible distortions, in meeting the constraints of a comparative summary table. The studies listed have a variety of different theoretical aims and assumptions, several of them having no primary interest in the two competing hypotheses (which may, on the other hand, mean that their results provide a more objective, disinterested test between them!) The studies also vary widely in certain crucial aspects of their design and execution. It is clear from the discussion above that the use of different

Table 5.1 *Studies of repetition and liking*

	Subjects	Music	Repetition	Result
Verveer, Barry & Bousefield (1933)	psychology students	jazz selections	2 weeks, many times/week	inverted-U, pleasantness
Krugman (1943)	students	classical, swing	8 weeks, once/week	pleasantness↑
Mull (1957)	music students	modern serious music	2 weeks, once/week	liking↑, but remained low
Schuckert & McDonald (1968)	preschoolers	jazz, classical	4 days, once/day	j→c shift in preference = 2(c→j)
Bradley (1971)	7th graders	contemporary art music	14 weeks, 3 times/week	liking↑
Bartlett (1973)	psychology students	classical, best-liked	3 weeks, 3 times/week	classical↑, best-liked↓, liking
Heingartner & Hall (1974)	4th graders, psychology students	Pakistani folk music	1 session, 1,2,6 or 8 times	liking↑
Heyduk (1975)	students	specially composed piano pieces	1 session, 16 times	inverted-U, liking
Hargreaves (1984)	I adult education students	easy listening, avant-garde jass	1 session, 3 times	inverted-U, liking, within styles
	II psychology students	popular, classical, avant-garde jazz	3 weeks, 4 times/week	inverted–U, liking, within styles

subject populations, especially as far as their age and musical experience is concerned, can exert a powerful influence on levels of subjective familiarity, and thereby on the results. These are also directly affected, of course, by the selection of the *musical stimuli*, which can vary on a large number of relevant dimensions which determine familiarity and complexity levels. The *experimental repetition procedures* also vary widely amongst the studies, in terms of the number of repetitions and overall time-scale, for example.

The four studies whose results could broadly be interpreted as favouring the inverted-U theory are those of Verveer, Barry and Bousfield (1933), Schuckert and McDonald (1968), Heyduk (1975) and Hargreaves (1984). Schuckert and McDonald's evidence was indirect: they obtained initial preference judgements from twenty preschoolers about 'jazz' and 'classical' pieces, and then repeatedly played the *less* preferred musical type in four different play situations. A post-test showed that the shift in preference from jazz to classical music, though not statistically significant, occurred twice as often as the shift in the opposite direction. If we assume that the classical pieces were of higher complexity than the jazz selections, this result would follow from the inverted-U hypothesis. It cannot be taken as strong evidence in support, however, as, apart from the indirectness of the evidence, the study suffers from several methodological shortcomings, including the smallness of the sample size and the representativeness of the pieces used as 'jazz' and 'classical' music.

The other three studies mentioned above all provide direct support. Verveer *et al.* (1933) found an inverted-U curve for undergraduates' pleasantness ratings of two 'jazz selections' that were repeated in two testing-sessions one week apart. These ratings rose to an affective peak at an optimal level of familiarity, and then declined, within a single testing-session. After a one-week interval, the ratings rose again. The authors explain this in terms of the different affects of *continuous repetition* and *repetition at intervals*. Hargreaves (1984) also implemented this distinction in the second of two linked studies. In the first, excerpts of 'easy listening' music and avant-garde jazz were played to groups of adults three times during a single session; in the second, excerpts of avant-garde jazz, popular, and classical music were played to groups of undergraduate students four times per session over three sessions. Although the results of both studies broadly supported the inverted-U theory, this was contaminated by attitudinal stereotyping effects in that the predicted curves occurred only *within*, and not *between*, musical styles or genres. Heyduk (1975), however, obtained clear support for the theory from his analysis of the preference ratings of the specially constructed piano compositions, mentioned earlier, that were presented to his undergraduate subjects sixteen times.

The four studies whose results broadly support 'mere exposure' theory are those of Krugman (1943), Mull (1957), Bradley (1971), and Heingartner and Hall (1974). Krugman found that undergraduates' pleasantness ratings of 'classical' and 'swing' music tended to increase over eight repetitions, one per week, and Mull found a similar increase in music students' liking for pieces of 'modern serious music' (Hindemith and Schoenberg) over two sessions of one hour each in successive weeks, although she concluded that overall levels of liking were still not high even at the end of the experiment. This finding parallels that of Hargreaves (1984), in that subjects' dislike of certain styles (usually complex 'modern', 'serious', or 'avant-garde') seems to override any repetition effects. On the other hand, Bradley's repetitions of pieces of 'contemporary art music' (tonal, polytonal, atonal, and electronic) to seventh graders over a period of fourteen weeks produced significant increases in liking in all four categories. This discrepancy can almost certainly be explained in terms of differences between the studies in terms of subjects, stimuli, and levels of exposure. None of the three, unlike the fourth study by

Heingartner and Hall, was carried out in an explicitly Zajonc-type 'repeated exposure' paradigm. Accordingly, one feature of this latter study was that the fourth grade and college student subjects were exposed to very unfamiliar Pakistani folk music on *either* one, two, six, or eight occasions. The results provided direct support for mere exposure theory.

Finally, Bartlett's (1973) study, which provides very indirect support for this theory, is worth mentioning here. Bartlett was primarily concerned with the effects of the 'structural discrimination' that might take place during repeated listening to music. He investigated this by asking his experimental group of undergraduate students to verbalise their responses to the structural aspects of the music whilst it was playing: 'classical' (Schubert, Brahms) and 'best-liked' music (determined by means of a preference test) was played three times a week for three weeks. Experimental group subjects showed significantly greater increases in preference for classical music than did one group of controls who heard the repetitions without verbalisation instructions, and also than a second control group who received the classical music preference pre-test and post-test only. These increases were higher for the first than for the second control group, indicating that repetition led to an increase in liking.

The fifty–fifty split in support for the competing theories could easily be the result of differences between the experimental designs and procedures; the importance of sampling an appropriate range of the familiarity variable was made clear earlier. I am inclined to maintain that the inverted-U curve is the most general form of the relationship, and that mere exposure effects can be interpreted in terms of the rising part of the curve. This accords with the conclusions reached by Lundin (1967) in his earlier review of the repetition literature. Lundin suggested that certain consistent trends were evident in spite of some areas of disagreement between the studies, including 'Popular music tends to reach the maximum of pleasantness at an early repetition, whereas classical selections reach their affective height with later performances', and 'With repetition, compositions considered by experts to be of greatest musical aesthetic value show the greatest gain in affective reaction with repetition' (p. 176).

This question will probably only satisfactorily be resolved *within* studies in which either monotonic, or inverted-U, or both types of familiarity–liking function are predictable from the variation of experimental conditions (cf. Colman, Best and Austen's (1985) investigation, which employs non-musical stimuli). This whole area is one in which empirical evidence seems to lag behind theoretical speculation. Unequivocal empirical evidence for a given position is difficult to establish because of the complexities of working with musical stimuli. One of the most promising ways forward may be to carry out field tests of the experimentally derived hypotheses, in parallel with broadcasting and audience research. Wiebe (1940) made a start on this, and his lead deserves to be followed up.

Dimensional studies of responses to music

I suggested earlier that 'naturalistic' and 'experimental' methodological approaches could be regarded as opposite poles of a single scale, in that many studies use methods which incorporate aspects of both. It seems obvious that the experimental aesthetician must grasp the nettle and use real art works as stimuli; this must necessarily involve classifying works of art, and trying to identify the major dimensions on which the classes differ. Berlyne (1976) argues convincingly that it is unsatisfactory to adopt the taxonomies of experts such as art historians, as they are likely to vary considerably between different experts, to change rapidly with time, and to lack scientific rigour and precision. Psychologists must therefore develop taxonomies of their own, using representative samples of the art works and subject-populations in any given area of investigation.

Fortunately, numerous techniques for scaling complex stimuli are available (see e.g. Dunn-Rankin, 1983), and experimental aestheticians have begun to explore their application. *Cluster analysis* is a general term for those methods that group subjects or stimuli together on the basis of some aspect of their similarity; they are relatively simple, and make few assumptions about the data to which they are applied. *Multidimensional scaling* (MDS) is the generic term for a variety of rather more sophisticated techniques which attempt to represent spatially the proximities between stimuli in terms of a limited number of dimensions within a given 'conceptual space'. These dimensions should theoretically correspond to psychologically significant attributes, and the techniques also enable subjects to be located in the same conceptual, or psychological, space.

MDS techniques are currently probably the most widely used for the scaling of artistic stimuli (see e.g. Carroll and Wish, 1974; Berlyne, 1976). They seem to have become more popular and fashionable in this application than the techniques of *factor analysis*, which have been extensively used for several decades in research on individual differences in ability and personality. This may be partly because MDS techniques make fewer assumptions about the underlying data: metric distances between stimulus objects can be determined with only ordinal assumptions being made about the data. They are applicable to any data that can be regarded as measures of the *psychological distance* separating stimuli (e.g. similarity, preference, evaluation); and this data can be derived from a relatively small number of subjects.

The MDS technique that has been used most often in experimental aesthetics research is INDSCAL (see Carroll and Chang, 1970): Berlyne's (1976) application is fairly typical. His subjects were given every possible pair of stimuli in the study in random order, and asked to rate them on a 7-point 'similar–dissimilar' scale. These ratings formed the raw data for the INDSCAL analysis, and the dimensions which emerged were then interpreted in the light of other subjects' stylistic, structural, affective, or evaluative ratings of the same stimuli. Berlyne proposed that the task involves subjects in forming internal representations of the stimuli, and that those stimulus attributes which are most prominent in subjects' internal representations are those which exert the greatest influence on aesthetic behaviour. The dimensions that emerge from MDS analysis should thus represent a taxonomy that has psychological significance for the individual. Most of the applications of MDS techniques have been in the visual arts (e.g. O'Hare, 1979): I shall concentrate here on the studies that have been carried out on musical stimuli.

Hare (1975, 1977), working in Berlyne's laboratory in Toronto just before Berlyne's untimely death, carried out a sequence of six related experiments using sixteen excerpts of European tonal music composed between 1700 and 1900. The subjects were sixteen music students and sixteen non-musician psychology students. The six studies dealt with multidimensional similarity scaling, descriptive and affective scaling, stylistic and technical scaling, free listening time, exploratory choice, and multidimensional preference scaling. On the basis of the similarity scaling in the first experiment, Hare identified one central dimension that seemed to predominate in the judgements of both the musician and the non-musician subjects, and two further dimensions, each of which was important to only one subgroup. The scalings in the second and third studies enabled Hare to label these three dimensions as 'tempo/playfulness', 'potency' (salient amongst non-musicians) and 'musical period' (salient amongst musicians) respectively. In the fourth, fifth and sixth experiments, the dominant 'tempo/playfulness' dimension was found to be related to listening time, exploratory choice, and preference judgements.

Berlyne (1977) carried out an investigation of sixteen excerpts of 'exotic and folk music' that was closely modelled on Hare's research, both in the sequence of its six related experiments and in its use of music and non-music students as subjects. Two dimensions emerged from the initial multidimensional similarity scaling study, and from the second and third experiments (on collative and affective ratings, and stylistic ratings, respectively). The first appeared to resemble Hare's pervasive 'tempo/playfulness' factor, and the second to reflect 'familiarity/strangeness'. In the fourth, fifth and sixth experiments, exploratory choice and preference judgements were found to depend on both similarity dimensions, but listening time on 'familiarity/strangeness' only.

The research of Hare and Berlyne, whilst very exploratory, aims at a systematic and comprehensive approach to the scaling of musical works; a few other studies in the literature have tackled the same problem in various different ways. Nordenstreng (1968) compared semantic differential and similarity analyses of the responses of a group of broadcasting sound engineers to ten varied pieces of serious and popular music, and emerged with four factors which he labelled 'richness', 'power of serious music', 'relaxation of light music', and 'calmness' respectively. Wedin's (1972) MDS analysis of forty varied excerpts of 'serious', 'jazz' and 'popular' music gave rise to three proposed dimensions, which he labelled 'intensity–softness', 'pleasantness–unpleasantness' and 'solemnity–triviality' respectively. Cupchick, Rickert and Mendelson (1982) used MDS techniques to compare similarity and preference judgements of jazz improvisations (Experiment 1) and of excerpts of 'classical', 'pop-rock', and 'jazz' music (Experiment 2). They found that the same dimensions seemed to describe both the similarity and the preference judgements of the jazz improvisations in Experiment 1, namely 'tempo', 'dominant instrument' and 'articulation'. The dominant dimensions for the similarity judgements in Experiment 2 ('classical-contemporary', 'jazz-rock', and 'tempo') were found to be different from those for the preference judgements ('rock-classical', 'jazz-classical', and 'tempo'). Cupchick *et al.* concluded that similarity judgements seem to reflect greater shared standards than do preference judgements, and that different dimensions become salient in within-genre (Experiment 1) and between-genre (Experiment 2) comparisons.

It is not really surprising that no clear pattern of results emerges from these studies, given the diversity of their subject-matter. It would be easy to conclude, simply, that a great deal more research is needed; but we must also ask whether the application of MDS techniques has produced any specific insights that could not have been achieved by the more traditional methods, such as factor analysis. There are several well-known and pertinent criticisms of the use of factor analysis in the formulation of theoretical models of the structure of abilities (see e.g. Butcher, 1968; Vernon, 1979): a major criticism, in essence, is that 'you only get out what you put in'. In other words, the validity of any dimensional model rests on the assumption that the test scores on which the analysis is based are truly representative of the phenomena which the model seeks to explain. In the case of intelligence tests and the structure of human abilities, this is by no means a straightforward assumption to make.

I would argue that precisely the same constraints apply to multidimensional scaling analyses of pieces of music; any dimensional model that is proposed is ultimately restricted by the range of musical stimuli on which it is based, as well as on the subjects and response measures adopted. The psychological interpretation of the dimensions that emerge is just as dependent on the subjective judgements of the psychologist as in the case of factor analysis. It could even be, as has been argued in the case of models of intelligence, that over-zealous applications of powerful multivariate techniques can seriously blinker our thinking about the important theoretical issues. Hudson (1966), for example, writes of the drawbacks of 'sophisticated statistics poised on tests of rustic simplicity' (p. 13).

Hargreaves and Colman (1981) carried out a dimensional study which adopted a more open-ended methodological approach, in an attempt to overcome this problem. For the reasons mentioned above, it was considered important to use a range of musical styles that was as wide as possible. A group of musicians from various backgrounds (including rock, folk, jazz and classical), as well as some non-musicians, were first asked to list what they considered to be the main styles, or genres, of music. The divergence between these lists was fascinating in itself; the musicians tended to have a very detailed differentiation of styles within their own sphere of interest, but to lump together styles that were outside that sphere. A jazz musician might list 'traditional', 'be-bop', 'mainstream' and 'jazz-rock' as different styles, for example, and include Bach and Debussy within the category of 'classical'. Classical musicians might make hard and fast distinctions between baroque, classical, romantic and avant-garde symphonic music, on the other hand, and yet lump together 'reggae', 'heavy metal' and 'disco' music as 'pop'. A final composite list of eighteen styles was derived which seemed to be reasonably representative, and a single piece was chosen to represent each style, such as Webern's *String Quartet Op. 28* ('modern classical'); The Glitter Band's *Let's Get Together Again* ('pop'); Miles Davis's *Dr Jekyll* ('modern jazz'); Puccini's *Madame Butterfly* ('opera'); Muddy Waters' *Clouds in my Heart* ('blues'), and so on. The pieces were played in groups of three at a time to forty-four listeners, who were asked to 'think of some important way in which two are alike and thereby different from the third'.

This modified form of *repertory grid* technique (cf. Fransella and Bannister, 1977) produced a set of bipolar *constructs* for each listener, such as 'lively–dull' and 'vocal–instrumental', which were categorised into five types. (The development of this scheme of content analysis, which draws on the work of Bullogh (1921) and Wright (1975), is described in the original report.) *Categorical* responses classify the music in terms of a stylistic label such as 'pop', 'folk', or 'classical'. 'Objective' responses were defined as those referring to intrinsic qualities of the music itself, and two categories of these were distinguished. *Objective-Analytic* responses refer to specific 'technical' elements such as instrumentation or tempo (e.g. 'played by strings', 'fast', 'syncopated') and *Objective-Global* responses describe intrinsic qualities of the music as a whole rather than specific elements of it (e.g. 'American', 'religious', 'twentieth-century'). *Affective* responses were defined as those which are emotional and evaluative (e.g. 'cheerful', 'weird', 'horrible'), and *Associative* responses as those which refer to extra-musical associations evoked by the music (e.g. 'birds singing', 'the sea', 'a log cabin in Canada').

The main result was that there seemed to be a sharp distinction between what might be called objective, technical responses (i.e. principally those in the *Categorical*, *Objective-Global* and *Objective-Analytic* categories), and more subjective, personal ones (especially those in the *Affective* category). This distinction clearly emerged from the matrix of correlations between the frequencies with which each type of construct was produced by the subjects, and it was confirmed in a supplementary factor analysis. It also emerged that musically experienced listeners were more likely to produce constructs of the former type, and the less experienced to produce the latter.

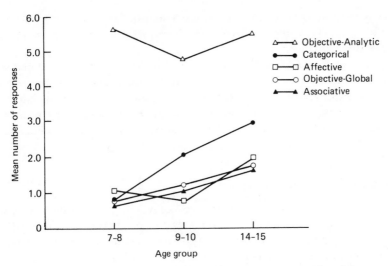

Fig. 5.5 *Descriptions of musical pieces by three age groups (reproduced from Hargreaves (1982a) by permission of the editor of* Psychology of Music)

This experiment formed the basis of a second one (Hargreaves, 1982a) in which the same scheme of content analysis was applied to the reactions of children of different ages to the same eighteen pieces of music. The pieces were played to forty-two children in each of three age groups: 7–8 years, 9–10 years, and 14–15 years. This time they were presented in nine pairs, and the children were asked to 'write down either in what way you think these two pieces are the same as one another, or how you think they are different from one another, in one sentence only'. The central *ideas* expressed in these sentences were categorised into the same five groups as in the previous study, and the results for each age group are shown in Figure 5.5. My hope was that restricting the children's replies to one sentence would mean that all three age groups should produce roughly equal numbers of ideas; unfortunately, that turned out not to be the case. Figure 5.5 shows that the children in the oldest age group produced significantly more ideas overall than did those in the other two, and the statistical analysis confirmed this. This means that any effects related to age in the results may have simply arisen from the fact that the older children were more fluent in producing classifiable responses; it may have had nothing to do with their reactions to the music as such.

Allowing for this problem, some interesting findings nevertheless emerged. Children in all three age groups seemed to produce a consistently high proportion of 'objective' reactions; the *Objective-Analytic* category occurred most frequently in each case. This is rather surprising in view of Gardner's (1973b) suggestion that such reactions should increase with age whilst more subjective ones should decline (see Chapter 2). However, Gardner's other suggestion, that sensitivity to musical style should increase with age, *is* borne out by the results. The tendency to use a stylistic label such as 'classical', 'rock', or 'folk', as represented by the *Categorical* responses, does indeed show a steady rise across the age groups.

It seems fairly obvious that this field of study is in its infancy, and that we are not yet in a position to draw any firm conclusions about the broad dimensions of responses to music. The application of the various different multidimensional scaling techniques does appear to hold some promise, especially if we are careful not to let the statistical tail wag the psychological dog.

Archival/historical approaches

Farnsworth (1969) carried out some well-known research on the nature of musical taste which was based on a *historical* analysis of the relative popularity of different composers, using a variety of different *archival* sources of information. These included the contents of orchestral programmes, radio programmes, musical encyclopaedias and reference books, which Farnsworth used alongside subjects' rankings of the composers on criteria such as eminence, enjoyment, and familiarity. One investigation, carried out in 1964, involved members of the American Musicological Association in nominating ten composers born in the 1870s or later who 'had the best chance subsequently of achieving great eminence, of producing compositions most worthy to be called to the attention of children and lay contemporaries, and so to be preserved as part of the musical heritage' (Farnsworth (1969) p. 101). Dividing the responses into two groups by alternate order of receipt revealed a very high degree of agreement amongst them. The first fourteen names chosen by the two groups were identical (Stravinsky, Bartok, Hindemith, Schoenberg, Berg, Prokoviev, Ravel, Britten, Copland, Webern, Vaughan Williams, Milhaud, Shostakovich, and Ives), and there were only minor variations in their rank orders.

Farnsworth carried out similar investigations based on eminence rankings over a period of some thirty years, which included rankings of classical composers born before 1870, and of composers of popular classics (e.g. George Gershwin, Cole Porter, Irving Berlin, Richard Rogers). His respondents included university students and subscribers to a Dutch symphony orchestra. Apart from the interest in the historical trends themselves, to which we return in Chapter 7, the overwhelming finding was that there exists very close agreement about the relative eminence of composers both between and within groups of expert and lay listeners. Farnsworth's investigations of his subjects' ratings of their *enjoyment* of different composers' works revealed that there was a great deal of overlap between enjoyment and eminence ratings, but that the size of the correlation between them was dependent on the degree of musical sophistication of the subjects. There were higher levels of agreement on composer preference rankings *within* groups of university students and symphony players, for example, than there were *between* the groups.

Historical analyses of more objective measures of popularity, such as the contents of orchestral programmes, and space allocations in musical reference books, also suggested that there is a good deal of agreement about musical taste. Farnsworth cites Mueller and Hevner's (1942) analysis of the programmes of seven leading U.S. symphony orchestras between 1936 and 1941: Beethoven, Brahms, Mozart, Wagner, Tchaikovsky, and Sibelius occurred most frequently on each orchestra's programme. Similarly, Farnsworth found that histories and encyclopaedias of music published from 1900 onwards all devoted almost the same relative amounts of space to the ninety-two composers that were most highly regarded by his sample of musicologists.

Farnsworth's research led him to two clear-cut conclusions. First, musical taste is lawful rather than whimsical: there is a strong degree of agreement about the relative merits of different composers within given groups of listeners. In some instances this agreement exists *between* as well as *within* groups of listeners, and it can often be stable over long periods of time. His own research demonstrated clearly that 'top billing' was given to a small, select group of composers by college and high school students as well as by experts, and that the different subjective assessments employed were confirmed by more objective measures. In this light Farnsworth's second conclusion may appear rather paradoxical, namely that musical taste is culturally *relative* rather than *absolute*. It cannot be explained in terms of the laws of natural science, or of any metaphysical rules, because it is based upon socially defined standards which vary from culture to culture and from period to period.

Another more recent researcher whose work is as original and innovative as Farnsworth's is Dean Keith Simonton of the University of California. His book *Genius, creativity and leadership* (1984) summarises his 'historiometric' investigations of what he calls the 'laws of genius' in a variety of different fields of endeavour, which he has carried out over the last two decades or so. I shall concentrate on his work on music, looking at its implications for the study of musical creativity in Chapter 6, and at its general approach to the experimental analysis of responses to music in this section.

Simonton has made extensive use of computerised content analysis techniques in order to code large numbers of musical themes drawn from the classical repertoire, and thence to carry out analyses of the relationships between measures derived from these thematic data bases. This *historiometric* approach is essentially *nomothetic*, in the sense that it uses the statistical sampling approach of empirical social science in seeking answers to universal questions. It contrasts with the more traditional approach of *psychohistory*, which is *idiographic* in its focus upon the in-depth analysis of the lives of important individuals.

Two studies (Simonton 1977, 1980a), for example, were based on 5,046 themes by ten extremely eminent composers (Bach, Handel, Haydn, Mozart, Beethoven, Schubert, Chopin, Wagner, Brahms, and Debussy), taken from thematic dictionaries by Barlow and Morgenstern (1948, 1976). These were selected as the 'top ten' composers on the basis of Farnsworth's research; although they represent less than 1 per cent of the available pool of composers, they have produced 39 per cent of all the music performed in the classical repertoire. In another study (Simonton, 1980b), the data base was extended to include some 15,618 themes by 479 classical composers. For all practical purposes, this could be taken to define the entire thematic repertoire of classical music. Paisley (1964) demonstrated that the first four notes of a given theme can usually serve to identify a composer's style, and Simonton chose to base his analyses on the first six notes of each, so as to gain additional information about melodic structure.

This approach has a number of clear advantages in comparison with the normal methods of experimental aesthetics (as well as some disadvantages, as we shall see later). It enjoys the benefit of very extensive (almost comprehensive) stimulus sampling; it would be impossible to utilise such a wide range of the stimulus domain in the course of conventional experimental research. The use of citation measures of aesthetic merit also has a high degree of face and content validity: Simonton is dealing with the consensus judgements of musical experts about real-life artistic works. He also points out that the mathematical character of musical notation means that themes can easily, quickly, and reliably be translated into a suitable form for computerised analysis.

The variables that Simonton derived in his analyses of the themes are divided into four types: 'esthetic', 'biographical', 'historical' and 'control' variables. The two main 'esthetic' variables are *thematic fame*, which is rated on the basis of music appreciation textbooks, record-buying guides, thematic dictionaries, etc., and *melodic originality*, which is operationally defined in terms of the aggregated statistical infrequency of the two-note permutations appearing in each of the theme's five transitions. 'Biographical' variables concern the composer's personal circumstances at the time when the theme was composed, and include *age* and *biographical stress* (defined by tabulating spouse death, separation, divorce, etc.: see Simonton, 1977). The single 'historical' variable is the composition date of each theme; and various 'control' variables are incorporated in order to assess the effects of potential artefacts. These include the composer's *lifetime productivity*, which allows for the potential influence of the total number of themes produced by a composer on the assessment of the melodic originality of any given theme; *year's competition*, which serves to assess the potential effects of the total number of themes composed by other composers in the same year; *work size*, which allows for variation in the number of cited themes within a given work; *medium*, which involves the coding of vocal separately from instrumental themes; *form*, which codes themes as being derived from chamber, church, or theatre works, as distinct from the normal concert repertoire; and *interactions* between all of these.

Simonton has tested a number of different hypotheses by carrying out multivariate analyses of these measures; in Chapter 6, we shall look in detail at his work on the creative productivity of composers, especially in relation to age, and historical time. I shall concentrate here on his analysis of the relationship between *thematic fame* and *melodic originality*, which has an important bearing on my earlier discussion of the relationship between familiarity and liking for music. This earlier discussion was set in the context of experimental aesthetics – Simonton's research represents a complementary approach to some of the same issues. His 'thematic fame' variable is closely related to liking: indices of popularity such as frequency of appearance in recording or citation guides could be thought of as real-life historical indicators of the likes and dislikes of the listening public as a whole; and he has shown (1983) that this variable does show positive correlations with actual frequency of performance.

Simonton (1980a) explicitly used Berlyne's 'optimal arousal' model to formulate the hypothesis that 'Thematic fame is a curvilinear inverted-U function of melodic originality' (p. 208), and tested it on his first data base of 5,046 themes. The results did not provide support; instead, a positive linear relationship was found between the two variables. Simonton suggests two possible explanations for this failure to confirm the hypothesis: first, that the use of themes by the ten most popular composers may have restricted the range of the originality variable that was sampled. This is very similar to Sluckin, Hargreaves and Colman's (1983) explanation of the appearance of Zajonc-type 'mere exposure' effects in some of the studies of familiarity and liking, given that Simonton's 'melodic originality' is one of the various manifestations of familiarity that could describe the abscissa of the inverted-U function. Simonton's second explanation is that the context of real-life music performance may be less likely to give rise to inverted-U relationships than laboratory studies, because the extensive repetition of themes in the classical repertoire does not take place in the laboratory. My earlier discussion of the effects of repetition on liking shows that this is by no means a straighforward issue.

In a subsequent study, Simonton (1980b) overcame the first of these potential sources of restriction by testing the same hypothesis on his more representative sample of 15,618 themes. He also incorporated a new theoretical distinction, between *repertoire* and *zeitgeist* melodic originality. Repertoire melodic originality is defined as the uncommonness, or statistical infrequency of a theme, in relation to the entire repertoire of music listening; zeitgeist melodic originality is defined in relation to other themes composed at about the same historical time. The ultimate fame of a melody may be a function of both. The results of this second study suggested that thematic fame is an inverted-J function of repertoire melodic originality, and a J-function of zeitgeist melodic originality. The first result reverses that obtained in the original (1980a) study; with a refined definition of originality, and a more representative sample of themes, a curvilinear relationship seems to obtain rather than a positive monotonic one. Simonton interprets this as support for the optimal arousal model upon which his initial hypothesis was based. Taking this along with the second result, we can conclude that, *at any given time*, that the most famous melodies are those which are most original, but that *over time*, that is, in long-term historical perspective, the most famous melodies are those of intermediate originality.

This theoretical distinction is an important one, which has a lot in common with that between the two applications of inverted-U theory to music which were proposed earlier in this chapter. It is virtually the same as that which forms the basis of the *preference-feedback* hypothesis, which I outline in Chapter 7 in an account of musical fashions. There is a good deal of scope for theoretical development here as well as for further empirical work.

Behavioural studies

One very promising line of current research on the assessment of responses to music stems from the behavioural approach. R.D. Greer and his associates, for example (e.g. Greer, 1978), have carried out a series of studies in which direct behavioural assessments of musical preference are made by using the *Operant Music Listening Recorder* (OMLR). This instrument, which was pioneered by Cotter and his associates (e.g. Cotter and Toombs, 1966; Cotter and Spradlin, 1971), could be described as a 'free operant episodic listening device'. It consists of a push-button switching box connected to an event recorder and timer; both functions can be readily carried out by modern laboratory microcomputers. Several music channels (typically four) are set to run simultaneously, and the subject selects any one of the channels by pressing the appropriate button. The precise length of time spent listening to each channel is automatically recorded, and so is the number of selections of each channel. This basic technique can be varied in many ways; the length of the session can be changed, the number of channels varied, and other listening options (e.g. silence, or white noise) can be incorporated. Greer built in the requirement that listeners must search the different channels if any single one was selected for a continuous period of two minutes.

The strength of this technique lies in the fact that it gives a direct and precise *behavioural* measure of the subject's music preference; it provides information that cannot be gained from verbal measures, and has thus been used successfully with groups of subjects including mental retardates, and children from preschool age upwards. The OMLR task also possesses a degree of face validity in the sense that people engage in analogous 'button-pushing' activities when listening to their car radios, for example.

Greer argues that the length of time spent listening to a particular musical stimulus is a direct measurement of its reinforcement value, and that this in turn is a direct indicator of its aesthetic value. The research evidence suggests that listening time is a fairly stable and reliable behavioural measure (e.g. Cotter and Spradlin, 1971), and shows positive correlations with measures such as attentiveness during concerts (Dorow, 1977). Other measures of reinforcement have also been devised, including information-seeking about music (Clarke, 1970), selective attention to the tuning (key signature) of orchestral compositions (Geringer, 1976), to different musical instruments (Geringer, 1977), and to intonation and/or tone quality amongst trumpet players (Geringer and Madsen, 1981). There is plenty of scope for further applications along these lines.

The majority of studies reviewed in this chapter have employed verbal self-report measures of responses to music, and it is of considerable interest to compare them directly with behavioural indices. It may well be that what people say about their musical likes and dislikes is quite different from their real-life listening behaviour; social psychologists are well aware, in more general terms, that the relationship between attitudes and behaviour is by no means straightforward (see e.g. Fishbein, 1967). Kuhn, Sims and Shehan (1981), for example, found correlations of 0.09, 0.58 and 0.59 between a behavioural measure of preference and a rating scale measure of liking for three pieces of varying styles. This level of agreement seems to be fairly typical of other studies along similar lines (e.g. Morgan and Lindsley, 1966; Pantle, 1978; Geringer, 1982): the average correlation between verbal and operant measures of music listening is around 0.50. This is about the level that would be expected from the results of other non-musical studies in the field of attitude measurement (Noll and Scannell, 1972; Wapnick, 1976).

The main area of application of this approach to date has been in the investigation of age changes in listening preference. Greer, Dorow and Randall (1974) used the OMLR to study the preferences of 134 children, ranging from nursery school pupils to sixth graders. They found a growing preference with increasing age for 'rock' music (selections taken from a rock radio station's 'top twenty'), and a corresponding decline in preference for 'non-rock' music (including symphonic music, classical piano music, and Broadway show tunes). There were no significant rock/non-rock preferences in the nursery school and first grade subjects, though rock was consistently preferred above this age. In particular, there seemed to be a 'critical change' between the ages of eight and nine, so that listening time for the rock music increased significantly, and that for the non-rock music showed a corresponding decrease.

Geringer (1982) carried out a study of three age/training subject groups (randomly selected fifth and sixth graders, college education majors, and undergraduate and graduate music majors), and employed the OMLR alongside verbal measures of preference. The four OMLR channels played the music of two 'composers in the formal tradition' (Bach and Beethoven), and

two 'popular composers' (John Denver and Barry Manilow). These composers were chosen because they emerged as the two top-ranking members in
each category in a previous free-recall survey of the musical tastes of three
similarly selected subject groups (Geringer and McManus, 1979). The results
were very clear: college music students showed marked preferences for
composers in the formal tradition, and the two non-musician groups for
popular composers, on both the verbal and behavioural measures. This
confirmed the findings of the previous free-recall study (which was based on
preference rankings, record collections, and concert attendances). Geringer
and McManus also found that the preference rankings of their college music
major subjects resembled those of Farnsworth's musicologists, described
above.

Given this resemblance to Farnsworth's results, which emerged from a
decidedly non-behavioural perspective, we might justifiably ask what unique
insights can be gained from the view of music listening as reinforcement value
that cannot be gained from other approaches. One field of research which
stems directly from the behavioural approach is that on environmental effects
on the reinforcement value of music; Greer, Dorow and their associates at
Teachers College, Columbia University, have carried out a series of
investigations of the effects of adult approval on students' music selection
behaviour. Greer *et al.* (1973), for example, found that fifth graders who
received music lessons under conditions of high adult approval (verbally
conveyed phrases such as 'good, I like the way you listen') selected more of the
taught music on a post-treatment OMLR task than the subjects who received
the lessons under conditions of low approval (phrases such as 'do it like this').
Greer, Dorow and Hanser (1973), using similar techniques, found that second
and third grade children's pre-test preferences for rock music over symphonic
music could be eliminated by differential teacher approval; and the same pre-
test preference in nursery school children could be reversed in favour of
symphonic music under certain conditions. Further studies along similar lines
showed that post-treatment selection behaviour was positively correlated with the *level* of adult approval/disapproval experienced during the
treatment sessions – four approvals per minute over twelve five-minute
sessions was sufficient to make dramatic changes in the preferences of first
graders, for example (Dorow, 1977; Greer, Dorow and Wolpert, 1978).
Preference and reinforcement value were also found to be more amenable to
change with children aged between two and eight years than with those above
age eight (Greer, Dorow and Randall, 1974).

Although these effects are striking and reliable, it seems likely that the
experiments tell only part of the story of the development of children's
musical preferences. As we shall see in Chapter 7, some aspects of adolescent
musical taste are based on the *opposition* of authority; secondary school
pupils may self-consciously prefer music that is positively *disapproved* by
adults. Is a behavioural explanation of this phenomenon less appropriate

than, for example, a role theory account in terms of identification with peer group norms? Or is it simply the case that the most powerful reinforcements for adolescents are those provided by peers, rather than by adults? Here is not the place to debate this knotty theoretical question: I would simply suggest, pragmatically, that one can conduct research in this field without a prior commitment to one side or the other. The OMLR is a valuable and versatile instrument that can be used in many areas of research on response to music without the necessary adoption of a behaviouristic view.

Psychometric studies

Tests of musical preference
In this section I shall consider those tests which, in the broadest terms, are concerned with the psychometric assessment of individuals' aesthetic responses to music. Their common approach is to compare listeners' preference judgements about musical stimuli with external criterion judgements, and these are usually based on the consensual views of musical 'experts'. Boyle (1982) suggests that the term 'preference test' probably provides the most neutral and parsimonious description of what is actually being assessed, though the interpretations that have been put upon this preference behaviour vary widely. Authors have referred to the measures as tests of musical taste, appreciation, sensitivity, discrimination, interest, opinion, and so on: perhaps the most general and all-inclusive term, if not the most elegant, is Bullock's (1973) 'measures of musico-aesthetic attitude'. Bullock's review of some forty-five tests is very useful in that it provides a conceptual framework which can be related to the wider range of musical ability, achievement, and attitude tests: I shall return to this shortly.

Some test authors have employed preference tests within aptitude test batteries, and thereby implicitly regard them as measuring the affective components of musical ability. Colwell's (1967) measure of 'stylistic discrimination', for example, involves subjects in making accurate value judgements as to the inferiority and superiority of different renditions of the same musical pieces: he regards this as having cognitive (discriminative) as well as affective (taste) components. Other authors more explicitly and unambiguously regard them as measures of attitudes towards music, without any connotations concerning ability. Farnsworth (1969), for example, defined musical taste as the listener's 'overall attitudinal set' towards music; this represents the long-term patterning of individual short-term preferences. Even this is not clearly distinct from ability, of course, in that attitudes are widely acknowledged by social psychologists as having cognitive as well as affective components.

Farnsworth's (1969) survey of what he called 'measures of musical taste' adopted only the broadest of distinctions between 'auditory tests' and 'paper-and-pencil tests', which he discussed alongside the non-psychometric, archival/historical measures that were discussed earlier (eminence rankings, orchestral programmes, reference book listings, and so on). Bullock's (1973) review is much more explicit about the nature of the tasks themselves, and I shall follow his taxonomic system here. Bullock divides the forty-five tests into three broad types: the first, 'measures of perceptive ability', essentially tap what he calls the *evaluative* aspects of 'musico-aesthetic attitudes'. The next two types measure the *valuative* aspects: these are 'verbal measures of attitudinal disposition' and 'tonal measures of attitudinal response' respectively. This distinction between evaluative and valuative aspects corresponds to that between cognitive and affective components of responses, mentioned above.

The measures of perceptive ability can be further subdivided into two types. Those of the first type are specifically designated as tests of 'musical aptitude'. Thus, for example, the *Kwalwasser tests of melodic and harmonic sensitivity* (1927) require subjects to rate short melodies and chord progressions as 'good' or 'bad', and the subsequent *Kwalwasser-Dykema tests of melodic taste and tonal movement* (1930) require subjects to select the most appropriate conclusions to unfurnished musical phrases. Part 2 of the *Wing standardised tests of musical intelligence* (1968) similarly includes four subtests in which subjects are presented with pairs of renditions of melodies in which rhythmic accent, harmony, intensity, and phrasing are varied. They are asked to judge whether these pairs are 'same' or 'different', and if different, which is the better member of the pair in terms of the variable being measured. In the musical sensitivity part of Gordon's (1965) extensively used *Musical aptitude profile*, subjects are asked to decide which of two renditions of a musical excerpt 'makes better musical sense': the renditions are varied in their phrasing, balance, and style.

The second type of 'perceptive ability' test is based on the 'achievement of skill in appreciation' rather than specifically on aptitudes. These measures are based on the recognition and evaluation of specific musical elements, and are thus dependent on subjects' knowledge and experience. In the *Keston music recognition test* (1954), for example, subjects are asked to identify the composers of thirty short excerpts from a supplied list of thirty-four.

Bullock's 'verbal measures of attitudinal disposition' do not concern us greatly here since they rely on subjects' self-report statements about their attitudes to music rather than upon actual responses as such. Bullock reviews the main *music interest* inventories, such as the *Farnsworth rating scales for musical interests* (1949), and those *vocational interest* inventories, such as the *Strong vocational interest blank* (1945) that evaluate individuals' interests in music in terms of their suitability for a professional career in music.

Bullock's 'tonal measures of attitudinal response' are perhaps most central to our interests here. They are more 'aesthetically' oriented than the perceptive ability tests in that they specifically ask for affective reactions, though there may well be a good deal of overlap. Bullock identifies five main types. Tests of 'sensitivity to appropriateness of extramusical associations', such as the *Taylor test of dramatic feeling* (1963), require subjects to identify which extra-musical associations – in this case dramatic mood – are intended by the composer. Tests of 'preference for excerpts of diverse merit' typically require the subject to recognise an original excerpt as better than an altered, or 'mutilated' version of it. the *Adler music appreciation tests* (1929) contain 'dull', 'chaotic', and 'sentimental' mutilations of pieces by Brahms, Chopin, Mozart, Rameau, Ravel, and Weber, for example; and the *Indiana–Oregon music discrimination tests* (Long, 1965), which are derived from the original tests of Hevner and Landsbury, involve variations of melody, rhythm, and harmony. Tests of 'preference for various music styles' require subjects to make comparative evaluations *between* rather than *within* styles. The *Baumann music preference inventory* (1960) assesses subjects' relative preferences for popular, classical, and traditional music, for example, and the *Bradley music preference inventory* (1972) is concerned with relative preferences for tonal, polytonal, atonal, and electronic music. 'Tests' in this third category, including both the Baumann and Bradley measures, are often specially constructed to meet a specific experimental need, rather than to stand as widely applicable, comprehensive assessments of taste.

Bullock's fourth and fifth categories of tonal measure are 'multiple, predetermined attributes of appreciation' and 'clinical diagnosis and counseling tests' respectively. The former includes measures which attempt to break 'appreciation' down into its components and assess those separately, such as Crickmore's (1973) approach in terms of 'syndromes'; and the latter includes tests which use musical preferences as a vehicle for personality assessment, such as the *IPAT music preference test* (Cattell and Anderson, 1953).

The central question for all of these tests concerns their *validity*: what exactly are they trying to measure, and how well do they manage to do it? The validity of a psychological test is usually measured in terms of the size of the correlation between subjects' scores and scores on some external criterion measure. We could, in the case of these tests, work on the assumption that the criterion consists of the consensual views of experts: test validity can then be straightforwardly and easily assessed, for example, as the correlation between the rankings of the same musical pieces by test-subjects and experts. The problem is that this criterion is essentially *culture-bound*: there is plenty of evidence (notably that of Farnsworth, 1969) that the views of experts are subject to change. This means that the tests are essentially measuring something like 'acculturation', or conformity to the established norms of preference, rather than 'appreciation' or 'sensitivity' in any objective or independent sense. Since many of the great composers have achieved their greatness precisely by breaking down and reconstructing these norms, this may or may not be an ability that should be cultivated!

The inadequacy of this approach to validity is brought out very clearly in a measure such as the *Keston music preference test* (Keston and Pinto, 1955).

In this, subjects are asked to make judgements about the relative worth of 120 musical excerpts, presented in groups of four. These judgements are assessed in terms of their degree of agreement with the ratings of twelve 'music authorities'. Now these authorities regard the twelve 'serious classics' excerpts as the best ones, for example, and the twelve 'swing' excerpts as the worst, and the implication is that their view somehow carries more weight than that of a test subject. This is clearly unsatisfactory, as there is no sense in which such a judgement could be determined 'right' or 'wrong' , regardless of one's personal preferences and prejudices. Davies (1978) puts this point succinctly in pointing out that 'nobody can tell the art critic he is wrong: they can only disagree' (p. 13).

Child's (1969) extensive discussion of 'expert reaction as a criterion of the esthetic' takes this point further, showing that it is by no means clear that experts (or to use his term, 'connoisseurs') *do* agree about standards of aesthetic merit, either within or between cultures. It may even be that what Child calls 'average reaction', that is, that of the population at large, is a more reliable reference point (cf. Beebe-Center, 1932). This was the basis of the postulation of a general factor of aesthetic appreciation, for example, by Eysenck (1940), which does not seem to have received much subsequent research attention, Konečni (1984), in some typically fascinating and quirky research, found that making major changes to the forms of presentation of different art works, thereby destroying the 'messages' intended by their creators, had virtually no effect upon the enjoyment of lay audiences. These changes included mirror image reversals and rotations of twentieth-century paintings; drastic stylistic alterations of literary texts; and alterations in the sequences of movements in Beethoven quartets. The relationship between the aesthetic preferences of expert and lay audiences is obviously not simple or straightforward, and it is almost certainly wrong to make the implicit assumption that the latter can be regarded as inferior versions of the former.

Even that most limited approach to the assessment of validity in which subjects' test scores are compared with those on similar tests of the same attribute yields poor results in this area. Boyle's (1982) study of the 'comparative validity' of three of the preference tests mentioned earlier (the appreciation subtests of the Wing Tests, the musical sensitivity portion of Gordon's MAP, and the Indiana–Oregon Tests) revealed not a single statistically significant inter-test correlation: the coefficients 'ranged from low to negligible' (p. 14). Boyle puts these disappointing results down to the smallness and restricted nature of his subject-sample: I am more inclined to think that they arise because the whole conceptual basis for this type of test is probably invalid.

Individual differences in responses to music
The research literature in this area is scattered and diverse; experimenters have looked at the effects of a wide variety of personal variables on responses

to music. Some studies have been based explicitly on psychometric tests, and others have followed the broad tradition of differential psychology in that their approach has been essentially nomothetic. Some have simultaneously considered the effects of several different demographic and personal variables: Schuessler (1948), for example, investigated the effects of age, sex, occupation, and social background on musical taste, and Keston and Pinto (1955) investigated intelligence, sex, age, personality, and musical training. There is no theoretical coherence about the various findings in this area; all I can reasonably attempt to do here is to identify the main individual difference variables that have been investigated, and to summarise the conclusions about their effects. Those studies which have looked at the effects of social background, and especially at social class, will be left until Chapter 7. In this section I shall briefly outline the literature concerning three other variables, namely age, ability/training, and personality.

Age is of course the variable that is most central to a developmental perspective, and three approaches to the development of responses to music have already been covered in this chapter. Some work in *experimental aesthetics* specifically looked at age in relation to stimulus familiarity; some *dimensional studies* were concerned with the changing patterns of dimensional salience with age; some of the work within the *behavioural* approach was specifically concerned with changes in the 'reinforcement value' of music at different ages. There are a few studies of individual differences in age that do not fit into any of these three categories. Rubin-Rabson (1940) found a negative correlation between age, and liking for pieces of 'classic' and 'modern' music; but neither Fisher (1951), nor Keston and Pinto (1955) found that age had any effect on preferences in their respective studies. Crowther and Durkin (1982) were concerned with the effects of age on *attitudes towards music* in their sample of 232 12–18-year-old secondary school students. They found that there was a general increase in positive attitudes over this age range, and also that girls were generally more likely to hold positive attitudes than boys. It seems likely that the influence of external cultural values and attitudes, especially those of the peer group, are at their most powerful in the secondary school years, and I shall develop this point in Chapter 7. In general, the only consistent finding to emerge from the various studies of age effects seems to be that there is a pronounced and fairly sudden increase in liking for popular music at the onset of adolescence.

I have rather arbitrarily conflated 'ability' and 'training' as the second area of individual differences research, as their effects upon aesthetic responses to music appear to be broadly similar. Listeners of high ability, and with high levels of training, are likely to prefer more complex forms of music than are those with low levels of ability and training respectively. This is of course only part of the story, as we saw in the previous section on experimental aesthetics research, but it is a prevalent finding in the (rather scanty) differential literature. Rubin-Rabson (1940) found that level of musical training was positively correlated with preference for 'modern' music; and Fay and Middleton (1941) found that subjects who preferred 'swing' music were 'decidedly inferior in sense of pitch, rhythm, and time' to those who preferred 'classical' music. Hargreaves, Messerschmidt and Rubert (1980) found that 'trained' subjects gave higher overall preference ratings than 'untrained' subjects to the excerpts used in their study, though there was a significant interaction with musical style in that the effect was more pronounced for 'classical' than for 'popular' excerpts.

The dimension of individual differences that has perhaps received the most experimental attention is that of personality. Some of the earliest work in experimental aesthetics was concerned with identifying distinct individual styles of artistic appreciation, which were called 'types of apperception', or 'apprehension'. Whilst these early typologies were not intended as descriptions of personality in the strictest sense, they nevertheless implicitly describe relatively stable and consistent aspects of behaviour which could in some sense presumably be regarded as components of personality. Bullogh's (1921) review shows that some of the leading British psychologists of the time, such as C.S. Myers and C.W. Valentine (and later P.E. Vernon), were working in this area, and he also comments in detail on the parallel research reported by Binet (1903) in *The Experimental Study of Intelligence*. Numerous other early writers had similar concerns, including Ortmann (1927), the composer Aaron Copland (1939), and Watson (1942).

I shall describe Bullogh's four-fold typology since it is fairly typical: it is closely related to the work of Myers (1922, 1927). The *objective* type of apperception is an impersonal one, which concentrates on the properties of the stimulus itself. The *intra-subjective* type is based on the personal, idiosyncratic moods that are evoked by the stimulus, and the *associative* type is based on associations, or memory images of past experiences. The fourth, *character* type, attributes a mood, or emotional character to the stimulus. The implication seems to be that one of these types will predominate in the aesthetic responses of any individual, although people are presumably capable of displaying other types when the conditions are appropriate. Research interest in this type of approach has declined since the 1930s, though a recent 'dimensional' study described earlier in this chapter (Hargreaves and Colman, 1981), draws upon Bullogh's typology as well as on some more contemporary ones.

Some other investigations of personality differences in responses to music have taken a more conventional correlational approach. The *IPAT music preference test* (Cattell and Anderson, 1953; Cattell and Saunders, 1954), mentioned above, attempts to measure personality traits and behaviour disorders in terms of subjects' liking ratings of a set of brief musical excerpts. Cattell and Saunders played 120 20-second excerpts to 188 mental hospital patients and to 196 normal subjects: factor analysis of their ratings produced eleven factors, such as 'liking for popular jazzlike structure', 'an attachment to classical music', and 'liking for warmth and gentleness'. The authors intend the test to be a clinical instrument in that it is supposed to discriminate between normal and abnormal subjects, as well as between different abnormal groups. Some limited independent evidence suggests that the test may have a reasonable degree of reliability and validity (Steenberg, 1959; Schultz and Lang, 1968).

Keston and Pinto (1955) found a relatively high correlation between scores on the *Keston music preference test* and 'intellectual introversion', and a correspondingly low correlation with 'social extroversion'. Payne (1967) hypothesised that people with stable temperaments should prefer classical music, with its emphasis on form, whereas those with neurotic temperaments should correspondingly prefer romantic music, which has more of an emphasis on feeling. She produced some positive evidence for this, based on scores of the *Maudsley personality inventory* and a questionnaire measure of composer preference, in samples of musically sophisticated college students and adult members of 'music and gramophone societies'.

Probably the most promising line of research in this area is on the interplay between the cognitive and affective determinants of aesthetic judgements; this has centred on the distinction between so-called 'warm' and 'cool', or 'hot' and 'cold' judgements. It could be thought of as 'personality' research in a broad sense, though it has implications which extend well beyond the bounds of individual differences. Machotka's (1982) study, on which I shall focus, used visual stimuli, but his conclusions could apply equally well to responses to music.

Machotka's study was based on Child's (1965) test of aesthetic judgement which, like the 'musical preference tests' reviewed earlier, involves subjects in making preference judgements between pairs of stimuli (in this case slides of artworks), one of which has reliably been judged by experts as better than the other. Machotka administered the test under two different sets of instructions, which emphasised either *subjective preference* or *objective judgement*: his subjects had no difficulty in making this distinction. Those subjects who obtained high scores under the first condition were described as 'warm' judges; they were seen as being 'open to emotional experience and search for emotional challenge in life and in art'. 'Cool' judges, who obtained high scores under the second instruction, were correspondingly seen to be more concerned with applying abstract, impersonal, standards of evaluation.

Machotka used this distinction as the basis for a four-way typology of styles of aesthetic judgement. Those who scored high under both instructions, that is, who were capable of being both 'warm' and 'cool', were termed 'esthetic' subjects: they were seen as 'emotionally open, challenged by art, and guided by evaluative standards'. Those with low scores under both conditions were described as 'nonartistic; as 'emotionally constricted, and without belief in evaluative standards'. 'Emotional' subjects were those who performed well under subjective preference instructions only, exemplifying the 'warm' style;

and 'discriminating' subjects performed well under evaluative instructions only, thereby exemplifying the 'cool' style.

Machotka's scheme is potentially important because it is in tune with current thinking in the field of social cognition (see Chapter 2); it has potential applications for art forms other than the visual; and it has clear parallels with the early work on 'apperceptive types'. It is almost certainly too simple, as indeed is any approach to the identification of individual differences which involves the arbitrary dichotomisation of subject groups. It is also somewhat confusing, conceptually, in that the proposed 'warm' and 'cool' styles are used as the basis for the definition of the four proposed groups, and yet simultaneously appear to provide the main defining characteristics of two of the four. Machotka's approach clearly deserves further empirical testing, and this should lead to theoretical refinement.

Taft (1971) proposed that 'hot' (emotional, uncontrolled) and 'cold' (evaluative, rational) styles of *creative thinking* can be identified, as we shall see in Chapter 6, and the distinction could probably be applied to other areas of thinking as well. It provides a way of looking directly at the interplay between affect and cognition. This is an important development in that the two have previously been studied quite independently from one another. The same argument applies to research on the development of social cognition, which is gradually breaking down a similar artificial barrier between 'social' and 'cognitive' development. Zajonc (1980) seems to swim against this tide in arguing 'that affect and cognition are under the control of separate and partially independent systems that can influence each other in a variety of ways, and that both constitute independent sources of effects in information processing' (p. 151). He thinks that many aesthetic judgements take place in two quite distinct stages, in that an initial affective reaction precedes, and is relatively independent of, the perceptual and cognitive operations that are normally assumed to underlie such judgements. Thus, it may be that 'preferences need no inferences'.

Only time and experimental data will tell whether Zajonc's iconoclastic view is correct; most researchers would argue that the two cannot be separated. Even Piaget, who has been severely criticised for failing to take adequate account of social and affective factors in his theory of cognitive development, argued long ago that 'the decentering of cognitive constructions necessary for the development of the operations is inseparable from the decentering of affective and social constructions' (Piaget and Inhelder, 1969, p. 95).

This debate goes well beyond the bounds of 'individual differences in responses to music', but the issues raised are fundamental to our understanding of personality, and the outcome will probably determine the direction of future research. In the next chapter I shall continue to explore the relationship between personality and music by looking at the complex question of creativity.

6

Creativity, personality, and musical development

Creativity is one of the most complex, mysterious, and fascinating aspects of human behaviour. It has attracted the attention of philosophers, artists, historians, and other thinkers for many years, and its complexity presents difficult, if not intractable problems to the experimental psychologist. Nevertheless, psychological studies of creativity have proliferated in recent years. A clear landmark was J.P. Guilford's Presidential Address to the American Psychological Association in 1950 on 'Creativity'. A wealth of research has been carried out since then; the *Journal of Creative Behavior* was established in 1967, and is still flourishing. Early signs that the empirical study of creativity represented a 'bandwagon' or 'cult' topic, which would become yet another educational fad, were not borne out. Instead, as Freeman, Butcher and Christie (1971) pointed out, 'It is now accepted in erudite and conservative circles: a review of the appropriate major learned journals and abstracts in education and psychology shows that a significant number of sub-sections have been established under the general heading "creativity"' (p. 74). Two of the twelve subscales of the *British ability scales* (Elliott, Murray and Pearson, 1978) are designed to assess different creative abilities, which is an indication of the way in which the topic has been assimilated into the mainstream of psychology.

Unfortunately, this rapid growth of research has not occurred in any organised or systematic way. Yamamoto's (1965) view of the field is what he calls a 'blind man's view of the elephant', implying that researchers' differing presuppositions about and definitions of creativity are not co-ordinated with one another. The term 'creativity' is perhaps best regarded as a convenient shorthand term in psychology – as an 'umbrella' encompassing different aspects of ability, personality, affect, and motivation. To complicate the matter still further, the interest in creativity has been equally strong in education, especially in the context of 'child-centred' and informal teaching methods; and the same term carries yet more different connotations in this context.

In this chapter I review those areas of this sprawling field that have particular relevance for developmental questions, and concentrate, wherever possible, on specific examples from and applications to the field of music. I begin by considering the difficult concept of creativity and how it might be defined and measured, and in what sense it can be applied to everyday life as well as to the works of the great, acknowledged creators. The creative process is perhaps the most elusive phenomenon of all for empirical investigation; though some preliminary attempts have been made, the main progress has been theoretical rather than empirical. I outline some of the theories of the creative process that have been advanced, consider some introspections about creativity that have been made by famous musical creators, and look at some work which is beginning to study the cognitive processes involved in composition and improvisation. Another approach has been to try to identify the typical characteristics of the creative person; I consider the characteristics of some famous musical prodigies, and review the empirical research on personality, cognitive style and creativity, and on the personalities of musicians. The largest single area of creativity research has been that based on the psychometric approach, where the focus has been on the relationships between measures of divergent thinking, intelligence, and educational attainment. I consider some of the factors that affect these relationships, and look in particular at the effects of age. Finally, I look briefly at some of the attempts that have been made to devise tests of musical creativity.

The concept of creativity

'Creativity' is a term that psychologists define in many different ways, as we saw above; it is also a term that is widely misused in everyday life. Hudson (1966) was quite right to say that 'In some circles "creative" does duty as a word of general approbation – meaning, approximately, "good" – it "covers everything from the answers to a particular kind of psychological test, to forming a good relationship with one's wife" (p. 119). The adjective's use can now even take on a pejorative connotation, as in 'creative' accounting, that is, that which may be less than 100 per cent honest in certain respects. In trying to establish an adequate definition of the concept, it is useful to distinguish between *originality* and creativity. The former, strictly speaking, can simply be defined in terms of novelty, or statistical infrequency: an 'original' response to a question, for example, is one which no one else has thought of. For a response to be creative, however, it needs to be in some way useful as well as original. 'Thus, 7,363,474 is quite an original answer to the problem "How much is 12 + 12?" However, it is only when conditions are such that this answer is useful that we can also call it creative' (Mednick, 1962, p. 221).

It is obviously important for the psychologist to establish a *criterion* for creativity, especially if the aim is to devise valid procedures for its measurement. Two main types of criterion have been used: those which are based on the nature of the *product*, and those based on the characteristics of the *person*.

One example of the former approach is simply to analyse the individual's creative products; the creativity of scientists, for example, could be measured by summing up the number of their patents, publications, research reports, and so on. McPherson (1963) has found some problems with this approach, as different products vary in their creative worth, and many scientific products remain unpublished or unpatented. He suggests a scheme for assessing the creative qualities of different products so they can be compared on the same basis: this is adapted from an existing patent law, designed to determine the 'inventivlevel' of patent applications. Products are judged in terms of their 'creative strength', their usefulness, and their novelty. These criteria resemble those suggested by Jackson and Messick (1965), who propose that a creative product should possess the properties of *transformation*, that is, the overcoming of constraints such that reality is seen in a new way, and *condensation*, which implies that the product can be interpreted in a multiplicity of ways, that is, that it possesses a high degree of summary power.

This approach has a good deal to commend it, and it has recently been taken up by Amabile (1982) as part of her contention that a social psychology of creativity must necessarily complement the differential approach. She proposes a 'consensual' definition of creativity according to which 'A product or response is creative to the extent that appropriate observers independently agree it is creative' (p. 1001), and a corresponding 'consensual assessment' technique which is based on the agreement between independent judges about the creativity of products within a given domain. The main limitation of this approach is that the operational definitions of creativity are restricted to the particular class of creative products under consideration, and therefore lack generality.

Person-based approaches do not suffer from this particular disadvantage, since they implicitly regard creativity as an individual trait which is predictive of real-life productivity; in other words, they try to assess what might be called 'creative potential'. By far the most common approach has been to employ *divergent thinking tests*, which are designed to assess those characteristics of thinking which are hypothesised to be predictive of real-life creativity. *Fluency* and *originality* are the characteristics which have received the most attention, though procedures have also been devised for the assessment of *flexibility* and *elaboration* (see e.g. Torrance, 1962). Finding out whether these actually do predict real-life creativity, and establishing the appropriate criteria of this, is of course the central *validation* problem. I shall return to this psychometric research area in the last section of this chapter.

An important feature of person-based approaches is that creativity is regarded as being a normally distributed trait; everyone is seen as creative to a greater or lesser extent, and as expressing this in different ways according to individual interests. This is an appealing feature for empirical researchers in that it possesses generality, not being tied to particular products, and also in that it 'demystifies' creativity. Creativity is seen as a mundane, everyday aspect of behaviour which can be observed in the activities of young children, for example, just as in the works of great artists. Nicholls (1972) argues against this view: 'To ensure that a trait of creativity has essentially the same meaning for normal subjects and eminent creators, we must isolate the distinctive characteristics of eminent creators and show that they are related positively in unselected samples' (p. 718). Nicholls' brief review of the literature leads him to the conclusion that this is not the case, and that a product-based approach is therefore much more appropriate.

This apparent conflict almost certainly arises from the misuse of the term 'creativity' when applied to persons. We can provide valid definitions of creative products, and we can assess individual differences in ideational fluency or originality, but we cannot make the inference, as have those psychologists who have referred to 'creativity tests', that creativity *per se* is a normally distributed trait. We can only approach it via the inference that what the tests measure might predict creativity, and so the implication is that more neutral, accurate descriptions of the measures should be used.

Having established this point as far as the psychometric criteria are concerned, there is nevertheless a lot to be said in favour of the idea of 'everyday creativity' as a quality which is possessed by all. Anecdotally, I can think of numerous examples of people who inhibit themselves from drawing, painting, writing, or playing an instrument because they *think* that they lack the ability, rather than because they necessarily really do. Students feel inhibited about devising their own research projects because they feel overawed by what they feel to be the superiority of learned journals and learned professors; and there is no doubt that musical composition possesses such a mystique that many aspiring musicians (with the exception of young children!) feel very unwilling to 'have a go', especially if the results are in any way public. I suspect that this 'mystification' prevents many people from embarking on creative activities, and thereby from fulfilling their potential. Perhaps we should be encouraged by Picasso's view of his own work: 'Paintings are but research and experiment. I never do a painting as a work of art' (Liberman, 1960, p. 33).

The creative process

'When people ask me what comes first, the tune or the lyrics', said the well-known popular songwriter Sammy Kahn, 'I say the thing that comes first is the phone call.' This is a down-to-earth, mundane view of the creative process that is held by many hard-bitten writers of popular music, and probably by quite a high proportion of 'serious' composers as well. Creative work is seen as an everyday affair, involving a good deal of persistence and hard work; it is ordinary and rational. Many writers take this view of their work, time-tabling their writing in a daily routine. Creativity in this sense is literally an 'everyday' activity like eating or sleeping. This is just the opposite of the rather romantic view that many people have of the creative artist; he is popularly perceived as a sensitive, intense individual, probably starving in a garret. When the Muse is upon him, he works frantically, without food or sleep, until the work has been produced. According to this view, creativity is mysterious, unconscious, irrational, and anything but ordinary.

These two apparently opposite views, that creativity largely involves either 'perspiration' or 'inspiration', have fascinated psychologists, philosphers, and creative artists themselves for many years. Because of this, there is a good deal of introspective evidence that provides revealing insights into the working methods of different creators. Almost certainly, the majority view is that creation involves inspiration as well as perspiration – that it is both irrational *and* rational – but there are some artists who report working predominantly in one mode rather than the other. The painter Max Ernst claimed to exert no conscious control over his work, for example, whereas the writer Edgar Allan Poe insisted that creative work involves no more than conscious planning and rational decision-making (Winner, 1982).

Similar differences in approach are to be found amongst composers. Haydn, Schumann, and Mozart, for example, all seemed able to compose with very little effort, whereas Beethoven and Bach expended a great deal of toil and sweat on the details of successive revisions. The American composer Roger Sessions reports how Beethoven's sketches for the last movement of his 'Hammerklavier Sonata'

show him carefully modelling, then testing in systematic and apparently cold-blooded fashion, the theme of the fugue. Where, one might ask, is the inspiration here? Yet if the word has any meaning at all, it is certainly appropriate to this movement, with its irresistible and titanic energy of expression, already present in the theme. The inspiration takes the form, however, not of a sudden flash of music, but a clearly envisaged impulse toward a certain goal for which the composer was obliged to strive.

(Ghiselin, 1952, p. 47)

Compare this with Mozart's account of his own composing:

When I am, as it were, completely myself, entirely alone, and of good cheer – say, travelling in a carriage, or walking after a good meal, or during the night when I cannot sleep; it is on such occasions that my ideas flow best and most abundantly. *Whence* and *how* they come, I know not; nor can I force them. Those ideas that please me I retain in memory, and am accustomed, as I have been told, to hum them to myself ... my subject enlarges itself, becomes methodised and defined, and the whole, though it be long, stands almost complete and finished in my mind, so that I can survey it, like a fine picture or a beautiful statue, at a glance. Nor do I hear in my imagination the parts *successively*, but I hear them, as it were, all at once (*gleich alles zusammen*). What a delight this is I cannot tell! All this inventing, this producing, takes place in a pleasing lively dream.

(Ghiselin, 1952, pp. 44–5. There is apparently some doubt about the authenticity of this letter)

Similarly contrasting styles of composition can also be observed in popular music. Songwriter Paul McCartney, for example, works 'on the run', drawing ideas and inspiration from his immediate environment at any given time. Duke Ellington, almost certainly the most eminent of all jazz composers, also wrote 'on the run', in dressing-rooms, trains, and buses. In his case, this was probably an inevitable consequence of life 'on the road' as a travelling musician. It is interesting to speculate whether Ellington would or would not have produced the work that he did without the pressures of the touring bandleader. Paul McCartney is presumably subject to none of these pressures, long since having amassed such a fortune from his work that he is in no way dependent on it for a living, and yet he continues to perform and compose. Equally successful is the American songwriter Paul Simon, although the process in his case is very much more laborious:

I find that by putting in time every day – if I am in a writing period – I can get more done than if I just sit around and wait for a song to happen. One of the benefits of working like this is that one can see the entire germ of a song develop from start to finish. Working steadily, it generally takes me about four to six weeks to complete a song, but if I am not working steadily it can take from four to six months.

(Martin, 1983, p. 67)

Although these composers' ways of working are quite diverse, there are elements of unconscious inspiration as well as of conscious effort that can be discerned in them all. Wallas (1926) attempted to suggest how these elements might be drawn together in proposing a four-stage theory of the creative process which has been widely quoted. The first stage, *preparation*, involves the collection of information relevant to the problem; this is probably best done in a flexible, open-ended manner. The British microelectronics inventor Clive Sinclair has commented that it is unwise to over-prepare for work on a new project, as too much advance preparation can constrain one's thinking, leading too far down paths that have already been explored by others. In the second, *incubation*, stage, conscious attention is turned away from the problem, and unconscious processes predominate. Many creators have commented upon the importance of seemingly irrelevant conditions and stimuli, which seem to act as catalysts at this point. Travel was important to Mozart; Wagner insisted upon perfumes, silks, and other 'feminine' articles; and in the non-musical world, Freud's cheroots and Coleridge's opium, for example, are equally well known.

Illumination, the third and perhaps the most difficult stage to predict, is the 'Eureka' experience in which a specific creative solution is defined: it appears with suddenness and a sense of certainty. In an often-quoted introspection, the mathematician Henri Poincaré describes his discovery of Fuchsian functions:

For fifteen days I strove to prove that there could not be any functions like those I have since called Fuchsian functions. I was then very ignorant: every day I seated myself at my work table, stayed an hour or two, tried a great number of combinations and reached no results. One evening, contrary to my custom, I drank black coffee and could not sleep. Ideas rose in crowds; I felt them collide until pairs interlocked, so to speak, making a stable combination. By the next morning I had established the existence of a class of Fuchsian functions, those which come from the hypergeometric series; I had only to write out the results, which took but a few hours.

(Ghiselin, 1952, p. 36)

We can clearly identify illumination here, as well as Wallas's fourth proposed stage, that of *verification*. Verification involves the 'working out' or formalisation of the solution: it is refined, and adapted to meet practical constraints. The theatre composer Stephen Sondheim, for example, uses aids such as dictionaries of rhymes and slang terms in order to tailor his songs to the practical constraints of a stage production (see Martin, 1983). Similarly, split-second timing is of vital importance in writing film scores, as film composer Carl Davis explains:

I frequently start to compose by improvising and playing. Then I take my time sheet and my piece of manuscript paper and work out whether the piece is slow or fast or medium, and it is then possible to measure it because the way to write out music is to work in bars: you can measure how many seconds there will be in a bar and then you just multiply so that you know how many bars are going to get you to the end of the cue. This may seem very primitive, but I can think of no better method.

(Martin, 1983, p. 92)

These introspective accounts seem to provide a good deal of anecdotal support for the existence of Wallas's stages, but this cannot of course be considered to be anything like conclusive proof of them. It would indeed be very difficult to establish any such proof, as the stages manifest themselves in very different ways according to the individual personality of the creator, the field of creative activity, and so on, but some attempts at empirical study have nevertheless been made.

Patrick (1935, 1937, 1955) investigated the writing of a poem, the painting of a picture, and the solving of a scientific problem. Groups of subjects including poets, painters, and scientists, as well as non-specialists, were given stimulus objects such as a Milton poem, and the activity with which they responded to these stimuli was observed and recorded in various ways. The results were interpreted as supporting the existence of the stages, and included some tentative evidence of incubation in that ideas which occurred early on were forgotten and then returned to later. Bahle (1936) carried out an empirical study in the musical domain by sending a set of poems to a number of eminent composers, and asking them to set them to music. The most interesting outcome was the variety of different approaches that were adopted. Some composers based melodies literally on the poems; some used the poems as springboards to relatively unrelated melodies; and some completed the task, but ignored the poems altogether.

Perhaps the most elusive and fascinating of Wallas's four stages is the second: what actually goes on during incubation? One common feature of the introspections is *imagery*; Mozart's account of his vivid mental representations of music (quoted earlier) is quite compelling, although Sloboda (1985) suggests that the composer's prodigious feats of musical memory may be better explained in terms of the superiority of his encoding skills than in terms of 'eidetic imagery'. The composer Henry Cowell trained himself to form novel images of different timbres, and was later able to use these in his compositions, and Benham's (1929) reports of the strength of his own auditory images whilst composing also support this idea (see Farnsworth, 1969, p. 176). Another prominent view is that novel associations are formed between previously unrelated cognitive elements during incubation: I return to this 'associative' theory of creativity later in the chapter.

Imagery and incubation no doubt figure prominently in a good deal of creative thinking, but neither of them can provide a comprehensive explanation of it. Such an explanation is almost certainly impossible to formulate, not least because there is no single 'creative process'. It is very likely to be the case that the creative thinking of the artist is different from that of the scientist, for example, and, at a more detailed level, that there are as many different styles of creativity as there are individual creators. Each person goes about things in a way that is unique, and this is presumably determined by temperament, past experience, environmental pressures, and so on. This brings us back to the idea of every individual possessing 'everyday creativity' to a greater or a lesser extent, although we are not consciously aware of behaving in any stylistically consistent manner. Once again it is Mozart who captures this idea: 'But why my productions take from my hand that particular form and style that makes them *Mozartish*, and different from the works of other composers, is probably owing to the same cause which renders my nose so large or so aquiline, or, in short, makes it Mozart's, and different from those of other people. For I really do not study or aim at any originality' (Ghiselin, 1952, p. 45).

Cognitive processes in composition and improvisation

Some cognitive psychologists have begun to study the complex processes underlying musical composition and improvisation by drawing analogies with other areas of skilled human performance. Sloboda (1985) suggests that these processes have two important characteristics. First, the formulation of *superordinate plans* seems to be an important starting-point; a plan for a composition or an improvisation then guides its detailed note-by-note working out. Secondly, these plans often seem to be *provisional*; they can readily be changed according to the way in which the working out proceeds, and this may be akin to the idea of *feedback* in skilled performance.

Superordinate plans have been described in different ways. The idea of a mental *scheme*, or *schema*, was discussed in Chapter 1: schemes are mental representations, or constructions, to which new information is assimilated, and which are modified as a result. They are also presumably used to guide the generation of new information. We organise activities in our everyday lives according to such schemes: shopping trips, meals, or holidays, for example, are planned by reference to general strategies based on our past experience of similar activities. We could think of these plans as 'scaffolds', that is, as empty frameworks which are filled in on different occasions with details that are appropriate to a specific situation. Minsky's (1977) notion of a 'frame' is somewhat similar to this.

In the case of musical creation there are certain scaffolds, or frames, that are pre-defined by the structures of particular musical idioms. A jazz solo based on a 12-bar blues sequence or on a 32-bar A-A-B-A 'standard' sequence, for example, has well-defined parameters that are known by all jazz performers, and these form the common language that enables musicians to 'sit in' with unfamiliar others with minimum rehearsal or preparation. In the case of more formal compositions, however (including a good deal of jazz music that is not based on the common chord sequences), the structure can itself be created and shaped by the composer: the blueprint, or skeleton, is not pre-formed.

One way of studying the nature of these blueprints, and the ways in which they are developed by composers, is to look at composers' sketches and manuscripts. Beethoven is known to have made extensive use of sketches, and to have written many successive drafts and revisions; Haydn and Mozart, on the other hand, wrote very little before the final draft. Evidence from the different colours of ink used by Mozart in his manuscripts has led musicologists to the conclusion that he worked 'top-down': he first captured the essence of a given piece (i.e. his superordinate plan of it) by writing its principal theme and its bass melody, and then subsequently 'filled in' the subordinate harmony parts at a later stage. This contradicts the popular idea that he virtually 'transcribed' the piece in all its detail from a fully formed 'camera-ready' mental image, but it is by no means conclusive proof of his way of working. It remains possible that Mozart *did* have such an image in his head, and that he chose to write this out in a 'top-down' fashion. The most likely explanation is that he probably had a clear and fully articulated plan of the essential organisation and structure of the piece in his mind, the parts of which he could indeed hear 'gleich alles zusammen', rather than a kind of mental tape-recording that he could switch on and off at will.

Sloboda (1985) has discussed the evidence from manuscripts in some detail, and points out that researchers have tended to regard composers as working *either* by 'sketching', that is, by detailed work on successive revisions, *or* by 'dictation' from an inspired vision of the work, as in the popular view of Mozart's way of working. His view is that this is a gross oversimplification, since many composers exhibit both processes: his analysis of the sketches of Stravinsky illustrates this point. He also reviews three other sources of data available to the cognitive psychologist, namely composers' introspective writings (several of which have already been discussed), observations of composers at work (including a detailed account of the writing of a section of one of his own choral compositions), and improvisation. Sloboda describes the classical pianist David Sudnow's (1978) account of the painful process of his learning jazz improvisation, which shows how increasingly complex patterns, such as chords, scales, and arpeggios, are gradually built into a coherent improvisational repertoire.

Improvisation is potentially an exceedingly fruitful medium for empirical investigation, which in a sense provides direct and instant access to the creative process, though with the exception of some work on the development of song (see Chapter 3), there has been virtually no research on the musical improvisations of children or adults. Pressing (1984) has sketched a very broad and general outline of the role of improvisation in different artistic traditions, ranging from traditional Japanese music (virtually no improvisation) to free jazz (highly improvised), with many forms in between. He proposes a model of improvisational performance which is derived from human skills research. Information is perceptually *coded*, potential responses are *evaluated*, and 'motor action units' are then *executed* in relation to cognitive 'referents', which are akin to the 'schemes' or plans described above. 'A simple description of the process might run as follows: ideas are generated and realised into sound via technique. This produces continuous aural and proprioceptive feedback, which allows continuous evaluation, on the basis of which current ideas are either repeated, developed or discarded. In this way a long-term improvisation can be built up' (p. 353). Pressing applies a 'resource allocation' model of attention (cf. Kahneman, 1973) which is based on the idea that conscious, central cognitive processing proceeds in parallel with unconscious, peripheral processing in improvisation; with training and experience, increasingly complex 'action units' shift from the control of the former to the latter. Pressing's stimulating chapter raises many more questions than it answers, and his model needs further clarification and elaboration, but it is quite clear that these issues deserve urgent attention.

Theories of creativity

The behaviouristic approach
Various distinctions between different types of learning theory were made in Chapter 1, and it seems clear that the application of behavioural principles is an extremely effective approach to improving the basic skills of music

learning. It is most effective for those skills which are easy to identify and observe, such as pitch discrimination and notation. Musical creativity is notoriously difficult to identify and observe, however, as we have seen, and it is probably for this reason that behaviouristic theories have had little success in explaining creativity. Skinner's (1972) attempt is a simple, straightforward account in terms of the artist's reinforcement history, and of the environmental consequences of creative behaviour. 'The artist puts paint on canvas and is or is not reinforced by the results. If he is reinforced, he goes on painting' (p. 335). No account is taken of the internal processes or emotional states involved in creativity; Skinner is purely concerned with the associations between observable creative behaviour and external reinforcements.

It is easy to criticise this approach for its drastic oversimplification of the phenomena under investigation: it simply cannot account for many of the phenomena that arise in the introspections of artists mentioned earlier, for example. It cannot explain how creative individuals take an active part in shaping their own course of creative development, rather than being driven by external events. It cannot account for the internal rules and strategies that are consciously used by creative artists, still less for the unconscious processes of incubation. The essence of a creative piece of work is its novelty in the context of existing environmental constraints; yet, by definition, no creator can possibly have been reinforced for producing the behaviour that led to this piece of work in his previous history.

These are all extremely difficult arguments for behaviouristic theories to handle without recourse to some form of mentalistic intervening constructs, such as those adopted in social learning theory, for example (see Chapter 1). Now it may be that the behaviouristic approach is inadequate for the explanation of creativity because it is inherently unable to deal with the phenomena, as my last point above suggests. It may be, on the other hand, that the approach *could* ultimately explain creativity if only its principles could be applied with sufficient complexity and detail. In other words, we need to decide whether the problem is more than one of operationalisation. Winner (1982) makes two further criticisms concerning difficulties with the explanation of individual differences in creativity, which confirm my own view that the problem probably *is* more serious than this:

First, the theory cannot explain why some artists but not others are reinforced for their work. What is it about the plays of the creative playwright that audience members like and which causes them to reinforce the author by attending his plays and writing positive reviews? . . . Second, why does the creative playwright persist when he is less reinforced than the hack, who may well be more popular? . . . Skinner would answer that some artists are reinforced not by popularity but by the praise of a select few or by pride in their independence. But then why does the less creative artist not find the same things reinforcing and thereby become more creative? Skinner could only reply that one artist is reinforced by a sense of independence because a sense of independence is reinforcing to him: another is reinforced by the praise of many because it is the praise of many that reinforces him. Such answers reveal the circularity and lack of predictiveness of the theory.   (p. 28)

The psychoanalytic approach

In complete contrast to the explicitly mundane and parsimonious behaviouristic view, Freud's account of artistic creativity stems from his fundamental view of the titanic struggle which takes place in each individual between powerful unconscious instinctual drives and the forces of socialisation. It would be inappropriate to expound the general aspects of the theory here: many excellent accounts exist elsewhere (e.g. Miller, 1983). In brief, a central concept is that normal psychological health can be maintained if the individual can find socially acceptable ways of releasing this instinctual energy, but that various types of neurotic disturbance may develop if this does not happen. The individual employs various *defence mechanisms* in order to regulate the conflict, which are manifested in domains such as play, dreams, daydreams, and also in artistic work. One aspect of the conflict that emerges in childhood is the well-known *Oedipus complex*, in which the child sexually desires the opposite-sex parent (see Hargreaves, 1986, for a full account). Freud suggested that one way of resolving this conflict was through artistic creativity: that artistic creation was in fact a *sublimation* of the socially unacceptable desires involved in the Oedipus conflict. His use of the work of Leonardo da Vinci as a case study to support this theory (Freud, 1910) is well known.

As far as the workings of the creative process are concerned, an important distinction is that between *primary process* and *secondary process* thinking. Freud defined primary process thinking as that which is irrational, diffuse, and undirected, as in dreams and hallucinations; it is essentially global or *syncretic* such that apparently contradictory, illogical, or unrelated ideas can co-exist, and possibly combine. Secondary process thinking is defined as the regulated, focussed activity which governs everyday, rational activity in the real world. The admittance of primary process material into an individual's thinking, which is otherwise predominated by secondary process, is seen as being regulated by the ego. If the conflicting ideas comprising primary process material are unacceptable to the ego, they are repressed, and neurotic distortions can occur (Kubie, 1958). Creative thinking occurs in individuals whose ego-strength is sufficient to admit this material without being overwhelmed by it – creativity is thus characterised by 'regression in the service of the ego' (Kris, 1950).

Pine and Holt (1960) attempted an empirical test of this theory by assessing the amount as well as the control of primary process expression by individuals on the Rorschach test, and by comparing this with creativity test scores. They found that the quality of imaginative productions, as evidenced by creativity test scores, was related to the control of primary process material (socially acceptable statements) as well as to the amount of expression of it (sexual, aggressive, or illogical statements) on the projective test. Creative thinking thus seems to require a balance between primary and secondary processes; it requires the capacity to 'suspend logical operations temporarily and to think in novel and possibly nonlogical and unconventional ways, and the capacity voluntarily to stop this regressive mode of functioning and to return to more secondary process modes of functioning where the novel thoughts are placed in appropriate and realistic contexts' (Blatt, Allison and Feirstein, 1969, p. 286).

This formulation is clearly cognitive in orientation, even though it originates from the psychoanalytic viewpoint; we could say that it operates at the interface between emotion and cognition. I pointed out in Chapter 5, in the context of aesthetic judgements, that psychologists have only recently begun to consider the interactions between these domains; and that one way forward has been to employ the distinction between 'hot' and 'cold' cognition. Taft (1971) has made an explicit attempt to apply this distinction to creative thinking. Taft draws on Freud's primary/secondary process distinction as well as on some related distinctions that have been proposed, such as that between realistic and autistic thinking (McKellar, 1957) and between sequential and multiple processing (Neisser, 1963). He synthesises all of these ideas in proposing that there are two styles of creativity: 'one a measured, problem-solving approach to the development of new knowledge; and the other, an emotional, and comparatively uncontrolled, free expression' (p. 345). Taft reports two empirical studies in which he attempts to identify these styles on an 'ego permissiveness' questionnaire and on projective tests, and relates individuals' tendencies to display one or the other style to self-reported creativity and divergent thinking. His results suggest that the two styles *can* be demonstrated empirically, and that they are unrelated to the convergent/ divergent distinction as well as to that between artistic and scientific creativity. Taft's evidence for these proposals is far from conclusive, but there can be no doubt that their implications for the direction of future research are very important. We need replications of Taft's research, further empirical tests of the validity of 'hot' and 'cold' creativity, as well as research on how the distinction relates to real-life creative thinking in the arts and the sciences.

Associative theories

One central idea that runs through the introspections mentioned earlier, as well as through the theories that we have discussed so far, is that the formation of *associations* is an integral part of creative thinking. Einstein spoke of the importance of 'combinatory play' and 'associative play' as essential features of his work, and the same features can be seen in the introspections of Mozart and Poincaré that were quoted earlier. The point is made eloquently in the context of popular songwriting by the British pop musician and composer Sting:

Our logical minds are in compartmented boxes and when those boxes are disturbed, when one is asleep for instance and not being logical, an idea can flow from one rigid box into another and that's where you get a spark. If you take a basic idea out of its environment and put it into another frame of reference, that's when you get magic. And when you 'wake up' and cement the ideas together with hard work and graft, clocking on in the morning and doing the job, the process is completed.

(Martin, 1983, p. 72)

This quotation captures the essence of primary/secondary process thinking and verification, as well as of association.

Mednick (1962) has developed an associative theory of creativity, which he defines as 'the forming of associative elements into new combinations which either meet specified requirements or are in some way useful' (p. 221). This formation of new combinations can occur in three ways: by *serendipity* (accidental contiguities of stimuli), by *similarity* between the associative elements or the stimuli which elicit them, or by *mediation* by some common element. Mednick's implementation of this theory is based on individual differences in 'associative ability'. Given a stimulus such as the word 'table', it is possible to construct an individual's 'associative response hierarchy' according to the order, and the degree of originality, of the sequence of associates that is produced. The creative individual is seen as producing relatively unstereotyped associates initially, and as being able to continue generating more remote ones. Plotting the strength of these associates (as measured, for example, by speed of response) against their degree of uniqueness gives rise to a shallow slope, as shown in Figure 6.1. The less creative individual, however, is seen as having a steep associative hierarchy: relatively stereotyped associates are produced early in the sequence, and these inhibit the production of further, more original ones.

On this basis, Mednick has devised a test of creativity. In the *Remote associates test* (RAT), subjects are presented with sets of three words drawn from mutually remote associative clusters (e.g. 'rat', 'blue', 'cottage') and asked to provide a fourth word which serves as a specific associative link between them ('cheese'). Mednick claims to have standardised and validated the RAT; he reports positive correlations with faculty ratings of the creativity of students on an architectural design course, with ratings of the research creativity of postgraduate psychology students, and with interests in 'creative occupations' such as journalism and art. There is evidence, however (e.g. Cropley, 1966), that the abilities tapped by the RAT are closer to 'convergent', directed thinking than to those involved in creativity; Wallach and Kogan (1965) point out that the experimenter is in the rather unrealistic position of knowing a supposedly 'creative' response before it is given. Their own emphasis is on the *process* of producing associations rather than on the *product* of this activity; Wallach (1970) argues that the crux of the creativity issue 'revolves around the process of generating or producing associates without regard to evaluating them for relevance or applicability to a problem or task' (p. 1254).

Wallach's emphasis is thus upon ideational fluency, without the constraint

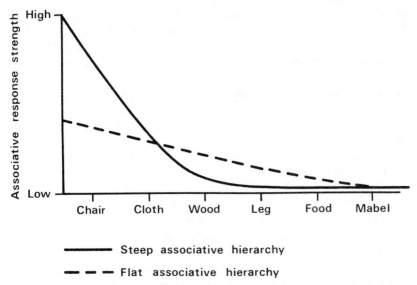

Fig. 6.1 *Mednick's 'associative response hierarchies' (from 'The associative basis of the creative process', S.A. Mednick, 1962, Psychological Review, 69, p. 223. © 1962 by the American Psychological Association. Adapted by permission of the author)*

that the ideas produced should meet any criterion of usefulness. He does not claim that such fluency is a *measure* of creativity *per se*, but rather that it is a good predictor. Mednick, on the other hand, *is* concerned with the usefulness of the product: the RAT *does* purport to be a test of creativity. Levin's (1978) study throws some light on this difference in emphasis: she examined the relationship between subjects' associative fluency on a continuous association task, and creativity as measured by a Hebrew version of the RAT. Analysis of undergraduates' orally produced continuous associations to a single stimulus word revealed two distinct modes of associative fluency, 'chains' and 'stars'. A star is a cluster of words all of which are related to the original stimulus word (e.g. 'swing, easy-chair, armchair, throne, bench, wheelchair' in response to 'table'), and a chain is a series in which each member is related to that which precedes it (e.g. 'table, wood, flowers, sea, sand, desert'). Levin found that chain fluency was related to creativity as assessed by the RAT, but that star fluency was not. We should interpret this result cautiously in view of the uncertainty as to what exactly is measured by the RAT; perhaps the most realistic conclusion is that the volume of associations produced by an individual (ideational fluency), the styles in which they are produced (chain, star, and maybe others), and the extent to which they adapt to external criteria (RAT peformance) are *all* components of creativity.

Mednick's associative theory is based on stimulus–response principles; Cropley (1967) classifies it as such, and much of Mednick's terminology derives from learning theory. It is by no means a 'behaviouristic' theory like that of Skinner, however: the elements that form associations are essentially cognitive, and the process of their formation cannot be attributed to any clearly identifiable external reinforcement. The theory has a lot more in common with that of Wallach (1970); although also 'associative', Wallach's theory is essentially one of cognitive functioning. Similarly, Koestler's (1964) orientation is also essentially cognitive, although his theory is based on associative principles. Koestler explains the creative act in terms of what he calls a 'bisociation' of two hitherto separate and habitually incompatible frames of reference, or 'matrices' of behaviour; this same idea is at the heart of all of the associative theories.

Cognitive theories

Apart from the associative theories discussed above, whose status is rather ambiguous, we can identify three further cognitive theories of creativity. The first is that of the Gestalt psychologists: Kohler's famous experiments with chimpanzees, for example, demonstrated how the restructuring of elements in their perceptual fields could produce a sudden 'insight' which led to a creative solution; this is akin to Wallas's notion of 'illumination'. The concept of re-organisation of the elements of problems was extensively studied by Duncker (1945), and Wertheimer (1945) suggested that productive thinking, which was based upon this concept, was a continuous process which formed the basis of the creations of great scientists as well as of children's attempts to solve simple geometric problems.

The second, and perhaps the best-known, cognitive theory of creativity is that of J.P. Guilford, which is squarely within the psychometric tradition. Guilford and his associates have carried out a long-running research programme at the University of Southern California which is devoted to the empirical validation of the 'structure of intellect' model (Guilford, 1967). This model, which is shown in Figure 6.2, is the result of factorial analyses of many subjects' scores on large numbers of psychological tests. Its basis is that there are 120 independent mental abilities in all, and Guilford has been able so far to produce tests measuring some 85 of them. The model incorporates five groups of intellectual *operation* (cognition, memory, divergent production, convergent production, and evaluation), which are carried out on four kinds of *content* (figural, symbolic, semantic, and behavioural), giving rise to six kinds of *product* (units, classes, relations, systems, transformations, and implications). It has been criticised for its omission of any mention of the interrelationships between the 120 cells (e.g. Eysenck, 1967), but has undoubtedly stimulated a good deal of research. As far as creativity is concerned, we can see that there are 24 cells in the divergent production category.

Divergent tests are concerned with the production of large numbers of new ideas from a given starting-point, as distinct from convergent tests in which

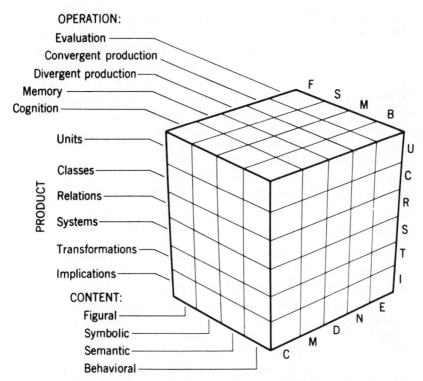

OPERATION:
Evaluation
Convergent production
Divergent production
Memory
Cognition

Units
Classes
PRODUCT
Relations
Systems
Transformations
Implications

CONTENT:
Figural
Symbolic
Semantic
Behavioral

Fig. 6.2 *Guilford's 'structure of intellect' model (reproduced from* The nature of human intelligence, *by J.P. Guilford (1967). New York: McGraw-Hill, by permission)*

subjects are required to converge on the one correct solution to a problem. Amongst Guilford's tests are *word fluency*, for example, which is assessed by asking the subject to give as many words as possible beginning with 's' or ending in '-tion': this represents the 'divergent production of symbolic units'. The parallel semantic activity, often termed 'ideational fluency', is tested by asking, for example, for as many objects as possible which are 'round' or 'red'. The trait of originality, which represents the 'divergent production of semantic transformations', is measured in three ways: by marking suggested titles for a short story for cleverness and unusualness, and by calling for remote associations. In summary, Guilford proposed that high scorers on divergent thinking tests display the qualities of fluency, flexibility, and originality; and that each of these is an important feature of creative thinking.

Guilford's theory is the major explanatory model within the psychometric approach; creativity is explained as the product of a particular pattern of cognitive *abilities*. The main empirical issue faced by this approach is that of validity, which I discussed earlier: how do we know that divergent thinking is predictive of real-life creativity? Is creativity a unitary dimension? What roles are played by other factors such as personality and motivation? How do these abilities relate to school attainment? These questions have received a considerable amount of empirical testing. I shall outline some of the conclusions, especially as they relate to music, later in this chapter.

One possible way round the problem of establishing a criterion for creativity is to evaluate the person rather than the product, as we saw earlier, and the third type of 'cognitive' approach might be identified as 'person-based'. The idea is to identify those cognitive features of the person that might predict creativity. Guilford's model is person-based in the sense that it concentrates on the trait of divergent thinking; the other traits that have been investigated are those of cognitive style and motivation, as well as personality characteristics themselves. I shall outline these in the next section.

The creative person

The main areas of empirical research on creativity from a person-based point of view have been those on personality characteristics and cognitive styles. Research in these areas has tended to be nomothetic: creativity has been treated as a normally distributed trait, which may manifest itself in different domains according to the interests and predilections of the individual. This is not necessarily a valid view, however; we saw earlier that the characteristics of 'everyday creators' may well be qualitatively, and not just quantitatively, different from those that mark out the great creators. Music, furthermore, is an area that seems to provide many exceptional cases. The phenomenon of the child prodigy seems to crop up more frequently than in many other fields; I shall consider some reasons why this might be so before outlining the work on personality and cognitive style.

The idea that there may be some kind of a link between madness and 'genius' has a long history (see Tysoe, 1984): is this particularly strong in the case of musical composition? Several of the great composers are known to have suffered from some kind of psychopathology. Storr (1972) refers to the obsessional personalities of Beethoven, Chopin, Rossini, and Stravinsky, suggesting that their creative activity may have provided a means of dealing with mental instability. An alternative view might hold that being creative *produces* stress and instability. This is a chicken-and-egg argument, of course; the causal relationship, if it exists at all, could work either way. Schumann suffered from depression and mania throughout his adult life, which ended in an asylum. Handel was a manic-depressive; his *Messiah* was composed in its entirety in just a few weeks, during a euphoric period of inspiration and creativity ('I thought I saw all heaven before me, and the Great God himself').

The predominant current view seems to be that these cases are the exception rather than the rule; that there is no convincing evidence that one has to be mad to be creative. Whether or not musicians have distinct personality styles remains an interesting empirical question, and I shall conclude this section by reviewing some studies of it.

Musical prodigies

Several of the great composers are known to have displayed remarkable talents at a very early age. Mozart was composing, performing, and improvising by the age of five; Haydn, Mendelssohn, and Britten showed similarly prodigious progress in composition and performance. Amongst performers, violinist Yehudi Menuhin was performing with symphony orchestras by the age of seven, and pianist Arthur Rubenstein, at the age of three, could faultlessly play back piano pieces that he had heard only once. Beethoven could play difficult scores at sight at the age of twelve, and had published three piano sonatas before he was thirteen.

Only one or two psychological studies have been made of child musical prodigies; by far the best known is that by Revesz (1925) of the Hungarian Erwin Nyiregyhazy. Nyiregyhazy was able to sing back songs that he heard at the age of one, and could accurately play on the piano any piece that he heard by the age of four. At the age of seven, when tested by Revesz, he could transpose pieces into a different key; analyse complex chords with exceptional accuracy; sight-read difficult pieces; and memorise melodies and complex pieces of music with more accuracy than some adult professional musicians. He began to compose at six years of age, toured Europe as a professional performer at the age of eleven, and continued in a successful career as a pianist. Yehudi Menuhin is another notable example of a child prodigy whose talent continued to develop throughout his life; but there are those who do not fulfil their early promise. Winn (1979) has suggested that a critical period of transition occurs in the lives of musical prodigies at adolescence. Some successfully manage to make the transition from early precociousness to mature artistry, whereas others flounder, sometimes giving up full-time music-making.

Why do prodigies occur in the field of music? Winner (1982) has pointed out that while all infants master the extraordinarily complex rules and structures of language, which enable them to produce an infinite number of novel, grammatical, sentences, only a few are able to do the same with music. The range of individual differences in musical expression is greater than that in many other domains, and this seems to be independent of training (Gesell and Ilg, 1946). Musical talent appears in children from non-musical families (Gardner, 1973a); and there are numerous examples of so-called 'idiots savants' who are mentally defective in most respects, and yet who display higher than average musical talents (see Shuter-Dyson and Gabriel, 1981, Chapter 11). All of these features lead Winner to the conclusion that

musical ability is a separate and innate neurological capacity requiring comparatively little external stimulation in order to emerge. In this sense, musical ability may be much like the physical ability to walk, or the ability to master the syntax of language . . . The difference is that the capacity to walk or to speak is possessed by the average human: only the exceptional human possesses the capacity to make music.   (p. 238)

The higher than average occurrence of prodigies in the field of music may be because most music is based on a circumscribed set of formal rules, which can be mastered independently of other forms of human experience: Gardner (1982) characterises it as a domain which is 'self-contained'. Mathematics and chess are two other fields of activity that fit into this pattern; there are numerous examples of extremely young chess masters, and most of the great discoveries in mathematics have been made early on in the careers of their originators. Human experience and personal relationships are more essential to the novelist, for example, than are formal rule systems; and this may well explain the absence of child prodigies in literature. It may also explain why musical prodigies tend to excel in performance, and in the mastery of compositional *technique*, and only in later maturity to produce profound, expressive masterpieces.

There are many features of 'musical genius' that are not so mysterious. There is little doubt that even the most gifted prodigies can only succeed productively with a great deal of discipline, training, and hard work, and of course there are many examples of famous composers who were not prodigious, coming to music relatively late in life after other careers (Borodin was a chemist; Mussorgsky a military man; Chabrier a civil servant, and so on). The phenomenon is nevertheless a fascinating one, which seems to present unique psychological features.

Personality, cognitive style, and creativity

Some reviewers (e.g. Dellas and Gaier, 1970) have concluded that individual differences in creativity are more closely related to personality characteristics than to cognitive traits. This appeared to be true in the pioneering work of Roe (1951, 1952, 1953), who made detailed studies of the personalities of scientists (biologists, physicists, and social scientists) who were acknowledged as highly creative. Using a variety of interview, projective, and psychometric techniques, she found that high levels of motivation and persistence were more characteristic of eminent scientists than were high levels of intelligence. She found that biologists and physical scientists tended, unlike social scientists, to show emotional 'withdrawal'; they had little interest in interpersonal relations, often appearing 'shy' or 'isolated'. One characteristic possessed by all the creative scientists was a marked degree of independence, often allied with a willingness to work hard.

Another well-known series of studies of the characteristics of creative adults was carried out by MacKinnon and his associates at the Institute of Personality Assessment and Research (IPAR) at the University of California (e.g. MacKinnon, 1962: Barron, 1965). MacKinnon subscribes to the view that biographical, temperamental, and motivational factors are more important in creativity than cognitive ones; perhaps his best-known study was that of 124 American architects. These were divided into three groups, representing different levels of creative talent, on the basis of expert ratings; they were given an extensive range of personality tests over a 'living-in' weekend.

MacKinnon found that the more creative groups tended to emphasise their inventiveness, individuality, enthusiasm, and independence, whereas the less creative stressed good character, rationality, and concern for others. The creative groups were more emotionally 'open', less hidebound by conventional beliefs and restraints, and were found to be generally higher than the population norms on scales measuring the tendency towards neurotic or psychotic symptoms.

Barron (1953), also working at the IPAR, identified a bipolar factor which he called 'preference for complexity', which emerged from subjects' responses to the *Barron–Welsh art scale* (Barron and Welsh, 1952). This consists of a series of complex and simple drawings to which subjects simply respond 'like' or 'don't like'. He found that preference for the complex drawings was related to a wide range of traits such as personal tempo, verbal fluency, impulsiveness, expansiveness, originality, sensuality, sentience, aesthetic interest, femininity in men, and independence of judgement. In a later paper (Barron, 1955) these were linked directly with creativity. The importance of independence of judgement in creativity was confirmed in a study using the small group techniques of Asch (e.g. Asch, 1956). In Asch's studies, 'naive' subjects are placed in a conflict situation in which a group of experimental 'stooges' (confederates of the experimenter) unanimously defend a proposition which is evidently erroneous. Naive subjects either stick to their own opinions ('independents', who usually form about one-quarter of the sample), or conform to group pressure ('yielders', who form the remaining three-quarters). Barron found that 'independents' described themselves as 'artistic', 'emotional', and 'original' on the *Gough adjective checklist* (Gough, 1960), and that they showed a preference for complexity on the *Barron–Welsh art scale*.

Various other researchers (e.g. Cattell and Drevdahl, 1955; Cross, Cattell and Butcher, 1967) have worked along similar lines and have come to similar conclusions: ego strength, dominance and non-conformity emerge as common characteristics of creative artists and scientists. Hudson's (1966, 1968) research is important here because it represents a fusion of ideas about personality with those concerning cognitive styles and abilities. Hudson's definitions of the 'converger' and the 'diverger' are based on relative levels of performance on these two types of cognitive test; but he extended these definitions to refer to types of *people*, for whom a whole constellation of personality traits and aspects of life style could be predicted. Hudson's empirical results are largely based on a rather restricted sample of high-ability boys drawn from British secondary schools, but his findings may well have broader implications.

In *Contrary imaginations* (1966), Hudson found that there was a strong tendency for convergers to specialise in science subjects, and for divergers to tend towards the arts, and in *Frames of mind* (1968) he elaborated the view that these cognitive biases reflect a much more deep-seated difference between two emerging British subcultures, each with its own distinctive attitudes and behavioural style. Divergers are less likely to respect authority, and less likely to be rigidly sex-typed in their behaviour and attitudes; they are less defensive emotionally, and more likely to give vent to their impulses. Now this has the ring of the 'creative personality', as described above, but it does not follow from Hudson's work that divergent artists are creative, and that convergent scientists, correspondingly, are not. Rather, the creative thinker in either domain is probably the individual who possesses both convergent *and* divergent capacities, and who can use them in conjunction with one another. In the field of musical composition, certainly, there is no doubt that the 'convergent' skills involved in mastering the formal rules of music are just as indispensable as are the 'divergent' abilities from which new works originate.

It seems clear that real-life creativity involves a particular pattern of cognitive as well as of personality characteristics, and Hudson makes the interaction between them an integral part of his approach. In this respect his work is unlike most research in the literature, which maintains an artificial separation between the two. The main body of work on cognitive factors in creativity is that on divergent and convergent thinking abilities, and is discussed elsewhere in this chapter. Apart from this, attempts have been made to identify the cognitive *style* and *structure* of the creative thinker. It has been suggested that the ability to *discover* rather than to *solve* problems is a vital characteristic (Getzels and Csikszentmihalyi, 1976): that 'concern for discovery' is an important prerequisite for creative thinking. Another suggestion is that the *willingness to take risks* differentiates the creative from the non-creative (Anderson and Cropley, 1966). In a sense, these both refer to the motivational characteristics of different cognitive styles.

Wallach and Kogan (1965) found that high scores on divergent thinking tests were associated with broad categories on Pettigrew's *Category width test* (Pettigrew, 1958), and also with the tendency to use *inferential* and *relational* rather than *descriptive* conceptual styles in object-sorting tests (i.e. to base conceptual groupings on common usages or locations, or on common relationships, rather than on common concrete attributes.) Spotts and Mackler (1967) found that divergent thinkers tended to be field-independent rather than field-dependent, using Witkin *et al.*'s (1962) terminology; all of these are clear indices of cognitive *style*. As far as *structure* is concerned, it has been proposed (e.g. Scott, 1963; Schroder, Driver and Streufert, 1967) that individuals differ in terms of the differentiation, relatedness, and integration of their cognitive structures. Individuals with high levels of *integrative complexity* are seen as capable of greater adaptation to changes in the environment, of greater flexibility and non-stereotypy of thought, and of generating general, abstract laws about the environment. Tuckman (1966) found a positive relationship between integrative complexity and divergent test scores in his study of 126 naval cadets.

In summary, numerous individual traits have been associated with creativity. The two prominent personality characteristics to emerge are ego strength (non-conformity, independence) and preference for complexity (tolerance of ambiguity); and those of cognitive style could be summarised as flexibility (openness, breadth of categories, risk-taking) and complexity. These traits may involve, or be accompanied by, the motivational characteristics of intrinsic task involvement and problem-seeking. All of these traits intersect and interact at a variety of levels, and while all of them may be descriptive of some aspects of real creativity, none could be regarded as a necessary and/or sufficient condition for it. It will probably remain impossible to establish the characteristics of the creative person conclusively, since these may well vary according to the particular field of endeavour. A more fruitful line of enquiry might concentrate on specific fields; a start has been made on this daunting task in the field of music. We shall look next at some preliminary attempts to describe the personalities of composers, as well as those of other practising musicians.

The personalities of musicians

Perhaps the most comprehensive attempt to map out the personality structure of the musician is that reported in a series of articles by Kemp (1981a, 1981b, 1981c, 1982a, 1982b, 1982c, 1984). Kemp administered various personality inventories including Cattell's *16 PF questionnaire* (Cattell, Eber and Tatsuoka, 1970) and the *High school personality questionnaire* (Cattell and Cattell, 1969) to large samples of musicians including performers, composers, students, and teachers, as well as to non-musician control groups. His results led him to the view that there exists a common core of personality traits which characterise the musician in all spheres: *introversion, pathemia* (sensitivity and imagination), and *intelligence*. Kemp suggests that this 'central trait profile' is stable throughout the course of development of musicians from childhood through to professional life; the development of certain types of musicianship at certain stages may also require additional traits, such as superego strength and personal control, which reflect temporary needs and demands.

Another of his findings which crops up elsewhere in relation to creativity (see e.g. Hargreaves, 1979), is that musicians tend to show relatively low levels of sex-role stereotyping. Kemp (1984) administered the *Bem sex role inventory* (Bem, 1974) to eighty musicians and eighty non-musicians, with equal numbers of males and females in each group. He found that the female musicians scored higher on both masculinity and femininity than did female non-musicians, and that male musicians were more feminine and less masculine than their male non-musician counterparts.

Kemp's view is that his proposed 'central trait profile' is present in all musicians, taking the performer as the norm: and it is modified and complemented with other traits in other musical specialisms. Thus, in the composer, 'the introversion and pathemia of the performer becomes linked with independence, subjectivity and lower moral upbringing' (1982c, p. 4). In music teachers, on the other hand, the same core personality is modified in order to cope with the rough-and-tumble of the classroom; studies of student teachers and classroom teachers (Kemp, 1982a) showed them to be more extraverted and realistic, and to score lower on measures of sensitivity than their performing colleagues.

We should bear in mind that these personality descriptions are all based on the results of self-report inventories, and so the labelled dimensions may or may not have psychological validity. The psychologically unsophisticated composer may well object to being described as having a low moral upbringing, and the music teacher as lacking sensitivity! More seriously, modern-day personality theorists tend to describe personality in terms of the interaction between situations and behaviour, and of the ways in which people 'construct' or interpret behaviour, rather than in terms of stable, situation-free traits (see e.g. Hampson, 1982). Assuming that Kemp's descriptions do indeed correspond with reality, there can be no way of knowing whether certain personality types are attached to certain branches of music, or whether working in a particular branch of music moulds personality. Kemp implicitly adopts the former position, suggesting for example that 'Those with more highly stereotyped and rigid self-concepts in connection with sex-identity would seem misfitted in the music profession' (1982b, p. 54), but this does not necessarily rule out the complementary influence of the music profession upon individual personality.

Another common suggestion is that there are distinct personality styles associated with the performers of different instruments. In Kemp's (1981b) research, string and woodwind players showed higher levels of introversion than brass and keyboard players, and than singers: this is a theme which has been developed by Davies (1978). Davies investigated the personality stereotypes that musicians attribute to players of different instruments by arranging a series of unstructured group discussions with musicians from a Glasgow-based symphony orchestra. Davies's analysis of a research assistant's transcription of these discussions is impressionistic rather than systematic, but nevertheless it confirms and complements Kemp's findings. The main polarisation to emerge was that between brass and string players. The brass described the strings as 'precious', 'oversensitive and touchy', 'humourless', 'weaklings' and 'wets', whereas the strings regarded the brass as 'slightly oafish and uncouth', 'heavy boozers', 'loud-mouthed and coarse', 'the "jokers" of the orchestra', 'extraverts, big noises', and so on. Brass players described themselves as 'a group of honest, straightforward, no-messing-about, salt-of-the-earth, good blokes', and 'by contrast, the strings see themselves as hard-working, conscientious, aesthetic and sensitive individuals' (p. 203).

It is obvious from the relish and gusto of Davies's account that the musicians greatly enjoyed these discussions, and that they had strong feelings about the stereotypes as well as great interest in them. Davies found less consistent stereotypes for other instruments, but there were some interesting ideas. Oboe players were described as 'neurotic' by some musicians; horn players were seen as brass players with the additional arrogance and riskiness of the prima donna, perhaps because the instrument is supposed to be quirky and difficult to play. Some viola players saw themselves as 'violinists who have moved on', whereas violinists were more inclined to see them as 'failed violinists'. There is a rich vein of material here, which clearly deserves more systematic exploration. It may well be that some of Davies's stereotypes are specific to the U.K. – he hints at possible links between brass and strings, North and South, working and middle class, for example – and so it would be important to establish the validity of the stereotypes in other cultures. It would be useful to combine the approaches of Kemp and Davies by examining how objective assessments of musicians' personalities are related to their self-concepts, and to their views of the personalities of others. It would also be useful to look more specifically at the effects of personality on musicians' creativity, in musical as well as in non-musical spheres. This research area is virtually virgin territory, and there are many other questions waiting to be asked.

The psychometric approach

By far the biggest area of psychological research on creativity is that within the psychometric tradition which has centred on tests of convergent and divergent thinking. As I pointed out earlier, this is essentially a *person-based* approach, concentrating on patterns of cognitive *ability*, and its main theoretical model is that of J.P. Guilford, discussed earlier in this chapter. The distinction between convergent and divergent thinking was made long ago by William James and others, and the Reverend H.L. Hargreaves (1927) devised a number of 'tests of imagination' which were remarkably similar to current divergent tests. Hargreaves described imagination in terms of fluency, that is, the number of associations or ideas produced in a given context, and originality, that is, the 'rarity value' of these ideas. This description was conceived within the context of Spearman's (1927, 1930) 'two-factor' theory of intelligence, in which all abilities are seen as a combination of varying amounts of general intelligence ('g'), and some content-specific factor. Spearman thus saw individual differences in creativity as deriving from the varying amounts of 'g' possessed by individuals, as well as from their specific talents in different fields of creative activity.

So many researchers have investigated the relationship between putative indices of intelligence, creativity, and school attainment that I shall attempt no more than a brief outline of the main findings here. Having established this background, our primary interest will be in the development of creativity with age, and in the construction of tests of 'musical creativity'.

Creativity, intelligence, and educational attainment

Most of the studies in this large area of research have centred on three interrelated questions: whether 'creativity' can be regarded as a unitary trait as measured by divergent and non-divergent tests; what relationship this range of abilities bears to conventionally measured intelligence; and what parts both of them play in different areas of educational attainment. A well-known pioneering study was Getzels and Jackson's (1962) *Creativity and intelligence: explorations with gifted students.* Getzels and Jackson selected 'high creative' and 'high IQ' subgroups from their sample of 533 Chicago schoolchildren, and their most provocative finding was that these two subgroups were roughly equal in scholastic achievement, in spite of a mean IQ difference of 23 points. This led them to conclude that IQ was an inadequate measure of giftedness, and that creative abilities should receive much more emphasis. They also found that their 'high creative' children appeared to value a sense of humour more than the 'high IQ' group, that they held more unconventional views and beliefs, and (perhaps most significant of all) that they were regarded as less desirable as pupils by their class teachers.

This conclusion was of great educational significance, since a good deal of assessment was (and maybe still is) based on IQ and convergent-type abilities. Unfortunately, the subsequent wide discussion of Getzels and Jackson's research revealed that it was riddled with methodological flaws (see e.g. deMille and Merrifield, 1962). There were problems with the validity of the heterogeneous collection of 'creativity' tests, which displayed low intercorrelations with one another; with the representativeness of the subject-sample, whose mean IQ was 132; with the methodological procedures adopted in selecting the 'high creative' and 'high IQ' subgroups; and so on. In order to provide a convincing demonstration that 'creativity' is just as important as intelligence in the prediction of educational attainment, one first needs to be able to demonstrate that the intercorrelations amongst measures of creativity are significantly higher than those between creativity and intelligence: this was not the case in Getzels and Jackson's results.

A subsequent major study which managed to overcome most of the methodological problems of Getzels and Jackson's research was Wallach and Kogan's (1965) *Modes of thinking in young children.* Wallach and Kogan worked with a sample of 151 10–11-year-old subjects which was much more representative of the normal ability range, using a homogeneous set of divergent thinking tests as measures of creativity. They also insisted that a relaxed, anxiety free situation was much more appropriate for the assessment of creative abilities than were the formal, pressurised conditions under which divergent tests had been administered in most previous studies. Their own divergent tests were accordingly described as 'games' and administered individually, without time limits, by the children's class teachers. Under these conditions Wallach and Kogan found a high degree of intercorrelation amongst divergent thinking tests (mean coefficient = 0.41), and a correspondingly low correlation between divergent and intelligence tests (mean coefficient = 0.09). They claimed that this was clear evidence of the existence of a unitary trait of divergent thinking, independent of intelligence.

Many subsequent studies have followed up these issues, using a wide variety of tests, subject-samples, conditions of administration, techniques of analysis, and so on (see e.g. Hattie, 1977; Jacquish, 1983). On the one hand we have Wallach and Kogan's view of an independent, unitary dimension of creativity; on the other we have Guilford's multifactorial conception of twenty-four independent divergent-thinking abilities, which are conceived of as part of general intelligence. Experimental support for one or the other of these views is clearly dependent on the concomitant factors mentioned above; in particular, the IQ level of the sample and the formality of the testing conditions appear to exert powerful influences. My own research in this area led to the conclusion that '"creativity" implies an integrated range of abilities, represented by the divergent tests, which although related to general intelligence in subjects of average IQ, remains factorially distinct from it' (Hargreaves and Bolton, 1972, p. 459), and I would adhere to this statement today.

Probably the most sophisticated explanation of these relationships is given by the 'threshold hypothesis', which was first suggested by Torrance (1962). It is difficult to find a formal statement of this, but it appears to have two aspects. The first is that up to a 'threshold' level of about IQ 120, general intelligence is the most important factor in predicting school achievement; above this level, creative abilities begin to assume more importance (Barron, 1963; MacKinnon, 1962). The second is that the size of the correlation between intelligence and divergent thinking decreases as the IQ of the subjects increases, and that the relationship breaks down altogether at IQ levels above about 120: this is illustrated by the hypothetical 'triangular scatterplot' shown in Figure 6.3. Both aspects of the hypothesis have received some experimental support (e.g. Yamamoto, 1965; Haddon and Lytton, 1968; Guilford and Hoepfner, 1966), although there is some debate as to the precise level of the threshold. Beyond this minimum level of IQ, being more intelligent does not guarantee a corresponding increase in creativity or school achievement. This fits in with Hudson's (1966) observation that 'a knowledge of a boy's IQ is of little help *if you are faced with a formful of clever boys*' (p. 127), and with the idea that personality and motivational factors may well be more important than cognitive abilities in promoting real-life creativity.

Wallach and Wing (1969) were able to show that divergent test scores can predict certain academic and non-academic achievements, which could be regarded as evidence of the criterion validity of the tests. They found positive relationships with participation and accomplishment in art, science, and literature, although participation in music, social welfare, and drama appeared to be unrelated. Aspects of educational attainment seem appro-

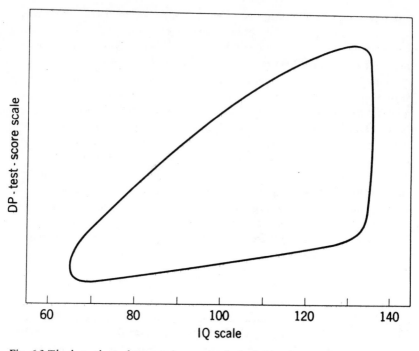

Fig. 6.3 The hypothetical 'triangular scatterplot' of the relationship between divergent thinking and intelligence (reproduced from The nature of human intelligence, *J.P. Guilford (1967). New York: McGraw-Hill, by permission)*

priate criteria for creativity in school-age subjects, and are relatively easy to quantify. Pinning down the development of creativity beyond adolescence is much more difficult, as we shall see next.

Age and creativity

Life-span developmental studies Applications of the life-span developmental perspective to the topic of creativity have given rise to two suggestions: there is a distinct and sudden decline in creativity at the age of approximately nine years (the 'fourth grade slump'); creative ability reaches a peak in early adulthood and thereafter declines with age.

The 'fourth grade slump' was first discovered by Torrance (1967): his analysis of the figural and verbal 'creative thinking test' scores of samples of children between the first and sixth grades in ten cultures gave rise to a generalised developmental curve as shown in Figure 6.4. Empirical confirmation of this result in a British sample comes from some of my own research (Hargreaves, 1982c); this confirmation is all the stronger because I was unaware of the existence of the fourth grade slump when I first reported the research! Five groups made up from 199 schoolchildren at one-year intervals between the ages of seven and twelve completed a figural and a verbal

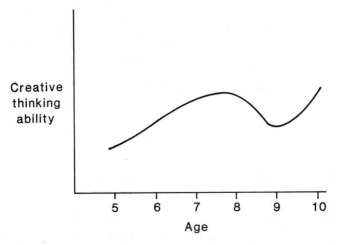

Fig. 6.4 *The 'fourth grade slump' in creative thinking*

divergent test along with the *Draw-a-man test* (Harris, 1963): there is a very clear dip in the scores on the verbal test ('Uses for Objects') of the 8–9-year-old group. Statistical age trend analysis showed that there was no significant difference between the mean fluency scores of the 7–8- and 8–9-year-olds on this test (9.47 and 7.10 respectively), and that there *was* a significant difference between the latter and the mean score of the 9–10-year-olds (11.58). This effect is arguably present, though much less clearly, on the figural test ('Circles').

Torrance explained the fourth-grade slump in terms of the personal stresses and strains that occur at this age, and his work for the U.S. Department of Health, Education, and Welfare aimed to find ways of 'holding it off'. The idea is that the pressures upon children to succeed at school, which come from parents, teachers, and peers, become particularly intense by the age of nine years, and the marked contrast between this pressure and the more liberal regime of the earlier years gives rise to a pronounced discontinuity in development. This shows itself in a generalised discouragement with the academic aspects of school life, and is therefore reflected in other domains as well as in creative thinking. Williams (1976) found that corresponding fourth grade slumps occurred in 'school motivation' and in 'school self-concept', both of which he measured by means of the Self Concept and Motivation Inventory (SCAMIN) in groups of American children from the second, third, and fourth grades. 'Personal self-concept', as measured by the Piers–Harris Self Concept Scale, did not show a corresponding slump, which supports the idea that the effect is school-specific.

The recovery in scores that occurs after the fourth grade presumably indicates children's adaptation to the competitive, achievement-oriented educational system. This is probably a less satisfactory explanation of my

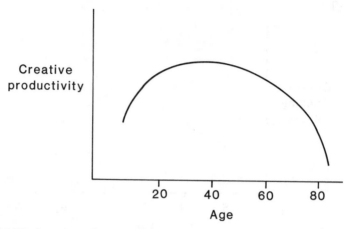

Creative
productivity

20   40   60   80

Age

Fig. 6.5 *The hypothetical age curve for creative productivity over the life span*

own demonstration of the fourth grade slump than of the American results, since the competitive pressures on British schoolchildren are almost certainly less intense than those on their American counterparts; the emphasis on regular assessment and evaluation is much less pronounced in the U.K. The clear presence of the effect in my own results must therefore mean either that pressures on British children *are* as intense, or that this explanation is inadequate: the slump may reflect a developmental phenomenon which is more dispositional than environmental. Williams suggests that the way to combat the slump is by:

building coping mechanisms so that people can better handle their behavior, preventing the development of mental problems that require treatment. While this is not a new concept in the field of mental health, it is rather a new approach to education, especially in that teachers and counselors are expected to use self-concept scales on a diagnostic basis by prescribing individual classroom exercises to develop children's feelings about themselves, others, and school.   (p. 17)

I cannot help thinking that there is something wrong with an educational system that produces the need for systematic 'primary prevention in mental health', and that it may be more profitable to remove the sources of stress than to devise methods of coping with it.

A widely accepted view of the later development of creative productivity is that it rises to a peak in the late thirties and declines thereafter, and the decline accelerates in old age. This hypothesised age curve is shown in Figure 6.5. It is grounded in two well-known historical studies of the productivity of eminent creators over their life span (Lehman, 1953; Dennis, 1966), and has received support from subsequent research (Simonton, 1984). Lehman assessed the number of outstanding works produced by prominent individuals in the fields of science, philosophy, music, art, and literature in successive five-year intervals; they were generally most productive in the decades of their twenties and thirties, with a subsequent decline. A similar pattern was found by Dennis, though he found the peak to occur slightly later.

The shape of this generalised age curve has been found to vary from discipline to discipline. Dennis found that creative individuals in the arts (composers, poets, and architects) and the sciences (biologists, chemists, and mathematicians) were at their peak in their forties, whereas those in 'scholarship' (historians and philosophers) did not show any appreciable decline in their fifties and sixties. *Within* the field of music, Simonton (1984) suggests that 'the peak for producing great instrumental selections occurs between 25 and 29, the peak for symphonies between 30 and 34, that for chamber music between 35 and 39, and that for light opera or musical comedy between 40 and 44' (p. 100). Simonton also points out that the peak for indices of creative *quality* tends to occur earlier than that for creative *quantity* in most fields of achievement.

I surmised earlier that child prodigies tend to occur in fields such as mathematics and music because of the highly abstract, impersonal rule systems involved; it may well be that the variation amongst disciplines in this respect might provide a more general explanation of the different ages at which peak productivity occurs. Presumably an individual's best work in a field such as history or philosophy depends on a lifetime of accumulated experience, and this may explain, translated into real-life terms, why political and national leaders tend to be old rather than young. Outstanding achievements in, say, mathematics, on the other hand, depend on path-breaking insights in much more abstract and circumscribed areas of thought; they are not dependent on accumulated experience to the same extent.

Romaniuk and Romaniuk (1981) have complained that there has been a good deal of confusion between creative *output* and creative *capacity* in interpreting research on this topic, and that there is a tendency to erroneously explain observed declines with age in the former in terms of the latter. They argue that creative capacity (or potential) may not decline with age, and that there are many other more plausible explanations of the results described above. Physical and sensory declines may inhibit creative productivity in some areas much more than in others. External pressures to produce, such as in academic publishing, may also follow very specific career-related age trends. The pressure to publish is probably at its peak in the thirties in academic careers, and may then decline in favour of an emphasis on administrative work. Romaniuk and Romaniuk come up with several other physical, psychological, and social factors that could provide alternative explanations of the decline in creative productivity, concluding that its attribution to a decline in capacity is 'unwarrantedly pessimistic'.

Evidence from direct studies of the cognitive processes involved ought to clarify this issue. Studies which have specifically looked at abilities rather than productivity do seem to confirm the idea of a corresponding age-related decline (e.g. Bromley, 1956; Alpaugh and Birren, 1977; Jaquish and Ripple,

1981), but Romaniuk and Romaniuk insist that these trends must be interpreted very cautiously. Age is essentially an index rather than an independent variable, and consistent age-related changes in performance on dependent variables could be attributed to a whole range of different possible causal factors. We saw in Chapter 2 that older children do better than younger ones on certain melodic discrimination tasks, for example, but that to attribute this unambiguously to the development of 'music conservation' is extremely risky. Concurrent developments in logical thinking, in the use of semantics, and in the control of attention could all contribute to the observed result, for example, and could even explain it entirely.

Romaniuk and Romaniuk point out that this gives rise to two methodological problems that must be faced in explaining the observed decline in creative productivity in terms of *ability*. Briefly, the first is that it is difficult to draw general conclusions about developmental processes from cross-sectional data, since different cohorts of subjects will inevitably have been exposed to qualitatively different learning environments. In particular, younger subjects in cross-sectional samples will be more likely to have been brought up in an educational environment geared to promote creative skills than will those from older generations. The second point is that creativity is susceptible to strong environmental influences: the course of an individual's creativity is shaped to a considerable extent by external events. This means that the long-term ecological changes (e.g. in social and political attitudes, or in economic conditions) which consistently affect individual creativity should be incorporated into any comprehensive life-span model.

These are general methodological issues which apply to all areas of developmental research, of course; we shall presumably only know whether or not Romaniuk and Romaniuk's optimism about the course of life-span creativity is justified when longitudinal data is available. In the meantime the work of Simonton, some of which was discussed in Chapter 5, has adopted what might be thought of as a longitudinal approach to *archival*, as distinct from *empirical*, data. I shall finish this section by reviewing that part of his work that has looked specifically at the effects of the age of the composer on musical creativity.

Archival/historical studies As we saw in Chapter 5, Simonton's research makes use of a sophisticated system of computer content analysis of classical music themes, taken from standard reference works. Three of the variables that he derived from his data base (composer's *lifetime productivity*, *melodic originality*, and *thematic fame*) seem to bear consistent relationships with the age of the composer.

Simonton (1977) assessed the productivity of ten classical composers born before 1870 by counting the total number of works and the total number of themes that they produced in five-year periods across the life span, and examined the relationships between these indices and a number of external factors including biographical stress, physical illness, social reinforcement, competition, war intensity, and internal disturbances, as well as age. He found that an 'inverted backwards-J' function best described the relationship between age and creative productivity. This is similar to the hypothesised age curve shown in Figure 6.5, with peaks of productivity occurring in the thirties for musical themes, and in the forties for complete works. With the (obvious) exception of physical illness, productivity seemed to be unrelated to the other environmental variables.

In probing this question further, Simonton (1980a) hypothesised that the *melodic originality* of themes should increase as a positive function of the composer's age at the time of their composition. This was tested using the 5,046 themes by the ten extremely eminent composers that were listed in Chapter 5. The inverted backwards-J function once again emerged from the results; in other words, there was a general increase in originality with age, but this tailed off toward the end of the composer's career. Another fascinating finding which emerged from this data was that melodic originality, over all composers, was a clear positive function of historical time. 'As time passes, each composer has to create ever more original themes in order to command the attention of music listeners. The baseline for melodic originality keeps moving higher and higher' (1980a, p. 216). This is an interesting finding which reinforces Romaniuk and Romaniuk's caution that the ecological context is very important in determining the development of individual life-span creativity.

In Simonton's (1980b) larger-scale follow-up study, which employed the distinction between *repertoire* and *zeitgeist* melodic originality as well as a much larger sample of 15,618 themes, he found that repertoire originality was a positive function of historical time and an inverted backwards-J function of the composer's age: both of these results corroborate those of the previous study. Zeitgeist melodic originality was a positive linear function of the composer's age, however; as composers develop, they apparently become increasingly independent from the prevailing musical trends. Simonton speculates that this may reflect the gradual development of an individual composer's unique approach over the life span, 'from mere imitation of role models to full-fledged self-actualization' (1980b, p. 982). Another related finding was that the *fame* of different melodies was found to be a positive function of the composer's concurrent creative productivity: the most famous melodies are produced during those years in which the composer is generally most productive. This seems to support the 'constant-probability-of-success' model (Dennis, 1966), according to which creative quality is seen as a direct probabilistic consequence of quantity. The more melodies that are produced, the higher are the odds of one or more of them becoming well known.

Simonton's work is pioneering and unique; it may well, as he claims, offer 'a general paradigm for examining the creative product within a more comprehensive context – within a framework that simultaneously incorpor-

Table 6.1 *Tests of musical creativity*

	Tasks	Measures	Positive correlates
Vaughan (1977)	Bisociation: rhythm Completion: rhythm Completion: melody Bisociation: melody Completion: synthesis	Fluency Rhythmic security Ideation Synthesis	Subtests of Bentley Measures of Musical Abilities and Torrance Tests of Creative Thinking

Webster (1979)	Composition (C):
	  Phrase for triangle
	  Variations on phrase
	  Extended composition on
	    phrase
	Analysis (A):
	  7-bar melody
	  2 duets
	  Complete composition
	Improvisation (I):
	  Rhythms on claves
	  Melody bells reproduction
	  Melody bells improvisation
		Fluency
		Flexibility
		Elaboration
		Originality
			Verbal creativity (A)
			Figural creativity (I,A)
			Music aptitude (I)
			Music achievement (I,C,A)
			IQ (I)
			Sex (I)
			Piano lessons (A)

Gorder (1980)	Improvisation:
	  Holes
	  Motive completion I
	  Contours
	  Motive completion II
		Fluency
		Flexibility
		Elaboration
		Originality
		Quality
			Subtests of Seashore
			Measures of Musical
			Talents, Colwell Music
			Achievement Tests and
			Torrance Tests of Creative
			Thinking
			Age
			IQ
			Musical experience
			Musical training
			Ability to improvise
			Musical creativity rating

ates aesthetics, individual differences, developmental changes, and sociocultural influences' (1980b, p. 982). This paradigm certainly possesses the dual advantages of ecological and face validity; but, in that Simonton's conclusions are all based on the works of eminent creators, they may have little applicability to the normal processes of 'everyday creativity'. There can nevertheless be no doubt that his is one that others may very profitably follow.

Tests of musical creativity

It is not surprising, given the prominence of the psychometric approach in music psychology, that various attempts have been made to devise 'measures of musical creativity'. Vidor (1931) and Vater (1934) asked their subjects to perform tasks such as building tunes upon tapped rhythmic patterns; subsequent tests, similarly, have been based on the assessment of small-scale, short-term improvisations. Three fairly recent such tests are summarised in

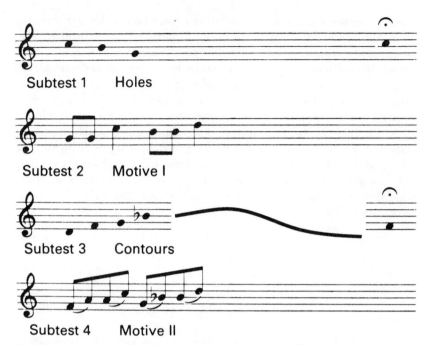

Subtest 1   Holes

Subtest 2   Motive I

Subtest 3   Contours

Subtest 4   Motive II

Fig. 6.6 Four subtests of Gorder's Measures of musical divergent production
(© 1980 by Music Educators National Conference. Reprinted by permission from
Journal of Research in Music Education*)*

Table 6.1 in terms of the tasks involved, the measures of creativity derived, and the other variables with which scores on the tests are positively correlated.

All three tests are essentially straightforward divergent thinking tasks using musical materials, and therefore presumably rest on the assumption that 'musical divergent thinking' is an important part of the potential for real musical creativity. The tasks mostly involve subjects in composing or improvising simple melodies or rhythmic sequences on the basis of different musical stimuli. In Vaughan's (1977) tests of musical creativity (which are apparently based on the earlier *Vaughan–Myers test of musical creativity*, 1971) and Webster's (1979) 'creativity criteria', they are asked to improvise responses to stimuli of varying complexity on percussion instruments such as melody bells, claves, and drums; and subjects on Gorder's (1980) *Measures of musical divergent production (MMDP)* respond by singing, whistling, or by playing a familiar instrument. Gorder's four subtests, which are reproduced in Figure 6.6, are fairly typical. The Webster and Gorder tests are scored, as are conventional divergent thinking tests, for fluency, flexibility, originality, and elaboration; and the latter also incorporates a more evaluative measure of the quality, or 'formal suitability', of the responses produced.

The list of variables that were found to show positive correlations with scores on these tests, in Table 6.1, is rather a hotch-potch; although there are some positive correlations with non-musical divergent tests, musical achievement and ability tests, expert ratings, and so on, there is no consistent overall pattern. This is hardly surprising, in view of the diversity of these variables as well as of the tests themselves. It is difficult to know whether any of the correlations could be regarded as evidence of criterion validity of the tests, since all of them represent indirect rather than direct measures of musical creativity. Presumably the only way that validity can be established with certainty is by employing a product-based approach, as suggested by Amabile (1982). My own view is that this is likely to prove more productive in the long run than one based on personal traits. But the problems of establishing the reliability and validity of 'musical creativity tests' may unfortunately turn out to be overwhelming.

7

Social psychology and musical development

The interaction between people and their social and cultural environment is at the heart of contemporary theories of development, as we saw in Chapter 1. Changes in behaviour produce changes in the environment, which in turn feed back to affect behaviour: it is thus impossible to study one without the other. This implies that one must necessarily study the 'musical environment' as an integral part of musical development. Some of the investigations described in Chapters 3 and 4 accomplished this in a fairly directly Piagetian manner: the research on the development of early song is a good case in point. Whereas this research is primarily concerned with the *production* of music, studies of its *perception* have tended to ignore the social context, as we saw in Chapter 5. Konečni (1982) has argued very convincingly that many studies in experimental aesthetics, for example, seem to regard music listening as taking place in a kind of social vacuum, and other authors (e.g. Arnheim, 1952; Munro, 1963) have made the same complaint about the psychology of art in general.

In this chapter I shall review the exceptions to this rule, and look at that research which deals specifically with social and cultural influences on musical behaviour. This literature, like that reviewed in Chapter 5, is scattered and diverse: it cuts across different areas of social and developmental psychology, as well as of sociology and education. Relatively small-scale empirical projects abound, especially in the form of U.S. doctoral dissertations (see Haack, 1980); but in the main these tend not to derive from any coherent theoretical framework. Various sociological theories of the social functions of music and art works have been proposed: I shall discuss those that aid our understanding of the developmental and social psychological research, and evaluate their usefulness in the light of the empirical evidence.

We start by considering the different theoretical approaches; it is fairly easy to distinguish between the broad sociological perspective on art and music, and the more fine-grained, social psychological explanations of processes of social influence. These theories have mainly been applied and tested in studies of popular culture, especially in research on teenage music preferences. We shall consider the mass culture debate, and the empirical work that has been carried out in testing the theories proposed; and look in particular at studies of the influences of the school, and of social class. We look next at two research areas in which direct social influences upon musical preferences have been studied experimentally, namely prestige and propaganda effects, and small-group studies of social interaction. Finally, I shall outline some of the broader cultural patterns of musical taste by identifying fashions in both 'classical' and 'popular' music, and try to show how they might be explained by the preference-feedback hypothesis.

Theories of social influence

The sociological perspective

Distinguished sociologists such as Adorno (1941) argued long ago that different musical forms and languages are a direct product of existing social divisions and structures. Bernstein's (1971) demonstration that ways of speaking and 'language codes' express a wealth of information about social divisions is very well known, and this applies equally to musical forms and codes. Wishart (1977), for example, makes a detailed comparison of the different meanings and values implicit in the written tradition of Western symphonic music, and those in oral–aural musics such as the blues. Shepherd (1977b) elaborates this argument much further in suggesting that musical scale systems, conventions of tonality, and so on are themselves the direct products of social stratification; he describes this as the 'musical coding of ideologies'.

To those who favour an 'absolutist' view of the meaning of music, which was discussed in Chapter 1, this turns the relationship between music and society on its head. They would argue that different forms of music exist which are clearly and objectively identifiable; and that these forms are preferred to varying degrees by different social subgroups. Shepherd, on the other hand, is suggesting that the social divisions are the most fundamental; that these form the primary framework around which musical forms are organised. This is almost certainly a chicken-and-egg argument, in that it is impossible to attribute any causal direction to the relationship. Musical forms do not create social divisions any more than vice versa: the two influence one another mutually.

When it comes to defining what constitutes a 'work of art', however, it seems that the social context *does* exert the primary influence. Crozier and Chapman (1981) cite various instances of paintings, for example, whose status as works of art is conferred on them by their 'art historical significance', that is, by their place in the social context of the 'artworld' (Blizek, 1974). Not only does the social context determine what constitutes a work of art, but it also determines how that work of art is valued. This line of argument has been pursued by the Marxist sociologist Pierre Bourdieu (e.g. Bourdieu, 1971). Bourdieu argues that social forces impose and shape norms of cultural taste; in particular, that the dominant social groups impose their standards of taste by 'legitimating' certain forms of art and not others.

One fairly obvious application of this argument to the development of musical taste lies in the dichotomy between 'serious' and 'popular' music, and the ways in which the former has traditionally been 'legitimated' by the musical establishment. Bourdieu's thesis would presumably be supported by a demonstration that these two forms of music show different patterns of preference amongst different social class groups: I review some of the research that has pursued this issue later in this chapter. This research makes it obvious that there is no simple, clear-cut relationship.

'Patterns of legitimation' are constantly changing; when Adorno (1941) analysed the entertainment industry's treatment of jazz and popular music, for example, it made sense to lump these two together under a single heading. This would certainly be invalid today, since most jazz music is regarded by all but the most conservative of commentators as 'serious' rather than 'popular'; in some respects at least, it has been 'legitimised'. Vulliamy (1977) has proposed a finer, more contemporary version of the same distinction in suggesting that 'rock' music has become an identifiable, 'legitimated' domain within the broader field of 'pop' music. He suggests that:

rock musicians seek to separate themselves from 'pop' musicians by making certain assumptions, which might be summarised as follows:

(a) Rock music is not commercial, whilst pop music is.
(b) The rock performer is a sincere, creative artist who has control over his product.
(c) The separation of composer, performer and producer in 'pop' music denies the possibility of creativity to the 'pop' performer.
(d) 'Pop' music is homogenous whilst rock music is subdivided into many different types which tend to appeal to differing sections of the audience for rock music.
(e) Rock music is neglected in the mass media; the latter concentrates on standardised ('singles') 'pop' music.
(f) Rock music is complex and musically developed (with respect to Afro-American musical criteria) whereas 'pop' music is standardised and musically clichéd.

(p. 191)

These 'patterns of legitimation' are obviously very complex, and subject to constant change; trying to explain their origins in different social class groupings is consequently a very hazardous undertaking. Nevertheless, this sociological perspective complements the points that I have made elsewhere about the conservatism of a great deal of research in music psychology, and especially about the desirability of including popular forms of music amongst the stimulus materials. Some of the sociological views mentioned above are concerned with the influences that shape musical forms themselves: my primary interest is in the ways in which social forces shape *psychological reactions* to music. In the next section we consider some of the theories that have been proposed.

Processes of social influence

We can distinguish between four main processes that have been proposed to explain how social structure might influence musical taste. These are complementary rather than mutually exclusive; they represent different, interrelated aspects of the same phenomenon. I have drawn on Crozier and Chapman's (1981) account in my attempt to capture the essence of each process fairly succinctly, and to outline the interrelationships between them.

The first, and probably the most prominent, view is that musical taste is shaped by the individual's conformity to reference group norms; this view is most closely associated with the work of Francès (1967), and has also been expounded by Child (1969). Francès argued that different works of art are assigned different values and attributes by different social groups, and that individuals tend to conform to these values according to their group membership. In particular, he proposed that 'high art' forms of culture are associated with higher socioeconomic status, so working-class people feel no identification with them.

This view receives clear support from the research on 'popular' and 'serious' culture that will be reviewed in the next section. In the case of teenagers, for example, musical preferences are an integral part of a network of likes and dislikes for fashions in dress and in hair styles, television shows, and so on. These preferences are formed in television viewing, reading, sports, hobbies, and many other work and leisure activities, and all of these are strongly patterned according to social class divisions. There is also some direct empirical evidence which demonstrates the powerful influence of peers on listening behaviour. Johnstone and Katz (1957) found that the preferences of groups of teenage girls were strongly patterned according to those agreed by small groups of friends; and that the preferences of the more popular girls in the sample for particular songs and disc jockeys were more like the neighbourhood norms than were those of the less popular girls. There is also a good deal of evidence for conformity effects on musical preferences from small-group experimental research, as we shall see later.

A second view, also propounded by Francès, is based on the analogy between the information transmission that occurs in the appreciation of works of art, and that which has been studied in research of 'persuasive communication'. Most of the latter derives from the well-known and systematic work of the Yale Communication Research Program (e.g. Hovland, Janis and Kelley, 1953). There are three specific parallels that can be drawn. First, the transmission of 'informative messages' has been shown to be affected to a considerable extent by the eminence and authority of their originators. This clearly applies to perceptions of works of art, as will be seen in our discussion of prestige and propaganda effects, later in this chapter. Secondly, the effectiveness of such communications has been found to depend on the variables intervening between the message and the receiver, such as the receiver's membership of different reference groups, and degree of integration into them. Thirdly, the transmission of the message is dependent on the relevant characteristics of the receiver; in the case of music perception, these might include training, personality, attitudes, and so on.

It is interesting to contrast this view with what Hirsch (1971) has called the 'hypodermic needle' theory of the effects of song lyrics on teenagers, according to which 'It is assumed that (implied or explicit) values expressed in popular hit protest songs are (a) clear to a majority of listeners, (b) subscribed to by a large proportion of listeners, and (c) likely to influence the attitudes and behavior of the uncommitted' (p. 376). This implies that the message contained in a song is more or less directly 'transmitted', and uncritically received, without any reference to those other parameters of the 'persuasive communication' mentioned above; and Hirsch claims that many analysts and observers of the popular music scene still subscribe to such a view. This view is akin to what has been called the 'massification hypothesis', which will be discussed in the next section; there is a good deal of evidence against both of them.

A third view, which has been proposed by Dimaggio and Useem (1978) is cast in terms of the competition between different social class groups for dominance and control over resources; this view is closely related to the idea of the 'legitimation' of different musical forms. Their premise is that the dominant upper- and middle-class groups want to defend and advance their relative standing in the cultural and social hierarchy, and they do this by regulating people's access to artistic training, their familiarity with the contexts within which different varieties of art works are presented, and so on. Dimaggio and Useem's review of the empirical literature on the social stratification of audiences showed clearly that 'high culture' (e.g. fine art, opera, classical music) tended overwhelmingly to be 'consumed' by upper- and middle-class audiences, and that education (rather than occupation or income level) was the best predictor of this. This kind of evidence is used in support of their view that 'cultural capital' (i.e. control over resources) is highest in upper-class groups which are relatively lacking in economic capital.

Whereas Dimaggio and Useem's analysis is very much a sociological one, the fourth perspective is essentially social psychological: it operates on the level of the individual. Kavolis (1963) makes the distinction between *expressive* and *instrumental* roles. Expressive roles are associated with the arts, and they concern those aspects of behaviour that are spontaneous, creative, and individual; Kavolis sees them as promoting affective spontaneity, and thereby the internal integration of the social system. Instrumental roles, on the other hand, are concerned with conforming to the external demands of the social system; they focus on those aspects of behaviour which are controlled, traditional, and affectively neutral. Kavolis has developed a fairly elaborate theory of how these roles, when either assigned or ascribed, can mediate social class differences in artistic preference. The line of reasoning by which he links expressive vs. instrumental and assigned vs. ascribed roles to artistic preferences (e.g. for abstraction, spontaneity, and simplicity vs. naturalism, control, and complexity respectively), and thence to middle- vs. working-class membership, is a tenuous and tortuous one which it is inappropriate to pursue here. It is hardly surprising that little direct empirical evidence has been gathered to support Kavolis's theory, though it nevertheless complements the other three in its emphasis upon the individual dimension of the process of social influence on musical taste.

Popular culture and the development of musical taste

The mass culture debate

In his influential work *Culture, industrialisation and education*, Bantock (1968) distinguished between three types of culture. *High culture* is seen as that which is operated (or 'legitimated') by the dominant cultural group or elite, and to which critical standards are applied which are independent of the characteristics of the consumer (Wilensky, 1964). *Folk culture* is that which traditionally exists in non-industrial societies; *mass culture*, or popular culture, is that which is specifically manufactured for the industrialised mass market. The latter is geared to the requirements of the mass media; and this results in a separation between those who create mass culture and those who consume it. Because of this, and because of the large financial rewards associated with the mass market, some theorists (e.g. Haag, 1959) have argued that certain aspects of high and of folk culture are exploited in popular culture, and that they consequently deteriorate. Mass culture is seen as sterile, homogenised, and lacking in artistic integrity; as pursuing the 'lowest common denominator' in its relentless quest for TV ratings, record and book sales, and so on. This has become known as the 'massification hypothesis' (e.g. Fox and Wince, 1975), and the question of its validity forms the mass culture debate.

Vulliamy (1977) has summarised the assumptions that might derive from the application of the massification hypothesis to music, namely:

(a) High culture ('serious' music) is not subject to commercial pressures; commercial gain must inevitably lead to inartistic works.
(b) High culture ('serious' music) results from the unique creative potential of the artist.
(c) Mass culture ('popular' music) is produced solely for a mass market. Its commercial nature therefore leads to standardisation of the product. This in turn denies the possibility of creativity to the artist.
(d) Mass culture ('popular' music) is a homogenous category whilst high culture ('serious' music) is subdivided into many different types with strict boundaries.

(e) Mass culture ('popular' music) inhibits the growth of high culture ('serious' music) mainly due to the former's sheer quantity in the mass media.

(f) Mass culture ('popular' music) is imposed from above and the audience (teenagers) are therefore exploited.   (pp.191–2)

It is easy to see how similar are these assumptions to those made by the rock musician about his own activity in relation to 'pop', which we outlined earlier.

The 'massification hypothesis' has met with a considerable amount of criticism; one of its main critics has been Gans (1974). Gans argues that Western culture is characterised by diversification rather than massification; that there exists a considerable degree of what he calls 'cultural pluralism'. This pluralism is described in terms of the concepts of 'taste cultures' and 'taste publics'. Taste cultures are the conscious, patterned values and preferences of different social groups; they serve to 'entertain, inform and beautify life and to express values and standards of taste and aesthetics' (Fox and Wince, 1975, p. 199). Taste publics are the groups of people who subscribe to a particular taste culture; and the separation of the two indicates that a taste culture is an abstracted concept which can presumably be defined independently from the people who subscribe to it (i.e. the taste public). Gans identifies five major taste cultures, which are associated with corresponding taste publics, in the U.S.A. These range along a social class continuum, that is, 'high culture', 'upper-middle culture', 'lower-middle culture', 'low culture', and 'quasi-folk low culture'. Taste cultures are thus seen to be rooted in the social structure; and Gans stresses the importance of the educational attitudes and values of different socioeconomic groups in this respect.

Fox and Wince's (1975) research was 'a modest attempt to examine empirically . . . the concepts of "taste culture" and "taste public"' (p. 198); it is of particular interest here in that it was carried out in the field of music. They asked 767 sociology undergraduates to rate their enjoyment of nine styles of music (current popular hits, folk music, classical music, blues, social protest music, rock music, easy listening, country and western music, and jazz), on 5-point rating scales for liking, and carried out factor analyses on the ratings. This produced five factors, which the authors interpret as reflecting distinct taste cultures; the factor scores obtained by each subject on each of these five were interpreted as an index of membership of the taste publics associated with the five cultures. This operationalisation of very broad and abstract sociological constructs in direct terms of factor scores derived from questionnaire responses is almost certainly premature and oversimplified, and some psychologists would undoubtedly disapprove of the skimpy empirical detail in Fox and Wince's report. Our primary interest here, however, is in their conclusions.

Fox and Wince amplified their description of the membership of the five musical taste publics by considering seven 'background characteristics' of the respondents, namely sex, age, size of home town, religious preference, father's education, father's occupation, and parental income. The first, *jazz-blues taste public*, is associated with an urban tradition: this manifested itself in strong relationships with hometown size (membership monotonically related to size of town), religious preference (atheists, agnostics, and Jews, not Catholics), and father's education and occupation (membership especially high amongst students whose fathers have a professional position). Membership of the second *popular hits taste public* was most strongly related to religious preference (Catholics, not atheists, agnostics, or Jews), and to a lesser extent to sex (women rather than men) and age (membership declines with increasing age).

Membership of the third *folk music taste public* was most strongly associated with sex (women rather than men), and to a lesser extent with age (students in early twenties much more involved than those of other ages), religious preference (high amongst Jews, low amongst Catholics) and father's education and occupation (positive relationship with socioeconomic status). Membership of the fourth *rock-protest taste public* was negatively and monotonically associated with age; members were very likely to be atheist or agnostic, they were likely to come from large cities rather than small towns, and from lower-income families. Finally, membership of the *country and western taste public* was related to sex (men rather than women), age (positive monotonic relationship), religious preference (Jewish rather than non-Jewish students) and father's education (membership greater amongst students with fathers at both extremes of the educational continuum).

Fox and Wince regard these results as a support for Gans' concepts of taste cultures and taste publics in the sense that they represent a diverse pattern rather than a common 'massified' musical taste; and the two background variables that seem to exert the strongest effects are religious preference and social class. Fox and Wince comment that the former may result from the importance of a 'religious factor' in American society, which is likely to affect many aspects of life style. Since this factor may have increased rather than decreased in importance in the ten or so years that have elapsed since the data was collected, the effect might be even more powerful today. I shall look at research on the effects of social class in more detail in the next section.

Dixon (1981) carried out a follow-up study using a similar approach to that of Fox and Wince, and incorporating various methodological improvements. His (undergraduate) subjects rated sixteen rather than nine musical genres, improved forms of the rating scales and factor analytic procedures were employed, and the analyses were carried out for black and for white subjects separately. Dixon found very different patterns of preference between his black and white subject-groups, and in general concluded that his results provided clear support for the taste culture/taste public hypothesis rather than for massification. In another study along the same lines, Skipper (1975) found no evidence for massification in the musical preferences of college students in Canada and the U.S.A. He found that these preferences were patterned according to sex, race, and social class, with classical and folk music, and hard rock and rhythm and blues being preferred by upper and lower social class students respectively. Social class apparently had a weaker effect on the preferences of the Canadian than of the U.S. students, and the former showed no evidence of 'Americanisation'.

The work of Robinson and Hirsch (1969, 1972; see also Hirsch, 1971) provides evidence for the diversity of musical taste from a different viewpoint. One of their primary interests lay in the extent to which the American popular song possessed universal or mass appeal, that is, whether or not popular song lyrics reflected the dominant values of American society, and directed their appeal to the broadest possible market. They carried out surveys of the attitudes of large groups of U.S. high school students to popular songs in general, and to 'popular social protest hits' in particular. Although 'current popular hits' seemed to be almost universally popular, there was a great deal of patterned variation within this category. Hirsch (1971) concluded from the results that 'The stratified teenage audience (usually viewed by adults as an undifferentiated horde) is an aggregate of individuals who form distinct popular music subaudiences – for protest hits, *or* other hits, *or* rhythm and blues hits – with little crossover in membership' (p. 379).

The massification hypothesis is unable to account for the rising popularity in the 1960s and 1970s of 'social protest' songs, whose lyrics explicitly rejected the values of the dominant Establishment culture; and it is interesting that U.S. 'progressive rock' radio stations that primarily featured these songs drew their audiences largely from the upper echelons of the socioeconomic scale. Denisoff and Levine (1972) carried out a study which looked in more detail at the 'sociopolitical functions' of these songs. They went about this by analysing the responses of sociology undergraduates to a questionnaire about their reactions to two such current songs: 'Eve of Destruction', by Barry McGuire, and 'Universal Soldier', by Buffy Sainte-Marie. The first of these was at the top of the U.S. national record charts in September 1965, when the survey was conducted. Amongst other findings, it emerged that over half of the undergraduates expressed a favourable attitude towards the sentiments expressed in these songs and in others of their type; and that a surprisingly high proportion (40 per cent or so) either would not or could not interpret the meaning of the songs correctly.

Denisoff and Levine conclude that these songs act neither as 'background noise' on the one hand, nor as vehicles for 'brainwashing', that is, attitudinal indoctrination, on the other; their function, rather, has elements of both. Konečni's (1984) investigation of listeners' comprehension of the lyrics of rock and roll songs confirmed that a very low proportion of them (only slightly higher than would be expected by chance) were able to correctly identify the message that was intended by the songwriter.

The problem with all the studies reported in this section is the lack of congruence between the extremely broad-ranging and abstract nature of the theories proposed, and the empirical methods employed to test them.

Comparisons of the responses of different subject-groups to musical preference questionnaires have a valuable descriptive, and potential explanatory, function; but they almost certainly cannot provide adequate tests of, for example, the 'massification' hypothesis as compared with the 'taste cultures' hypothesis. Fox and Wince, for example, imply that the emergence from their analysis of five distinct factors with eigenvalues greater than unity, rather than a single general factor, supports the latter rather than the former. This conclusion, however, depends on the precise operationalisation of the crucial test between the two hypotheses: on the level of analysis at which the test is made. It would almost certainly be possible, by choosing different subject-samples, musical stimuli, and factorial techniques, to obtain a single factor in a follow-up study.

In other words, my contention is that the empirical data collected in these studies function more as illustrations of the theories than as critical support for them. The level of generality of the theories may indeed be so broad that it is impossible to devise any adequate test. Hirsch (1971) makes a complaint which is closely related to this, suggesting that the 'fragmented and disordered' state of research on popular culture arises from the failure of sociologists to integrate four theoretical approaches, namely content analyses and the functional approach to the mass media; the impact of popular music on its audience; the impact of technological change on mass media programming; and organisational analysis of entertainment industries.

School influences

The research reported in the previous section was all based on subject-samples obtained in North America. We turn now to a project that was carried out in the U.K. under the auspices of the (now defunct) Schools Council: Murdock and Phelps' (1973) *Mass media and the secondary school*. This study has a great deal in common with those discussed already in that it is concerned with the diverse nature of teenage musical preferences, the origin of these preferences in social class groupings, and the relationship of the preferences with various other aspects of life style, attitudes, and behaviour. Its main difference, apart from its U.K. base, lies in the interest in the influence of the school.

Murdock and Phelps carried out separate studies of the teachers and pupils in 90 secondary schools in all, comprising 35 grammar schools, 19 comprehensives and 36 secondary modern schools. (The two-tier system of parallel *grammar* (academically oriented) and *secondary modern* (vocationally oriented, less academic) schools has gradually been replaced by universal *comprehensive* schools in the U.K.: Murdock and Phelps' study was carried out during the transitional period.) They adopted a research strategy in which coarse-grained questionnaire surveys of some 1,310 teachers and 1,071 pupils were complemented by a smaller number of individual case studies. Their central aim was to study the 'culture clash' that exists between the school curriculum on the one hand and the mass media on the other – especially in that the latter is likely to represent popular culture. The culture clash might manifest itself in a variety of different real-life forms. It could have an explicit social class basis in the case of a middle-class teacher of working-class pupils, for example; this is likely to be a commonly occurring situation. Murdock and Phelps compared indicators such as the newspapers read by teachers, and their patterns of television watching, with those of the general population. It was clear from this that teachers may have very limited awareness and knowledge of the newspapers, television and pop music programmes that form the staple diet of many of their pupils' leisure interests.

In the *teachers' study*, Murdock and Phelps investigated some general aspects of one side of the 'culture clash'; their questionnaire covered topics such as teachers' views of the job, and their use of audio-visual aids. The primary interest, however, was in teachers' specific attitudes to the role of the mass media; they were questioned about their perceptions of the influence of the media on their pupils, and about their own use of mass media materials in the classroom. Four basic types of approach were identified. Teachers could be either 'high' or 'low' in their *orientation* towards the media, that is, in the extent to which they used media material in their lessons, and they could be either 'favourable' or 'unfavourable' in their *attitude* towards the media. It is not too much of a generalisation to conclude from the authors' descriptions of their results that the general attitude towards the media was indifferent, if not actively hostile. Even some of those teachers whose attitudes were favourable tended to use media material to 'sugar the pill' by attracting their pupils' initial attention in a topic before giving it more serious attention.

On the other side of the 'culture clash', the *pupils' study* investigated a wide variety of attitudes to general and specific aspects of school, leisure activities, and pop culture (especially pop music). One variable that was investigated by means of a specially constructed attitude scale was the degree of pupils' commitment to or disengagement from school; this turned out, predictably, to be mediated to a considerable extent by social class. Hargreaves (1967) suggested that there are essentially two main peer group cultures amongst secondary school pupils – the 'academic' (committed to school), and the 'delinquescent' (anti-school). Murdock and Phelps elaborate this view, developing a further distinction between *school*, *pop*, and *street* cultures in explaining their own results. In the case of middle-class boys, there was a fairly clear polarisation between 'academic' and 'leisure' roles; factor analysis of a self-description questionnaire revealed that they perceived themselves *either* primarily in the pupil role, *or* in terms of roles offered by the leisure environment. In the case of lower-working-class boys, the pattern was not so clear. The main reason for this seems to be that there was a differentiation between the roles of 'rebel' and 'street peer' from that of 'pop fan' which was not present in the self-perceptions of the middle-class boys. The general patterns for girls, interestingly, seemed to be less affected by social class; as

	Mainstream.	Underground
Activity–potency (Negro based music stressing beat and rhythm)	*Cluster 1* Aretha Franklin (soul) Jackson Five ('Motown') Owen Gray (Reggae) Brotherhood of Man Creedence Clearwater	*Cluster 2* 'Heavy rock' (Rolling Stones) Progressive urban blues (Johnny Winter)
Understandability (music performed by whites stressing the lyrics)	*Cluster 3* The Beatles Simon and Garfunkel	*Cluster 4* Individual singer-songwriters (Leonard Cohen)

Fig. 7.1 *Four 'taste clusters' in pupils' descriptions of pop music (reproduced from Murdock and Phelps (1973) by permission of Macmillan Ltd)*

with middle-class boys, there was a fairly clear polarisation between 'pupil' and 'leisure' (primarily pop) roles.

These distinctions are fairly complex and tenuous, and the picture is complicated further by the pupils' attendance either at grammar, secondary modern, or comprehensive schools. What is most important about them from our point of view is that musical taste is obviously strongly influenced by subcultural peer-group pressures. Murdock and Phelps carried out some detailed analyses of the patterns of pop music preferences within the different groups. One study, based on the factor analysis of pupils' ratings of twelve different pop records on nine semantic differential-type rating scales (such as 'interesting–boring', 'unoriginal–original', and 'gentle–powerful'), led them to propose four basic 'taste clusters', which are shown in Figure 7.1. The two major interacting dimensions are 'mainstream vs. underground' (relating to whether or not the pop artists are perceived as pro- or anti-establishment), and 'activity-potency vs. understandability'. The latter is supposed to represent the difference between music with an emphasis on beat and rhythm, such as 'soul' or 'reggae', and that 'performed by whites stressing the lyrics' (p. 108). Exemplars of each of the four clusters are shown in Figure 7.1.

The results showed that preferences amongst these four were significantly influenced by *age*, *social class*, and *school commitment*. As far as age was concerned, there was a shift in preference away from 'mainstream' pop and towards 'underground' between the ages of twelve and fourteen. Although more than half of all the respondents expressed a preference for mainstream pop, those who opted for underground pop tended to be from middle-class rather than from working-class backgrounds. This is in line with some of the findings of the (North American) 'taste cultures' research that was mentioned earlier: Murdock and Phelps suggest that it may have emerged because middle-class pupils express their anti-school attitudes through pop rather than through street cultures. As far as school commitment is concerned, it is not very surprising that pupils who expressed low levels of commitment tended to prefer underground rather than mainstream pop.

I have discussed Murdock and Phelps' study at some length because it provides probably the most detailed and elaborate account so far of the complex process by which various social influences combine to shape the developing musical tastes of secondary school pupils. I have two reservations about an uncritical acceptance of their conclusions, however. First, and most important, it would in my view be wrong to regard youth subcultures as the *sole* determinants of teenage musical taste. The empirical results show that they are undeniably powerful; yet Murdock and Phelps devote no attention to the characteristics of the music itself. These characteristics exert their own, complementary influence, as we saw quite clearly in Chapter 5: and yet one almost gets the impression that Murdock and Phelps view music as malleable 'cultural material' whose perceived characteristics can be transformed almost to an infinite degree by social forces. Many studies in experimental aesthetics can be criticised for taking insufficient account of the social context; it may be that Murdock and Phelps err in the opposite direction.

My second reservation arises from the ephemeral and rapidly changing nature of teenage culture. Each fashion that arises is out of date more or less as soon as it becomes widely accepted (we shall return to the mechanisms of musical fashion later in this chapter), and so Murdock and Phelps' data could be regarded as a 'snapshot' of teenage life that could never be replicated: preferences have changed considerably in the fifteen years or so that have elapsed since their study. Their descriptions of the taste clusters of pop music preferences and of pupils' classifications of pop stars, though lacking in experimental rigour, are nevertheless fairly detailed; the crucial question is whether the *structure* of these descriptions would still be found in an equivalent study conducted today, even though the *content* of the analyses would of course have changed. My hunch is that they probably would not, because the *Zeitgeist* that made 'mainstream/underground' a critical distinction in the 1960s and 1970s has been replaced by a rather gloomier concern with questions of deprivation and unemployment in the 1980s. It is also impossible to assess the extent to which Murdock and Phelps' results are specific to teenagers in the U.K., or whether they might have wider cross-cultural validity.

These speculative doubts about the generality of the findings have a certain amount of empirical foundation. Brown and O'Leary (1971), for example, were unable to find any evidence for the existence of a class-based youth culture in their study of the pop music preferences of English secondary school pupils, although their study was based on a sample drawn from only three schools. Some of the behavioural studies of musical preference that were reviewed in Chapter 5 showed that teachers' approval of certain styles of music could increase the amount of time that pupils spent listening to these styles, which seems at variance with the idea of a 'culture clash', though the subjects in these studies were mostly pre-adolescent.

In spite of these reservations, there can be no doubt that Murdock and Phelps have performed a valuable service in documenting what they call the 'pervasiveness of pop'; in demonstrating quite clearly that musical taste must be viewed in the broader context of dress fashions, newspapers and magazines, television programmes, and so on. Their concern about the alienation experienced by many (especially working-class) teenagers leads them to make some recommendations about the uses of media materials in classroom practice which deserve to be widely read by teachers.

Social class influences

All of the research described in the two preceding sections has social class at its heart; this powerful variable manifests its influence in many different ways. In this section I shall briefly review those studies of the effects of social class that have not been covered already. Many of these focus on preferences for 'popular' as distinct from 'serious' music; and some consider social class in the context of other variables. Table 7.1 summarises the subject-populations, the particular musical preferences investigated, and the results of the studies.

Schuessler (1948) asked over 1,200 adults to express their preferences for recordings representing eight different musical styles; he found that these preferences were related to listeners' sex and age, as well to their occupation. In general, classical recordings were liked more by subjects of higher occupational status. This finding also appears in the results of Baumann (1960), who investigated teenage music preferences by means of a specially devised Music Preference Inventory. Baumann found that his teenage subjects enjoyed excerpts of 'popular' music more than equivalent excerpts of 'classical' or 'traditional' music overall; but that the 'classical' excerpts were enjoyed more by high than by low socioeconomic status groups within the sample. Another interesting result was that 'low status' subjects were twice as likely to express a preference for listening to music on a juke box as 'high status' subjects, who preferred to listen to records at home. This is easy to explain in terms of the differences between working-class 'street/pop' and middle-class 'academic/pop' cultures, which I described in the last section.

Rogers (1957) played pieces of 'seriously classical', 'popular classical', 'dinner music' and 'popular music' to 635 children in the age range 8–16 years. Once again, whilst the 'popular' music was preferred overall, the 'classical' pieces were liked relatively more by subjects of higher socioeconomic status. One study that does not seem to fit into this recurring pattern is that of Fisher (1951). Fisher obtained the preference rankings of 251 students for five little-known pieces of classical music whose identity was unknown to the subjects. She found no clear differences between the rankings of three different socioeconomic groups, and suggested that the factors that normally deter-

Table 7.1 *Studies of social class and musical taste*

	Subjects	Music	Results
Schuessler (1948)	adults	'old song', 'classical', 'jazz', 'modern classical', 'old waltz', 'light classical', 'popular', 'hill-billy'	higher occupational status Ss preferred classical
Fisher (1951)	school and university students	5 unidentified 'classical' pieces	no significant differences between socioeconomic status groups
Rogers (1957)	2nd–12th graders	'seriously classical', 'popular classical', 'dinner music', 'popular music'	'popular music' preferred overall: 'classical' preferred by high socioeconomic status Ss
Baumann (1960)	12–20 year-olds	'popular', 'classical', 'traditional'	'popular' preferred overall: 'classical' preferred by high socioeconomic status Ss

mine likes and dislikes for known pieces of music do not come into operation when the identity of the composers is unknown.

One other small area of research which throws some light on the relationship between social class and musical taste is that on political attitudes. Fox and Williams (1974) found that students' political orientation was associated with musical involvement (measured in terms of concert attendances and record purchasing), and with preferred musical styles (assessed by means of rating scales). They found that 'liberal' students tended to be more involved with music than did 'conservatives': and that the latter preferred current popular hits, whereas the former preferred folk music. Mashkin and Volgy (1975) studied the relationships between university students' preferences for 'rock', 'folk', and 'country/western' music, and their scores on measures of political alienation, as well as of social alienation, attitudes towards women, and post-bourgeois ideology. They found that folk listeners were most alienated, country/western listeners least alienated, and that rock listeners fell between the two extremes. They were uncertain as to the causal implications of these relationships, however: musical preferences may shape and determine social and political attitudes, as well as vice versa.

The studies outlined in this section demonstrate fairly conclusively that people from higher socioeconomic groups are more likely to prefer 'serious' music than are those from lower groups, and that people in general prefer 'popular' to 'serious' music. It does not necessarily follow from this that members of lower status groups tend to prefer popular music: as we saw earlier, there are fairly complex class-based differences in patterns of preference *within* pop music. We should bear in mind that most of this research is based on the musical tastes of teenage and college student subjects, and is thus by no means representative of the listening public in general. This particular subject-population is probably the focus of most studies because musical preferences are a salient feature of teenage and college life, and are therefore likely to give a clearer and more detailed picture of social influences than are the tastes of other age groups.

Experimental studies of social influence

Prestige and propaganda

Francès (1967) analogy between the perception of works of art and 'persuasive communications' was mentioned earlier in this chapter; it is well established in this context that the prestige of the person who sends a message has a considerable influence upon the way in which that message is perceived. A small body of empirical research has accumulated which has experiment- ally investigated such *prestige* effects upon aesthetic reactions to works in different art forms, and some other studies have approached the related question of the effects of *propaganda* about different artists and art works on reactions to them. The two influences are combined and/or indistinguishable in many of the experiments, and so I shall consider them both together. Crozier and Chapman (1981) have carried out a fairly comprehensive review of this research, which includes aesthetic reactions to poetry and radio plays amongst other art works. Farnsworth and Beaumont (1929), for example, found that students gave higher attractiveness ratings to pictures that were presented to them as being highly rated by art experts, and Sherif (1935) found that subjects' rankings of prose passages were influenced by their prior evaluations of the authors, when in fact the attributions of authors to the prose passages were false.

Before we look at the research on prestige and propaganda effects on reactions to music in particular, it may be useful to consider some general conclusions that Crozier and Chapman reached as a result of their own review across all art forms. Most importantly, they draw attention to the view of writers such as Asch (1948) and Child (1969) that because of the weaknesses in the design of many of the studies, prestige effects may be unimportant: they may be artefacts of particular experimental procedures and conditions. Crozier and Chapman identify four reasons why prestige effects may be small, unreplicable, and unstable. First, the *selection of the stimulus material* may exert a strong effect; familiar stimuli may be less susceptible to prestige effects than unfamiliar stimuli, for example, and Francès (1963) found that the selection of highly similar stimuli also seemed to enhance the likelihood of obtaining prestige effects. Secondly, the *selection of labels* is important: experimenters should ensure that their subjects attend to the labels which are assigned to art works in order to manipulate their prestige, and need to be able

Table 7.2 *Studies of prestige and propaganda effects*

	Subjects	Music	Results
Rigg (1948)	college students	Wagner, Beethoven, Franck, Sibelius	negative propaganda about Wagner had no negative effect on enjoyment ratings
Geiger (1950)	radio audiences	Haydn, Schubert Mozart, Beethoven, Mendelssohn	description of music programme as 'classical' rather than as 'popular' halved audience figures
Duerksen (1972)	college students	Beethoven	description of performance as by 'professional' rather than as by 'student' influenced quality ratings
Weick, Gilfillan & Keith (1973)	jazz orchestra musicians	new jazz pieces (to be performed)	pieces described as having 'serious' rather than 'non-serious' arranger better performed, remembered, and liked
Chapman & Williams (1976)	14–15-year-olds	stylistically ambiguous piece (Takemitsu)	significant differences between high status ('progressive pop') and low status ('modern serious music') groups on bipolar rating scales
Radocy (1976)	college music students	I Beethoven, Brahms, Corelli II baroque, twentieth-century, classical, romantic	bogus information about performance (I), composer identity and prior listener judgements (II) influenced performance evaluations and preference judgements
Castell & Hill (1985)	6–7, 8–9, 10–11, 14–15, 18–19-year-olds	4 stylistically ambiguous pieces	descriptions of pieces as 'contemporary classical' or 'modern progressive rock' influenced liking ratings: interactions with age

to account for subjects who try not to be influenced by them. Thirdly, it is important to establish the *reliability* of any prestige effects that are obtained: slight variations in the procedure of some studies (e.g. Das, Rath and Das, 1955) have been found to diminish the size of the effects, or even to eliminate them altogether. Fourthly, there may be *individual differences* in susceptibility to prestige effects, as a result of specific training or experience, for example: very few studies have taken this into account.

The studies of prestige and propaganda effects on responses to music are summarised in Table 7.2 in terms of their subject populations, the musical stimuli employed, and the results obtained. One of the best-known studies is that of Rigg (1948). Rigg played six pieces of music, including three by Wagner, to three groups of college students on two separate occasions; it is significant that the experiment was conducted just before the outbreak of World War Two. On the first occasion, no information was provided about the music to any of the subjects. On the second occasion, one group was told that Wagner was Hitler's favourite composer and that his music was used in

Nazi ceremonies. This negative propaganda did not produce a decline in enjoyment ratings for those two pieces, but a small increase (presumably a 'mere exposure' effect). This increase was greater in the control group, who once again received no information. The largest increases in enjoyment between the two conditions were reported by the third group, to whom the music was described in romantic terms. The propaganda was clearly of an emotive nature in this study, and it is rather surprising that it did not have a more powerful negative effect on the ratings.

Duerksen (1972) played a tape-recording of Beethoven's Piano Sonata No. 6 to two groups of college music and non-music student subjects on two separate occasions. The *control* group subjects were told that they would hear two performances of the same composition, and were asked to rate it on each occasion on eight scales concerned with different aspects of quality (rhythmic accuracy, pitch accuracy, appropriateness of tempo, appropriateness of accent, dynamic contrast, tone quality, interpretation, and overall quality of performance). The *experimental* group subjects were told that one perform- ance was by an eminent professional pianist, Wilhelm Backhaus, and that the other was taken from an audition tape submitted by a student seeking admission to a graduate music course; half of these subjects heard the 'professional' performance first and the other half heard the 'student' performance first. Duerksen found that members of the experimental group gave consistently higher ratings of the objective characteristics of the music as well as of the more subjective aspects under the 'professional' condition. Members of the control group consistently rated the second performance as better than the first; and Duerksen interpreted this as a 'mere exposure'-type effect. Two other interesting aspects of his results were that the music students in the experimental group were apparently just as susceptible to the prestige effect as were the non-music students; and that the ratings of the objective characteristics of the performances were affected to the same extent as were the more subjective aspects.

Radocy (1976) presented false information about identical performances of classical pieces for trumpet, orchestra, and piano, and about alleged composers and imaginary prior listeners' judgements of paired examples from four style periods (baroque, twentieth-century, classical, and romantic). He found that this information exerted a strong influence on the evaluative and preference ratings of his college music student subjects, in that they could be biased to conform to those of a teacher or other authority figure.

One powerful source of prestige effects is the way in which musical pieces are *stylistically* categorised. Chapman and Williams (1976) carried out a study on 14–15-year-old schoolchildren in which the perceived status of a stylistically ambiguous piece was manipulated by labelling it in one of two different ways. They first established, by means of a preliminary study, that the subjects in their sample were 'progressive pop' enthusiasts who were negatively disposed towards 'serious' music. All subjects were played part of a piece by a contemporary 'serious' composer, Toru Takemitsu, which bears some resemblances to 'progressive pop'; and asked to evaluate it on twelve bipolar rating scales ('interesting–boring', 'good–bad', 'serious–humorous', and so on), as well as on some open-ended preference measures. They were divided into three groups of equal size: the 'high status' group were told that the music was by a progressive pop composer (Roger Waters, of Pink Floyd); the 'low status' group heard a true description of the composer, as 'a leading Japanese composer of modern serious music'; and the control group received no description. The results revealed significant differences between the ratings of the 'high status' and 'low status' groups on three of the scales; the former group found the music more 'interesting', 'weird', and 'sorrowful' than the latter group. The ratings of the control group tended to lie outside, rather than between, those of the other two groups on most of the scales.

Castell and Hill (1985) followed up Chapman and Williams' investigation with a study which investigated the potential *developmental* aspects of prestige effects. A preliminary investigation (reported by Castell, 1984) had identified four pieces which were consistently labelled as either 'contemporary classical' music, or 'progressive rock', or both, by large groups of adults. These pieces were played to forty subjects at each of five age levels (6–7, 8–9, 10–11, 14–15, and 18–19 years), who rated them for 'liking' and 'quality': the testing of the two youngest groups took place over one year after that of the other three. Half the subjects at each age level heard the pieces described as 'contemporary classical music', and the other half as 'modern progressive rock'. Castell and Hill found that their 14–15-year-old subjects gave significantly higher liking ratings to pieces when they were described by the latter than by the former label, and that the reverse was true for the 6–7-year-olds. There were no significant effects for the other three age groups, nor for any of the 'quality' ratings. These interesting interactions between prestige effects and age were explained in terms of the increasing influence of peer-group norms in adolescence: they clearly deserve further study.

Finally, there are two studies which add a new dimension to those described already in that they both involve 'real-life' rather than laboratory based musical preferences. Geiger (1950) reports a Danish study in which 'a program of ear-appealing and not too difficult classical music' formed the content of a radio music programme which was introduced to the listeners as 'popular gramophone music'. The identical programme was repeated one week later, this time described as 'classical music'. This change resulted in a halving of the audience figures, which Geiger interpreted as an example of 'snobbism in reverse', implying that the listening public may have a more refined musical taste than it cares to admit.

Weick, Gilfillan and Keith's (1973) study employed the members of two jazz orchestras as subjects, and presented two new ('experimental') pieces to them that were by the same composer, and of similar difficulty and style, along with a third ('control') piece. The musicians were led to believe, by means of (bogus) accompanying press releases, that one of the experimental pieces was arranged by a 'serious' composer, and the other by a 'nonserious' composer. Weick *et al.* found that the latter was performed with more errors, and that it was recalled less well one day later, than the former. This is an impressive demonstration of a prestige effect because it possesses a considerable degree of ecological validity; and it shows that expert musicians can be just as susceptible to such effects as non-musicians.

The results of the studies reviewed in this section tend to confirm the importance of prestige and propaganda effects, in spite of the reservations, mentioned earlier, of authors such as Asch and Child. All but one of the studies summarised in Table 7.2 found social influences to have a significant effect on aesthetic judgements, and it may be that these are more powerful in the case of music than in other art forms. The effects are particularly striking in two of the studies because they appear in the reactions of musically experienced subjects; it seems intuitively quite likely that the power of social influences should be *inversely* related to the background knowledge of the listener.

If prestige and propaganda do exert such a powerful influence, how might their operation be explained? Asch (1948) argued that they involve complex perceptual reorganisations of the art works, rather than merely re-evaluations of constant stimuli. In other words, Asch was unhappy with the implicit assumption that the prestige and the content of a stimulus were independent factors that could be studied in isolation from one another, and considered instead that they were interdependent. Crozier and Chapman (1981) are inclined to support this view, since subjects in several of the experiments reported changes in their perceptions of the music alongside those in their subjective evaluations of it. The mediation of prestige and propaganda effects by perceptual reorganisation remains an interesting, though as yet unproven, theoretical lead. In a sense it represents an individual, 'cognitive', emphasis rather than a primarily 'social' one, although these are probably complementary rather than contradictory.

Social interaction

Very few laboratory based studies in experimental social psychology have investigated the effects of variations in the immediate social/interpersonal situation upon music behaviour, even though this approach is likely to prove very productive. By far the largest body of research that has been carried out is by Konečni and his associates at the University of California at San Diego, and comprehensively reviewed by Konečni (1979, 1982). Konečni's general complaints about music psychologists' failure to take adequate account of the social context of music listening were raised in Chapter 5: his original, pioneering, and sometimes bizarre research incorporates some valuable ways of tackling this issue. Konečni proposed a theoretical model which draws together the social environment, the listener's emotional state, and musical preference:

The model assumes that music, and aesthetic stimuli in general . . . are simply another aspect of a person's acoustic (or visual) environment and that they are chosen largely for the purpose of mood- and emotion-optimization. The model regards a person as being engaged in a constant exchange with the social and nonsocial environment, of which the acoustic stimuli are a part. The social behavior of others . . . is assumed to have a profound effect on a person's emotional states, which, in turn, affect aesthetic choices, including the choice of music, that a person will make in a given situation. The degree of enjoyment of the chosen piece presumably varies as a function of the concurrent social and nonsocial micro-environmental conditions . . . Listening to music is further assumed to produce changes in the listener's emotional state and thereby affect his or her behavior towards others in the situation. Since social behavior is by definition interactive, it is safe to assume that the behavior directed toward the listener by others will also change, leading to a further modification in the listener's emotional state, and possibly to different subsequent musical choices. The model thus contains a feedback-loop feature representing the ongoing nature of a person's interaction with the social and musical environment – a series of aesthetic episodes mediated by changes in emotional state and mood.   (1982, pp. 500–1)

Konečni and his colleagues have put this model into operation by experimentally manipulating the social situation in a variety of ways, thereby inducing various different emotional states in their subjects, and by assessing their liking for different pieces of music under these conditions. In the first part of Konečni, Crozier and Doob's (1976) experiment, for example, some of the subjects were repeatedly insulted by an accomplice of the experimenter, posing as a subject. Pilot work had already established that this reliably induced anger in experimental subjects, in terms of both physiological measures and subjective reports. In the second part of the experiment, subjects chose on each of fifty trials to listen to 10-second episodes of either one of two different types of computer-generated melody, by pressing one of two buttons. The two types of melody varied considerably in objective complexity: previous research had established that subjects listening under neutral (i.e. non-aroused) conditions typically showed no significant preference for the simpler or the more complex melodies.

Subjects were divided into three groups. Those in the 'annoy–wait' group were insulted, then waited alone in a room with nothing to do, and then listened to the melodies. They showed a strong preference for the simple melodies, choosing to listen to them on approximately 70 per cent of the trials. Subjects in the 'no annoy–wait' group, who were not insulted and who also waited, showed no such preference. (These subjects essentially acted as controls, and their lack of preference is predictable from the earlier findings.) Subjects in the third 'annoy–shock' group were insulted in the same way as the first experimental group, but were then given the chance to retaliate against the accomplice by delivering a fixed number of what they thought were electric shocks. Like the 'no annoy–wait' group, these subjects showed no pronounced preference for either type of melody.

Konečni *et al.* concluded from this experiment that the angry state of the 'annoy–wait' group represented a high level of arousal which was not present in the 'no annoy–wait' subjects; and that the former preferred to listen to simple rather than to complex melodies in order to minimise any further increases in arousal. The retaliatory aggression of the 'annoy–shock' group served to 'let off steam', that is, to bring the level of arousal back down to normal, such that their preferences once again resembled those of the 'no annoy–wait' group. The notion that high arousal gives rise to preferences for simple rather than complex melodies was confirmed by the results of some other studies (e.g. Konečni and Sargent-Pollock, 1976) that employed non-social means of inducing it, including exposure to bursts of a very loud squarewave tone, and the concurrent performance of cognitive tasks. Konečni suggests that this effect is probably mediated by a decrease in information processing capacity; highly aroused subjects minimise the demands on their system by preferring to listen to low- rather than high-information sequences.

This explanation hinges on the 'feedback loop' relating overt behaviour to internal states, and also involves the notion that collative stimulus variables, such as complexity, can influence the operation of the feedback loop. This latter connection perhaps represents the most original feature of Konečni *et al.*'s research. Although Berlyne's theory (see Chapter 5) implies that central states such as level of arousal ought to determine aspects of aesthetic preference, no previous work has attempted to put this notion into practice experimentally.

Ridgeway's (1976) study, though carried out from a completely different, sociological, point of view, nevertheless has a good deal in common with that of Konečni, Crozier and Doob. Ridgeway classified college students as 'high' or 'low absorption' listeners on the basis of several different measures, including self-reports and Thematic Apperception Test-type indices. She then put her subjects in six difficult interpersonal role-playing situations, three of which involved positive and three of which involved negative affect, and re-assessed their levels of absorption. The results showed that exposure to the difficult situations tended to further increase 'high absorption' listeners' involvement with the music, but not that of 'low absorption' listeners. Ridgeway explained her results by proposing that music listening provides a 'structural representation', or 'symbolic model' of social interaction processes, and that it becomes 'one means by which individuals may maintain psychological well-being whilst adapting to complex social structures' (p. 414).

It is difficult to know what to make of this rather elaborate interpretation, but Ridgeway's results are certainly in line with Konečni's demonstration that variations in the social situation can directly affect music listening preferences. His proposed feedback loop also implies that the direction of this causal relationship can be reversed, and in another study (Konečni, 1975) the effects of listening to different musical sequences on emotional states and behaviour were investigated. The general approach here was to manipulate subjects' arousal level by means of insults, as in the research described above, and then to further increment this level to varying degrees by playing melodies that were differentially aversive. This was accomplished by manipulating the *listening level* (i.e. loudness), as well as the *complexity*, of the melodies. The dependent variable, aggressive behaviour, was assessed by apparently giving subjects the opportunity to administer supposedly painful electric shocks to the accomplice on each of many trials. Thus the experiment was arranged so that subjects, having been insulted in some experimental groups and not in others, heard melodies varying in listening level and complexity while making the decision to shock the accomplice or not.

The results tended to corroborate the 'arousal' theory. With few exceptions, control groups of non-insulted subjects showed low levels of aggression towards the accomplice, and this was largely unaffected by the characteristics of the melodies. Insulted subjects, on the other hand, showed high levels of aggression, and this interacted with the characteristics of the melodies. The highest levels were observed in subjects who had heard loud, complex melodies; intermediate levels were displayed by those subjects who had heard complex melodies at low listening levels, and simple melodies at high listening levels. Those who heard simple melodies at low levels showed surprisingly little aggression; in fact, they were less aggressive than some non-insulted subjects, Konečni suggests that this may demonstrate the active soothing propensities of some melodies: they seemed to have been very effective in reducing arousal.

Konečni's experiments are bold and imaginative, and represent a genuine attempt to tackle the interactions between cognitive, social, and emotional aspects of aesthetic behaviour. The experimental operationalisations of these interactions, as in the study mentioned above, are necessarily elaborate and complex: establishing any clear relationships would appear to be quite a long shot. It is therefore surprising yet gratifying that the evidence presented by Konečni in favour of his theoretical model seems to be fairly clear-cut, if inevitably rather limited. It would be easy to criticise his research on several grounds. The experimental paradigms are based on those used in studies of authority and obedience, such as those of Milgram, and one could argue that these paradigms are inappropriate for the study of music listening. There are well-aired criticisms of the ethical aspects of these paradigms, and of their artificiality and contrivance. The proof of the pudding is nevertheless in the eating; Konečni has taken some important, pioneering steps towards what he sees as 'a psychology of music that recognizes the role of social, emotional and cognitive factors in music appreciation as well as the conditions under which music of all kinds is enjoyed in daily life' (p. 515).

One other small area of research which is based on a well-known paradigm in experimental social psychology is that on conformity effects on musical preferences. Three studies have been carried out which are based on Asch's famous experiment (Asch, 1956) in which subjects were found to make clearly erroneous judgements of the relative lengths of lines in order to conform with the apparent consensus judgements, which were in fact false, of other small-group members. Radocy's (1975) study was very clearly modelled on the Asch experiment: naive subjects were asked to make judgements on pitch and loudness matching tasks along with four peers who had been instructed beforehand to respond incorrectly. The naive subjects tended to conform to the incorrect responses of their peers on approximately 30 per cent of the pitch trials and 50 per cent of the loudness trials, which confirms Asch's findings about the power of group pressure. This result is convincing, as the subjects were college students majoring in music, who could be expected to perform well on the tasks under normal conditions, given that the tasks involved objective musical skills.

Inglefield (1968) carried out a study on ninth-graders in which the dependent variable was rather more subjective, that is, scores on a musical preference inventory. Experimental-group subjects who completed the inventory under different Asch-type peer-group pressure conditions were found to conform to the preferences of their peers, unlike a control group who completed the inventory under neutral conditions. Inglefield also found that conformity tended to be greatest for expressed jazz preferences, and least for classical music; and that it occurred to a greater degree in subjects who scored high on independent measures of other-directedness, need for social approval, and dependency.

Finally, Crowther (1985) carried out a study in this tradition which incorporated two important methodological improvements. Crutchfield (see Krech, Crutchfield and Ballachey, 1962) realised long ago that the traditional Asch experiment is inefficient in the sense that acquiring data from a single naive subject involves the recruitment of a whole small group, the other members of which are confederates of the experimenter. He developed a modified version of the experimental procedure in which subjects apparently signalled their task judgements by means of a panel of lights, which was visible to all subjects simultaneously. By simulating false 'group decisions' on the light panel, Crutchfield was able to assign every recruited subject to the 'naive' condition, thus saving a good deal of time and effort. Crowther employed this technique in his study, in ingenious conjunction with an operant music listening recorder (see Chapter 5), the measures from which served as the primary dependent variable.

Crowther carried out a preliminary study which revealed that his secondary school pupil subjects typically gave 'disco' and 'rock'n'roll' music higher ratings on a number of different seven-point preference scales than 'heavy metal' and 'reggae' music. His *control* group subjects listened to one of four OMLR channels at a time, one for each musical style; this confirmed subjects' preference for the 'disco' and 'rock'n'roll' music under normal listening conditions. When the *experimental* group subjects switched between the same four channels under the impression that a majority of their co-listeners were spending more time listening to the 'heavy metal' and 'reggae' music channels, as conveyed by the (bogus) display on the light panel, however, Crowther found that there was a significant tendency for them to conform by shifting to these two channels.

This is an elegant demonstration of the power of what Crowther calls *minority* influences on adolescents' musical taste. In his study, peer-group pressure was a minority influence which was able to override the *majority* influence of normative preferences; a clear shift was produced away from normally preferred musical styles. Patterns of majority influence are extremely complex within teenage musical taste, as we saw earlier in this chapter, and they are constantly changing. It is the patterns of change in musical taste over time that form the focus of the final section of this chapter.

Musical fashions

Regularities undoubtedly exist in patterns of change in musical taste over time; some of the evidence for this, in 'serious' as well as in 'popular' music, will be reviewed in this section. The most easily identifiable regular pattern is the inverted-U function, which has already been discussed at some length. As we shall see, plots of the 'popularity curves' of various different types of music reveal increases in popularity up to a peak, and then a subsequent decline: this pattern is sometimes followed by further fluctuations. The precise shapes of the inverted-U functions are dependent on a host of other factors, including the nature and complexity of the music, the length of the time-scale (hours, weeks, or decades?), the characteristics of the listeners, the measures of popularity, and so on. It may indeed be surprising that any regularities do emerge, given the numerous variables which might influence and override them.

I shall outline the *preference-feedback hypothesis* of cyclical vogues and fashions (Colman, Sluckin and Hargreaves, 1981), which is based on inverted-U theory principles, after a description of some of the real-life manifestations of the curve. I shall also consider some other social and cultural factors that affect these patterns of musical taste. We have already looked at the effects of social class, the mass media and the school, for example; these can be thought of as complementary influences upon the familiarity–liking model. There are clear examples of pieces of music which do *not* follow inverted-U patterns of popularity over time. Some pieces never gain any popularity and some emerge as perennial 'classics'. These outcomes almost certainly derive from idiosyncratic social, cultural, or musical factors rather than from any general considerations of familiarity. Familiarity is nevertheless one of the most important factors, and its importance is enhanced by the absence of any competing, or comparable, theory.

Fashions in 'classical' music
In this field, the research of Farnsworth (1969) is deservedly well known. Farnsworth investigated fashions in the popularity of the works of the great

Table 7.3 *Eminence rankings of composers by musicologists*

Rank	1938	Rank	1944	Rank	1951	Rank	1964
1	Bach	1	Bach	1	Beethoven	1	Bach
2	Beethoven	2	Beethoven	2	Bach	2	Beethoven
3	Wagner	3	Mozart	3	Brahms	3	Mozart
4	Mozart	4	Wagner	4	Haydn	4	Haydn
5	Palestrina	5	Haydn	5	Mozart	5	Brahms
6	Haydn	6.5	Brahms	6.5	Schubert	6	Handel
7	Brahms	6.5	Palestrina	6.5	Debussy	7	Debussy
8	Monteverdi	8	Schubert	8	Handel	8	Schubert
9	Debussy	9	Handel	9	Wagner	9	Wagner
10	Schubert	10	Debussy	10	Palestrina	10	Chopin
11	Handel	11	Chopin	11	Chopin	11	Monteverdi
12	Chopin	25	Monteverdi	15	Monteverdi	12	Palestrina

(Reproduced from Farnsworth (1969) by permission of Iowa State University Press)

symphonic composers by devising various different indices. In Chapter 5 I mentioned his surveys in which groups of subjects including university students, members of the American Musicological Society and Dutch symphony subscribers were asked to rank the eminence of the 'top twelve' composers at different times over a period of some thirty years or so. Table 7.3 shows, for example, the mean rankings of the musicologists in 1938, 1944, 1951, and 1964. Although there are generally high correlations between the rank orders, with Bach and Beethoven in the top two places on all four occasions, there are also some interesting upward and downward trends. Palestrina's positions were 5, 6.5, 10 and 12, for example, whilst those of Haydn were 6, 5, 4, and 4. If we look at the positions of Brahms in the table, we can discern something like an inverted-U curve which peaks in 1951, and a similar pattern holds for Schubert, a few places lower. Farnsworth's calculation of the correlations between these sets of rankings shows that there are indeed significant changes in ranking patterns over time. The 1964 rankings correlate 0.95 with the 1951 rankings, but only 0.78 with the 1938 rankings, for example.

Another popular notion that Farnsworth was able to test by analysing these rankings was that of 'reverence for the past'. According to this idea, the eminence of composers increases in proportion to the length of time that has elapsed since their death; many a contemporary composer has ruefully pointed out that one has to die in order to achieve eminence! Farnsworth tested this idea by comparing the eminence rankings with the composers' dates of birth, and he also studied the relationship between composers' dates of birth and their presence in or absence from two current music encyclopaedias. His analysis showed very clearly that there was little or no evidence for a 'reverence for the past' effect in the data, but that something like an intermediate recency effect was operating. Neither contemporary composers nor those longest dead received the highest rankings, but rather those in between. In the case of Farnsworth's sample, these were the composers of the eighteenth and early nineteenth centuries. This, once again, is something like an inverted-U effect; the highest eminence rankings seem to be associated with intermediate levels of familiarity, expressed in this case in terms of historical recency.

Another index of popularity that was studied by Farnsworth, as well as by Mueller and Hevner (1942), was the amount of time devoted to the works of different composers in the programmes of major symphony orchestras. One study looked at the frequencies with which ninety-two composers were listed in the programmes of the Boston Symphony Orchestra over each of the five decades from 1915 to 1965. The most striking finding was the degree of similarity between the top names on these five lists: Beethoven, Brahms, Mozart, and Wagner figured most prominently. This accords with Mueller and Hevner's analysis of the programmes of seven leading U.S. orchestras over the period from 1936 to 1941: the consistency amongst them was discussed in Chapter 5. Similar consistency was found in Farnsworth's analysis of the 'serious music' programmes broadcast by the Pacific Gas and Electric Company over the period from 1941 to 1943.

Although the general pattern is one of consistency and stability, slow changes nevertheless do occur. Correlations between the rankings in different decades in Mueller and Hevner's data, for example, showed that the resemblances between programmes were greatest in contiguous decades. That between the decades starting in 1915 and 1925 (1915/25) was 0.98, for example, whereas the equivalent figures for 1915/35, 1915/45 and 1915/55 were 0.90, 0.90, and 0.89. In a study of the programmes of several American orchestras over the period from 1876 to 1941, Mueller and Hevner found evidence of curve fluctuation and plateaux in the changing positions of different composers, rather than consistent climbs or falls. Wagner started high in popularity and declined in the late 1880s, for example; he ascended once again to second place in 1910, and then declined again. Tchaikovsky's rankings showed a similar pattern, though at a lower level of popularity.

These are clear musical examples of *cyclical vogues*, which can be observed in the popularity of other cultural objects, and which I shall attempt to explain later. There are obvious resemblances between the patterns mentioned above and those which describe changes over time in the popularity of the different Christian names that parents select for their children, for example (see Fig. 7.4). Mueller and Hevner also found that the popularity patterns of individual works, such as the Beethoven symphonies, could be described in a similar way. One of their interesting findings was that the shapes of these popularity curves were constant between different cultural groups, but their phasing might vary. For example, whilst Beethoven's popularity curve was the same shape in the programmes of the major London and New York orchestras, there was a time-lag of some five years between the former and the latter.

It is worth recalling Simonton's (1980a, 1980b) analysis of the relationship between thematic fame and melodic originality at this point. In Chapter 5 we discussed his conclusion that at any given time the best-known melodies are

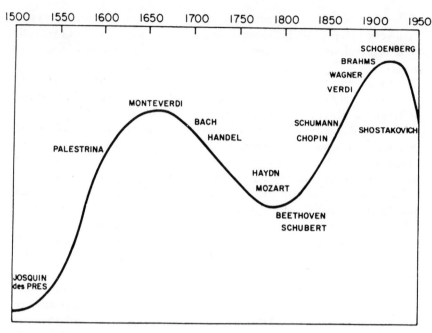

Fig. 7.2 Transhistorical trend line for repertoire melodic originality (from 'Thematic fame, melodic originality, and musical zeitgeist: A biographical and transhistorical content analysis', D.K. Simonton, 1980, Journal of Personality and Social Psychology, 39, *p. 976. © 1980 by the American Psychological Association. Reprinted by permission of the author)*

those which are most original ('zeitgeist originality'), but that over time the most famous melodies are those of intermediate originality ('repertoire originality'). Simonton carried out a historical trend analysis of the 15,618 themes in his 1980b study, and the result is shown in Figure 7.2. There is a general increase in repertoire melodic originality over time, with cycles superimposed over this broad tendency. I should prefer to leave the explanation of these trends to music historians: what is significant in the present context is the clear presence of the cyclical pattern. This applies to melodic originality in Simonton's results, and it is difficult to know whether there may be a causal relationship with the popularity patterns discussed above: but the similarity is striking.

There seems to be little doubt that fashions do exist in classical music, and that the patterns of change move fairly slowly. This is probably because the 'establishment' that promotes classical music is by definition conservative: and, in terms of inverted-U theory, because the music itself possesses a high degree of subjective complexity for most listeners. Popular music, on the other hand, is simple rather than complex; it is promoted by the mass media, which are guided by commercial pressures rather than by the artistic values of the

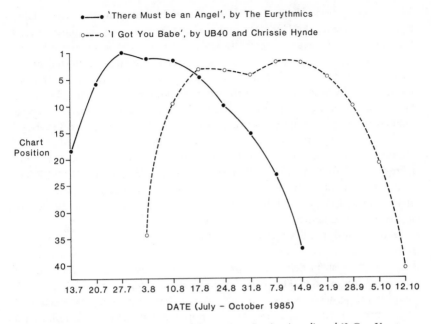

Fig. 7.3 Weekly chart positions of 'There Must Be An Angel' and 'I Got You Babe' between July and October 1985

establishment. It is therefore not surprising that fashions in pop music, as evidenced by indices such as record sales, are much more ephemeral and rapidly changing. The central point of interest for our theory is to establish whether the patterns of change in classical and pop music show similar characteristics, even though their time-scales are altogether different.

Fashions in 'popular' music

Fortunately for music researchers, a wealth of detailed information about pop record popularity is available in the form of the 'charts' that are produced, usually weekly, by various agencies in the pop music industry. It is almost certainly the case that the inverted-U curve provides the best general description of the changing chart positions of many pop records over time: this is shown very clearly in Figure 7.3. The curves describe the weekly chart positions of two songs, 'There Must Be An Angel' by the Eurythmics and 'I Got You Babe' by UB40 and Chrissie Hynde, in the British *Melody Maker* singles charts between July and October 1985. It does not seem too far-fetched to suggest that these typical patterns may resemble those identified by Farnsworth for classical works, even though the time-scale is very much shorter.

Dixon (1982) carried out detailed correlation and regression analyses of the 'chart careers' of the 234 records listed in *Billboard's Top 200 LP & Tape*

Chart over the period September–December 1979, in conjunction with related information about the *Hot 100* singles. These are the main popularity charts for singles and LP records in the U.S.A., and positions on them are largely based on sales volume and airplay exposure. Dixon was interested in the patterns of waxing and waning such as that shown in Figure 7.3: his analysis focussed on the *intensity* and *duration* of the popularity of individual records. He devised operational measures of each of these variables: CHARTOP was defined as the highest chart position attained by a given record, and TIMEON as the total number of weeks it remained on the chart. The main aim of Dixon's analysis was to establish the predictability of these two variables from the position at which records entered the chart (defined as ENTRYPOS), as well as from other 'halo' variables such as sales volume, the presence in the chart of other LPs by the same artist, and the simultaneous presence in the *Hot 100* of singles taken from the LP in question.

Dixon found that ENTRYPOS was the most powerful predictor variable. Rank at chart entry was a good predictor of how high records ascended, of how long they sustained peak popularity, and of how long they remained in the chart after peaking. However, 'an unanticipated finding was that LPs took roughly the same amounts of time to attain peak popularity irrespective of chart entry position, and then waned in popularity in direct accordance with chart entry position. This finding tempted the interpretation that (strength of) "front end" performance is a crucial determinant of LP chart tenure' (p. 40). More specifically, it emerged that CHARTOP was best predicted by the third-week chart position; and that this predictability was strongest for records which entered the chart in one of the upper 100 rather than of the lower 100 positions. TIMEON was not clearly determined by any of the predictor variables, and there was no clear pattern of relationships between any of the 'halo effect' variables mentioned above, and ENTRYPOS, CHARTOP, or TIMEON.

Dixon's pioneering efforts show that some regularities and rules *can* be observed in these record charts, and should serve to inspire further investigations, but it is hardly surprising that the patterns are by no means clear-cut. There are various social and cultural influences that may override or at least influence familiarity based patterns of popularity; some of these are easy to identify in the case of pop music preferences.

The motives of the mass media-based music industry are primarily commercial rather than artistic, and the popularity of a given song, record or artist can to a certain extent be 'manufactured'. The Monkees, a successful 1960s pop group who were modelled on the Beatles, were entirely manufactured by the industry; they were essentially a business concern that was conceived, organised, and packaged without any initiative from the musicians themselves. Disc jockeys have also been shown to exert a considerable influence in shaping teenage musical taste, even though they openly declare their allegiance to commercial rather than to artistic standards, and though teachers regard them as a bad influence (Booker, 1968; Tanner, 1976).

Hirsch (1969) has described how the filtering and selection of records for the 'top 40' format on U.S. radio stations has a crucial influence in 'making or breaking' a given record in terms of its subsequent popularity and sales. The top 40 records are used as the basis for 'playlists' that form the staple broadcasting diet of the network of pop music radio stations; these lists are drawn up according to a preset combination of styles which is designed to appeal to a maximum proportion of the mass audience. Similar playlists form the basis of pop music programming by the BBC in Great Britain.

Once a song has got over the initial hurdle of appearing on a playlist, its exposure can lead to further popularity in the form of television appearances and much greater mass media coverage. In this sense the industry determines who shall become 'a star overnight', and so it is hardly surprising that dubious practices have been employed by record companies in order to ensure that their products reach the playlist stage. Denisoff (1975) has documented the (now illegal) 'payola' practices by which disc jockeys and radio programmers received payments for 'plugging' certain discs; the widespread current practice of record companies buying up large numbers of their own products in order to secure a chart position, known as 'hyping', is no less dubious.

Though these influences are undoubtedly powerful, we can by no means conclude that they are *entirely* responsible for the creation of hit records. Jolly's (1967) study enabled him to identify no single agency as the main creator or predictor of hits; his own discussion was in terms of exposure and familiarity. This reinforces my earlier point that familiarity may well be one of the most important determinants of musical taste, and that its effects can probably be predicted more accurately than those of other social and cultural factors.

Musical fashions and the preference-feedback hypothesis

The *preference-feedback hypothesis* derives from a programme of research on the relationship between familiarity and liking for non-musical stimuli carried out by myself and my colleagues in the Leicester Aesthetics Research Group (see reviews by Sluckin, Hargreaves and Colman, 1982, 1983). In Chapter 5 I explained how our adaptation of the inverted-U hypothesis ought to be able to encompass 'mere exposure' theories in which liking is seen as a positive monotonic function of familiarity, as well those which propose a negative monotonic relationship. The methodological approach used in most of our studies involved subjects rating large numbers of different classes of stimuli for *either* familiarity *or* liking, and our analyses focussed on the properties of the correlation scattergrams describing the relationships between these sets of ratings.

Some of our studies of names produced apparently contradictory results. Scattergrams of the familiarity–liking relationships for ratings of Christian names, derived from samples of subjects in England and Australia, showed strong positive monotonic relationships: the best-liked Christian names (e.g. *David, Sarah*) were those which were most familiar to the subjects, and the least-liked names (e.g. *Oswald, Gertrude*) were those which were least familiar (see Colman, Hargreaves and Sluckin, 1981). A similar investigation of surnames, however, revealed a corresponding inverted-U relationship: very familiar and very unfamiliar surnames tended to be disliked (e.g. *Smith, Brown; Bamkin, Nall*), and those of intermediate familiarity (e.g. *Burton, Cassell*) were liked best (see Colman, Sluckin and Hargreaves, 1981).

This apparent contradiction between a 'mere exposure' result for Christian names and an 'inverted-U' result for surnames led to the formulation of the preference-feedback hypothesis, which has implications well beyond the study of names. We start by assuming that all classes of stimuli are potentially subject to the inverted-U effect; providing they are exposed to people sufficiently often, liking for them will follow a curve that increases up to a peak of optimum familiarity, and then declines with further increases in familiarity. In the case of music, we saw in Chapter 5 that this ought to apply to subjects' liking for pieces varying in familiarity at any given time, as well as to their liking for any given piece at different points in time.

With this in mind, we can now distinguish between two broad classes of stimuli: those whose exposure depends on voluntary choice, such as designs in furniture and styles of dress (Class A), and those whose exposure is virtually beyond voluntary control, such as geometrical shapes and letters of the alphabet (Class B). The basis of the hypothesis is that stimuli in Class B may become so familiar that liking for them passes well beyond the peak of the inverted U, but that those in Class A are prevented from reaching such high levels of familiarity by a cultural feedback mechanism; the frequency of exposure of the latter is reduced by voluntary choice as soon as they show signs of declining popularity, that is, of going beyond the peak of the inverted-U curve.

It is very clear that Christian names fall into Class A. Parents choose best-liked Christian names for their children, and the preference-feedback mechanism should come into operation. If a given Christian name begins to decline in popularity through over-exposure, parents will be likely to avoid it, and its frequency of exposure and thence familiarity in the culture will decrease. This decrease in familiarity may in due course lead once again to an increase in liking, so the name may return once again to fashion. Thus, *at any given time*, the hypothesis predicts a positive, monotonic relationship between familiarity and liking for Class A stimuli. *Over a period of time*, however, the hypothesis predicts a cyclical pattern of waxing and waning in popularity. This pattern is clearly identifiable in the frequencies of occurrence of Christian names, as shown in Figure 7.4. This shows the number of times the boys' name *Alexander* and the girls' name *Laura* were chosen in every 10,000 same-sex births in eight different years between 1850 and 1975: this data is taken from the Index of Births in England and Wales (see Dunkling, 1977).

Most people exercise no control over their surname, and so surnames

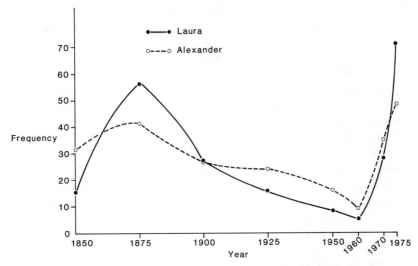

Fig. 7.4 Frequencies of occurrence per 10,000 same-sex births of the names
Alexander *and* Laura *between 1850 and 1975*

belong to Class B. No cultural feedback mechanism comes into operation; some surnames therefore become so common that they pass well beyond the peak of the inverted U. The hypothesis therefore predicts that an inverted-U familiarity–liking relationship should be found for surnames at any given point in time, and that this should remain stable over time. The results of our surnames study confirm this prediction, therefore the preference-feedback hypothesis enables us to reconcile the apparent contradictions between the results of the studies on names, as well as to account for the existence of cyclical vogues and fashions in certain classes of stimuli.

The hypothesis will need a good deal of development and refinement before it can be applied more generally, for example, to the explanation of consumer behaviour. A recent attempt to test it directly by simultaneously employing examples of Class A and Class B stimuli in the same experimental design (Colman, Best and Austen, 1985) met with only limited success, and there are various possible reasons for this. It is almost certainly the case that stimuli exist which are intermediate between Class A and Class B, for example, and that other cultural factors mediate the familiarity–liking relationship to varying degrees for different classes of stimuli, and for different subject-groups. My main interest here is in trying to apply the theory to the musical fashions that have been described.

Strictly speaking, all musical stimuli can be thought of as belonging to Class A in that they are subject to the voluntary control of the listeners. The hypothesis therefore predicts that there should be a positive monotonic familiarity–liking relationship for musical stimuli at any given point in time. The evidence from our own work tends to support this; Hargreaves,

Messerschmidt and Rubert (1980), for example, found that familiar excerpts of both 'classical' and 'popular' music were significantly better liked by undergraduate subjects than were unfamiliar excerpts. Hargreaves and Castell (1986) found that familiar melodies were better liked by groups of subjects ranging from preschoolers to adults than were unfamiliar melodies, and statistical approximations to music.

The other prediction that the hypothesis makes about Class A stimuli is much more difficult to subject to a clear test; can we conclude that the serious and popular music fashions that were discussed earlier conform to the description of cyclical vogues and fashions? Some of Farnsworth's conclusions about long-term trends in the popularity of composers, and in orchestral programming, do seem to fit this description. Pop records do not continue to wax and wane, however; we saw that the typical chart career of a record consists of a single rise and fall, without any further variation. In this sense, it may be that classical music fashions do follow different rules from those in pop music, which may be the result, for example, of the relative complexities of the musical forms.

Changes over time in the popularity of the works of the great composers are probably more akin to *movements* in pop music than to the chart careers of individual pop records. A broader historical view of pop music reveals that 'revivals' of earlier styles are a prominent feature of current trends. At the time of writing (1984–5), pop music programmes feature artists representing earlier styles, such as 1930s swing jazz (e.g. Harvey and the Wallbangers; Manhattan Transfer) and 1950s rock'n'roll (e.g. Shakin' Stevens; Showaddywaddy); and some movements are explicitly marketed in revivalist terms (e.g. the trad jazz revival of the 1960s; the 'new romantic' movement of the 1980s). This view of cyclical vogues in 'pop', the definition of which is broadened to include other cultural artefacts, is of course quite different from preference-feedback predictions about the popularity trends of individual classical works, or composers. The comparison nevertheless brings us back to the point that familiarity is only one factor affecting musical fashion: its effects can only realistically be interpreted in the broader cultural perspective.

8

Developmental psychology and music education

The aim of this book has been to draw together those parts of developmental psychology that can explain the phenomena of musical development: these explanations should form the natural foundation for music education. In this final chapter I try to identify some of the specific areas of music education in which my aim might be accomplished. This is in no sense intended to be a comprehensive review of music education, but rather a fairly brief outline of the salient issues to which developmental psychology ought to be able to make a contribution.

The term 'music education' has different definitions and connotations within different disciplines, as well as in different countries, and so it is difficult to know whether or not a particular theoretical idea is likely to be universally applicable. Because different countries have radically different educational philosophies, institutions, and policies, there are wide variations in the ways in which theory is translated into practice. There are also wide variations in the importance of music and music education relative to other subjects on the curriculum. A glance at the 9th Yearbook of the International Society for Music Education (Dobbs, 1982) soon conveys this diversity: the contributions come from many countries across four continents, each with its individual traditions and emphases. My own account of the scope of music education has an admittedly parochial emphasis upon practices in the U.K. and the U.S.A., but most of the issues that I shall raise are universal.

I consider some controversial questions about the curriculum which are especially topical in the light of some recent, fairly radical recommendations by schools inspectors in the U.K. For convenience, I have rather uneasily divided my outline of the different methods of instruction into what I have called behavioural, pedagogical, and programmed approaches; in practice, there is a good deal of overlap between these. The questions of assessment and evaluation are also controversial; although some aspects of musical skill are easy to quantify, and although tests and examinations predominate in many children's own musical development, there are some important aspects of it which may be impossible to assess.

The scope of music education

It is a salutary thought that most of the currently controversial issues in music education have been debated for many years. Well over 200 years ago, for example, Jean Jacques Rousseau (1762) formulated some guidelines for music education which would be identified as fairly 'progressive' by today's standards. He considered that intuitive musical experience was an essential precursor of musical literacy; that children should create, as well as receive music; and that music should be enjoyable. These ideas are echoed in the philosophy of Emile Jacques-Dalcroze, who believed that the development of musical feeling was as important as the acquisition of formal knowledge. This same philosophy is central to the British Schools Council Project *Music in the secondary school curriculum* (see Paynter, 1982), and it remains controversial; the hostility of some school music examiners, expressed in their comments on the Project's assessment proposals, is surprisingly vehement.

This is a musical variant of the general educational debate about the pros and cons of different aspects of so-called 'traditional' and 'progressive', or 'formal' and 'informal' methods. These seemed to be quite distinct from one another in the 1960s and early 1970s, when the debate was at its height: teachers were prepared to identify with one 'side' or the other. This is no longer the case, and the labels are now recognised as covering a multitude of dimensions of teaching – today's attitudes are not clearly polarised in the same way. Research on teaching styles (e.g. Bennett and Jordan, 1975; Galton and Simon, 1980) has produced typologies in which different styles can be identified as 'progressive' in some respects but 'traditional' in others. 'Discovery learning' or 'enquiry learning' methods derive from the educational philosophies of Froebel, Dewey, and Montessori, and have been given added impetus by the developmental theories of Piaget and Bruner. Put very simply, the idea is that children have the freedom to proceed at their own rate of learning, and to choose their own preferred activities; they thereby discover important principles and skills; and they 'learn by doing', that is, through concrete activity, rather than merely following the instructions of the teacher. The emphasis upon each one of these three central dimensions of *freedom*, *discovery*, and *activity* varies in the styles of different teachers, and also in the styles used by the same teacher in different settings.

Simpson (1976) and Taylor (1979) have outlined the history of music education in the U.K., documenting the influence of methods such as Curwen's tonic sol-fa, 'payment by results', Dolmetsch's introduction of the descant recorder, Jacques-Dalcroze eurhythmics (exercises emphasising the physical aspects of musical experience, especially through rhythm), and the appreciation movement of Macpherson, Read, and Scholes. Two fairly recent reviews of the state of British music education (Burnett, 1977; Burnett and Lawrence, 1979) make it clear that this rich legacy is woefully under-exploited. In the foreword to the first of the reviews, Swanwick (1977) writes that 'It resembles a patchwork quilt roughly sewn together with some squares of the finest material and others of thin sacking. We can find isolated bits of work of a highly imaginative and professional quality in schools, colleges and universities, but, to be frank, we have to know where to look for them' (p.iii). He also complains that this unevenness results in a lack of communication and conceptual common ground between those music educators who *are* carrying out innovative work, so 'We clutch at the straws hanging from a dozen bandwagons and snatch up flags marked "literacy", "creativity", and "pop culture" (p. 64).

Music is undoubtedly a low-status subject in British schools, often regarded as an 'optional extra' rather than as a 'proper' part of the academic curriculum. This is of course quite wrong; and a very encouraging step in the right direction is the publication of *Music from 5 to 16*, the fourth in the discussion series Curriculum Matters, by Her Majesty's Inspectorate (DES, 1985). This is an enlightened document which has widespread implications. One of its central concerns is that music should not be isolated from the rest of the school curriculum, and that it could and should be integrated with teaching in science and social studies, for example, as well as with other arts subjects. Paynter (1977) makes the same point in suggesting that *music in education*, that is, as an integral part of the general school curriculum, is just as important as the *musical education* of the relatively few pupils who intend to follow musical careers.

Another important philosophical foundation of the HMI document relates to the distinction made earlier between 'intuitive' and 'formal' musical understandings. Along with Rousseau, Jacques-Dalcroze and more recently Paynter, the Inspectors consider that 'the mastery of techniques should be subservient to experiencing the music itself' (p. 1). The intuitive experience and enjoyment of music should come first, such that the later acquisition of formal musical skills occurs *inductively*, that is, as an integral growth of the child's experience. A good deal of traditional music education has worked *deductively*: the formal rules have been taught in the abstract, for example, through verbal description or written notation, rather than in the practical context of making the sounds themselves. To Paynter (1982), this is putting the cart before the horse. An over-emphasis upon the 'academic' aspects of music, for example upon the rules of notation, harmony, counterpoint, and so on, has probably stifled interest in the subject for many pupils, especially those who have had no intention of following careers in music.

Whereas the undoubted potential of British music education seems to be unfulfilled through institutional inertia, and through the desperate lack of resources, its counterpart in the U.S.A. appears to be better established within the general curriculum, and to be more generously provided for. As I mentioned in Chapter 1, the American use of the term normally *includes* music psychology, in contrast with the British gulf between theory and practice. *Music therapy* also comes under the same umbrella in the U.S.A.; this is a discipline which is largely regulated by the National Association of Music Therapy, and which has a good deal of overlap with developmental and clinical psychology. British music therapy is 'musical' rather than 'psychological' in its orientation, as a comparison of the *British Journal of Music Therapy* and the (U.S.) *Journal of Music Therapy* will quickly illustrate.

Several American music education textbooks are oriented towards practical aspects of the classroom situation (e.g. Nye and Nye, 1977; Madsen and Kuhn, 1978; Hoffer, 1983); Leonhard and House (1972) provide a sound and solid guide to the historical, philosophical, psychological, and sociological foundations of the subject, and Mark's (1978) text is written from the practising musician's point of view. Another feature which is much less pronounced in the British textbooks is the strong emphasis on evaluation and assessment, and in particular on the application of behavioural principles to music learning (e.g. Greer, 1980; Madsen and Yarbrough, 1980). There is a prevalent concern with the detailed analysis and specification of objective goals and skills in music learning, and with the need to demonstrate that teaching can achieve these goals. Madsen and Yarbrough call this 'competency-based' music education, which is very much in line with current thinking in other areas of North American education.

The curriculum

Curriculum planning in music starts from a broad and fairly abstract analysis of the overall objectives of music teaching, and psychological theories ought to be able to contribute towards this. Most theorists seem to agree that music teaching should cover much more than just the learning of specific musical skills: amongst the broader objectives might be included an understanding and appreciation of the artistic qualities of music; transmission of the cultural heritage; fostering of creativity; social education; provision of worthy recreation; improvement of physical and mental health; development of intellectual capacities; and so on. In other words, music education ought to contribute to intellectual, emotional, sensory-motor and social development, and no doubt further dimensions could be added to this list.

Some music educators have tried to formulate models of the objectives of their discipline, and Bloom's *Taxonomy of educational objectives* (Bloom, 1956; Krathwohl, Bloom and Masia, 1964) is a useful reference point. Bloom's division of these general objectives into the three basic *cognitive*, *affective*, and *psychomotor* categories is paralleled in Regelski's (1975) analysis of the components of musical behaviour. Regelski makes a primary distinction between its *overt* and *covert* aspects, and the educator's job is presumably to work on both of these levels. There are three main types of the former: verbal behaviour (speaking and writing), making behaviour (composing, creating, arranging, rearranging, organising into something new, notating), and performance behaviour (playing instruments, singing, conducting, moving to music, dancing).

Much more difficult to specify and isolate, of course, are the covert aspects of musical behaviour, and it is here that Regelski's model follows the lines of the Bloom taxonomy, with the delineation of three main categories. *Cognitive* variables are those involved in understanding music, such as 'perceiving', 'comprehending', 'analyzing', 'identifying', and 'synthesizing'. *Affective* variables represent the subjective, emotional response to music, including 'intuitive responding', 'free interpretation', 'preferring', 'enjoying', and so on. *Psychomotor* variables are those involved in the organisation and co-ordination of skilled musical behaviour, such as 'attending to cues', 'imitating and repeating', 'monitoring oneself', and 'following instructions'. It may be that the psychomotor variables tend to be over-emphasised at the expense of the others by music teachers, given the complex nature of musical skills; but Regelski stresses that there are close interrelationships between the three domains. His model is very detailed; in fact it may almost be too detailed to be applicable in any rigorous manner. Swanwick's (1979) CLASP model of the parameters of musical experience is probably more amenable to practical application by virtue of its greater simplicity. This incorporates Composition, Literature studies, Audition, Skill acquisition and Performance; three of these (C, A and P) are directly related to music, and the other two (L and S) have 'supporting and enabling roles'.

Alongside such broad, generalised models of the objectives of music education must presumably go some degree of specification of the achievements and skills to be expected of children at different ages: and the British HMI document succinctly spells out the objectives, contents and methods for music teaching at four age levels (up to ages seven, eleven, fourteen, and sixteen). Now it could well be argued that these guidelines are *over-prescriptive*: that the needs of individual children are more varied than can be dealt with in any generalised set of detailed recommendations. Nevertheless, they seem to me to point in the right direction, and they incorporate two general features which are likely to be fairly controversial.

The first of these concerns the problem of the relative importance of intuitive and formal skills, which I discussed earlier. The Inspectors quite unambiguously recommend that although music education should ultimately aim to develop both, the latter should be subservient to the former, especially in younger children. The practical implementation of this is that composition and improvisation are recommended as integral parts of the curriculum: creative music-making and playing by ear are seen as central and indispensable parts of the syllabus. By the age of seven, for example, children are expected to 'take part in simple improvisations using voices and instruments', and to 'play by ear on percussion instruments or recorders or both' (p. 3): and by sixteen, they should be able to 'demonstrate the ability to devise original statements in music (using voices, instruments and simple electronics) both for individual and group performance; work at such compositions using various systems (scalic, harmonic, aleatoric, ethnic, etc), forms (dance, song, variation, binary, ternary, rondo etc) and media (vocal, instrumental, voice(s) and instrument(s) combined, electronics etc)' (p. 15).

The inclusion of playing by ear and improvising represents a major expansion of the view of 'performance' that has traditionally been taken in British music education, and the consequent incorporation of composition into the new national General Certificate in Secondary Education (GCSE) examinations, to be taken at the age of sixteen, is likely to have a significant impact on secondary school music teaching in the U.K. These innovations are backed up by an explicit acknowledgement that formal notational skills may be unnecessary in certain forms of music. 'Playing by ear and improvising, sometimes believed to be forms of self-indulgence, can have a liberating effect on singers and players alike. For pop, jazz, folk and ethnic musicians, such approaches are fundamental to their art. Performance as taught and examined in schools should take full account of the rich variety of vocal and instrumental music making in contemporary society' (pp. 16–17).

This latter point conveys the second feature of the HMI proposals which is likely to be controversial, namely the inclusion of forms of music outside the Western symphonic tradition, and in particular pop music. I have discussed this question elsewhere (Hargreaves, 1982b), complaining of the conservatism that exists in music education as well as in music psychology in the U.K. Various British commentators (e.g. Vulliamy and Lee, 1976; Burnett, 1977; Swanwick, 1968, 1979; Burnett and Lawrence, 1979) seem to agree that 'classical' music forms the staple diet of most courses. These writers suggest that many British music teachers fail to capitalise upon the intrinsic motivation that is involved in learning to play and appreciate pop music because their own training and background is usually restricted to the classical tradition. Teachers are suspicious about the role of pop music in the school curriculum, perhaps because they know very little about it. Now the argument that Afro-American music should be given equal status in the school curriculum is frequently set in the broader context of a sociological critique of music education (e.g. Vulliamy, 1980). The essence of the argument is that classical music is more or less arbitrarily 'legitimated' by the musical establishment, and that this cultural association tends to alienate teenage pupils (see Chapter 7). Even when attempts *are* made to introduce pop, teachers' misunderstanding of it means that inappropriate standards of performance and aesthetic judgement are frequently applied.

Swanwick (1982) argues that there are some fundamental misconceptions in such critiques; his article raises several important issues which deserve further debate, and which it would be inappropriate to elaborate here. His central argument, however, is that disposing of the traditional Western procedures of musical analysis would not in itself 'legitimize' pop music in schools. Afro-American musics have their own constraints and restrictions which can be dealt with by the normal analytical techniques; what we lack is the realisation that different criteria must be applied in judgements of different musical traditions. Pop music should be integrated into the syllabus alongside classical music, argues Swanwick, rather than set up in opposition to it.

We should not get sidetracked by the 'pop' issue, since the argument about the inclusion of 'non-classical' musics goes well beyond this. Her Majesty's Inspectors make the refreshing assumption that '*what* music is taught is only slightly more important than the *way* it is taught' (1985, p. 2); presumably different teaching techniques, and evaluative criteria, should be adopted according to the music in question. Formal notational skills will remain an essential tool for most forms of tonal music; experimental, aleatory, and electronic musics demand expertise in the technology of sound production and recording, especially in the light of recent advances in personal computing and electronic synthesis; folk, jazz, and pop music may well demand an emphasis on improvisational and aural skills; traditional and ethnic music and songs need to be set in the historical and social context of music-making; and so on. Now it may be that recommendations along these lines have been made before: and the HMI document has been criticised for paying insufficient attention to the means of their practical implementation. It is nevertheless almost certain that most music teaching in the U.K. falls well short of meeting these objectives, so that their enunciation ought to be welcomed.

Methods of instruction

Behavioural approaches
The origins and main features of behavioural approaches to music education were described in Chapter 1: their applications to classroom practice have mostly taken place in the U.S.A. (see e.g. Madsen and Kuhn, 1978). Madsen, Greer and Madsen's *Research in music behavior: Modifying music behavior in the classroom* (1975) is an extensive collection of studies that have employed this approach, and some of the general findings that have emerged from them were outlined in Chapter 1. Nearly all of this is 'practical' research in that it deals with learning in its real-life classroom context; the main emphases have been on the use of music itself as a reinforcer for learning, and on the use of other reinforcers in music learning.

Perhaps the most thorough and unequivocal statement of this approach to date is to be found in Greer's (1980) *Design for music learning*. Greer presents a comprehensive account of behavioural methods for the systematic observation of teaching and learning, devoting his attention (a) to the application of behavioural principles in obtaining students' attention, and (b) to 'teaching musical discriminations' through music performance, analysis and creation. He proposes a Personalised System of Instruction (PSI) whose characteristics are sevenfold:

(a) the model focusses on the actions and reactions (behaviors) of the learner in terms of the instructional objectives. (b) The learning tasks are analysed behaviorally and categorically by hierarchies. (c) Learning rates and levels are systematically monitored and measured in numerical terms. (d) Strategies of teaching are based on scientifically derived principles of learning. (e) Actual teacher techniques are derived from principles and systematically practised by the teacher in the classroom and rehearsal hall. (f) Strategies, principles and techniques, as well as student learning, are measured systematically, and there is an explicit system of accountability. (g) The teacher is responsible, within his or her power, for student learning. The instructional power of the teacher resides in the professions' systematic or research-based knowledge.   (1980, p. 9).

Greer goes on to outline how PSI models might be applied in settings such as the studio, the musical ensemble, and the actual music class, and discusses the issues that might arise in applications to specific age and ability groups. As is often the case in books written from a behavioural viewpoint, there are copious illustrations of different observation and recording techniques, credit systems, and other practical aids. This method is extremely rigorous in its precise specification of the progress to be made by the student: part of the philosophy of the approach is that concrete gains must be continuously and explicitly charted.

Another area of research which is not 'behavioural' in the strictest sense, but which ought to be mentioned in this context, is that on skill learning. Studies of the learning of skills such as typing have shown, for example, that 'distributed practice', in which new material is acquired in a number of discrete sessions, is more effective than 'massed practice', in which the same total amount of time is concentrated within a single learning session: this can readily be applied to the learning of a new piece of music. Another practical distinction is that between whole and part learning: is it better to practice a new piece of music 'as a whole', that is, to get the general sense of its unity without too much initial concern about the details, or is it better to analyse the piece and learn the parts of it separately before combining them again? Lundin's (1967) answer to this particular question is that the former method is best suited to short pieces and the latter to longer ones, although this is by no means a clear-cut issue.

Whether there are areas of 'musical behaviour' that are best *not* taught by behavioural methods is a question for future research to consider. It seems intuitively quite likely that they are much more appropriate for the teaching of lower-level performance skills than of those required in composition and improvisation, for example. If this were so, it could either be because the model is inherently unable to deal with higher-order skills, or because the methods are not yet sufficiently developed to deal with such levels of complexity. It probably makes more sense to use different theoretical approaches for different types and levels of instruction than to strain to cover everything from a single viewpoint.

Pedagogical approaches: Orff, Kodaly, and Suzuki

I have labelled these approaches 'pedagogical' because they originate from practical music teaching rather than from psychological theory; but each one nevertheless embodies an implicit view of the nature of child development, and of the role that music ought to play within it. The methods of Carl Orff, Zoltan Kodaly, and Shinichi Suzuki emphasise different aspects of the learning process, as we shall see, but they are at one in their insistence that all children can and should benefit from musical instruction, regardless of their level of talent, or 'musicality'.

Carl Orff, based in the Guentherschule in Munich, published his first volumes of *Orff-Schulwerk* in 1950 (available in English in Orff and Keetman, 1958). His approach is based on rhythmic and melodic improvisation, which was originally carried out on simple percussion instruments. The range of 'Orff instruments' now available includes xylophones, glockenspiels, metallophones, tom-toms, gongs, and cymbals, as well as stringed instruments. Orff insisted that many skills that are often thought of as advanced or difficult (e.g. playing syncopated rhythms, or modal and minor scales) are in fact an integral part of the child's musical experience, and that they can be expressed quite easily and naturally in creative improvisation.

Although the method is not intended to be rigorous or systematic, it does involve a graded series of 'musical models' that the teacher uses as the basis for improvisation, in five volumes of the *Schulwerk*. These start with simple rhythmic patterns and two-note 'cuckoo calls' based on descending minor thirds, and move through pentatonic and major scales to minor modes, and to more sophisticated harmonic patterns. Orff also emphasised the importance of building upon the natural 'singing voice' and 'spoken word' of the child, incorporating singing games, chants, and playground rhymes into his scheme. His approach is clearly 'child-centred', and amenable for use with very young children: perhaps for these reasons, it has become well known and widely adopted throughout the world.

Zoltan Kodaly was a Hungarian composer who created a system of music teaching which is still extremely influential in Hungarian education, and which has become well known further afield. It has been 'translated' for the U.S.A., for example, along with Orff's work. Kodaly based his system in the Hungarian folk song repertoire which he, along with Bela Bartok and others, had been compiling and studying for many years. It is a rigorous and elaborate scheme of instruction which places a strong emphasis on the *voice*. Kodaly's primary concern was with the development of aural imagination, or the 'inner ear', and he felt strongly that this should be accomplished through singing before there was any introduction to instrumental playing; in fact he objected to teachers' frequent over-reliance on the 'help' of an instrument in sight-reading.

Details of the *Kodaly choral method* (originally in twenty-two volumes) can be found in English translation in Szonyi (1973) and Choksy (1974). It is based on a graded system of tonic sol-fa training which (unlike the Orff method) must be rigorously and systematically applied. Nursery songs and singing games are used in the early years to build up the pentatonic scale; these are gradually replaced by folk songs, and then in carefully graded stages by increasingly complex musical forms. The details of what musical material may and may not be taught are rigorously specified, as are the details of the skills to be expected at each stage. Because of the importance of the system in relation to other school subjects in Hungary, the music curriculum starts at the age of three or thereabouts. An important feature of the method is that children learn to read and write music notation from the earliest years; this is seen as an integral part of learning to read and write. By the age of six or so they are expected to be able to write out simple pentatonic tunes from dictation or from memory; memorisation is also seen as an important part of musical literacy.

In some respects Kodaly's method may appear to be excessively intensive and inflexible, and to go against the idea that intuitive musical understanding should take precedence over the rigorous training of formal skills, particularly in the early years. Szemere (1982) points out that the formal aspects of the method have been unduly predominant in recent years, resulting in a somewhat elitist music pedagogy in Hungarian schools. She argues that this is quite at variance with the original aims of the method; the creative spirit and richness of traditional folk singing, which was a vital part of Kodaly's original conception, unfortunately seems to have got lost along the way.

The 'Suzuki method', which has received a considerable amount of publicity in recent years, is more limited in its scope and aims than those of Orff and Kodaly as it is primarily concerned with performance skills, and it has tended to concentrate on the violin. Suzuki's *Talent Education* movement began in 1945, and has involved many Japanese preschoolers in learning to play miniature, scaled-down violins. Suzuki (1969) expresses the fundamental belief that musical talent can be nurtured in any child, drawing an analogy with the learning of natural language. Since children very skilfully and rapidly learn their mother tongue at an early age, he argues that learning instrumental skills should also begin in the first few years of life.

A vital part of the method is the involvement of the mother, who also learns the violin herself in the early stages. Recordings of great performances, and of the twenty or so songs that will form the initial curriculum, are played to children daily over the first two years. At around the age of two, along with their mothers, they start to attend group lessons which involve games and exercises, and hear short performances by older pupils. In these early stages, each mother practices every day on a small violin in order to arouse her child's interest, and only when this interest and motivation are clearly established are children allowed to play themselves. Mother and child then work together intensively, and as the child progresses, the mother gradually drops out. The child then follows a graded curriculum which has been very carefully worked out: it is regarded as essential that each stage should be mastered before work begins on the next. The curriculum is based on playing by ear rather than on reading notated music, and success at each stage is evaluated in terms of the accuracy of pupils' reproduction of model performances. There is a strong emphasis on memory training, imitation, and repetition.

Although excellence in performance is not the ultimate aim of the method, its results can be spectacular: ordinary preschool childen can be and have been trained to play the violin like child prodigies. The method capitalises on the child's heightened adaptability and sensitivity in the early years, as well as on the extremely powerful influence of the mother–child relationship. On the debit side of the balance, it could be argued that a method which demands such intensive work and dedication ought perhaps to aim at fostering a wider range of skills and knowledge. Spectacular though the results may be, the child's performance is essentially imitative rather than creative, and rooted in a conventional 'classical' conception of what constitutes musical excellence. This seems to run counter to 'child-centred' ideals; the aims of the method are somewhat specialised and narrow, and clearly geared towards the development of 'formal' rather than 'intuitive' musical skills as I described these earlier. More generally, it could be argued that such intensive concentration on music might lead to the neglect of other important areas of development. Nevertheless, the method seems to be increasingly widely used in the U.K. (e.g. Rural Music Schools Association, 1977) and the U.S.A. (e.g. Mills and Murphy, 1974).

Programmed approaches

Under this heading can be included programmed instructional texts on music as well as the growing number of computer-assisted programmes, which are usually electronically administered programmed learning texts with a high capacity for branching. Programmes of both types are often designed according to behavioural principles, but this need not necessarily be the case.

Carlsen and Williams (1978) have prepared an extensive annotated bibliography of sixty-eight research reports on programmed music instruction between 1952-72: a perusal of this, and of the contents of U.S. doctoral dissertations in music and music education over the period 1972–77 (reported in the *Journal of Research in Music Education*, 1978) shows how rapidly this approach has been applied in many areas of music education. These include the teaching of music theory, analysis, and structure; of auditory skills such as rhythmic discrimination and timbre recognition; of performance skills such as snare drum technique, sight singing, and other choral and instrumental techniques; of score-reading; of jazz improvisation techniques; of melodic dictation; and so on. Some automated programmes have even been devised which incorporate the principles of pedagogical programmes like the Orff and Kodaly methods.

Computer-assisted techniques have the potential to take over a lot of the donkey-work of the music teacher. They may be most appropriate for the teaching of lower-level skills; freedom from the chores of routine exercises ought to enable the teacher to spend more time on those parts of the job that fully utilise his advanced skills and expertise. Another significant advantage is that self-instructed pupils are free to progress at their own rates: individuals are not held back or overstretched by the learning speed of their co-students, as they would be in a group teaching situation. Computer-assisted techniques provide privacy, and individual attention; immediate feedback of results is available at any time, and the student's progress is cumulatively recorded over a course of study. They also provide a high degree of convenience; the computer is always available for unlimited periods of practice, and never gets tired or impatient! Current developments, such as the provision of aural and graphic feedback, and the pooling of resources through linked computer networks, mean that future applications may have profound and far-reaching effects; they have the potential to radically affect the nature of music education.

Having said this, we must remember that these techniques are essentially tools to assist the teacher; they cannot in themselves determine the broader objectives of music education, or what should be taught in a given programme. This may seem an obvious point, but there is always a potential danger with powerful computer-based techniques that the 'tail can wag the dog' in the sense that the original and fundamental aims of a particular educational programme become overlooked, and swamped by technological considerations. One clear need in this respect is for more *evaluation* studies of computer-assisted techniques in comparison with the longer-standing approaches. Ideally, matched groups of pupils should be randomly assigned either to a computer-assisted teaching condition or to a conventional teaching control group; the groups should be pre- and post-tested on the appropriate criterion variable or variables, and their relative improvements compared. Much more effort has so far been expended on the development of the programmes than on their evaluation, though the two ought to go hand in hand.

Assessment and evaluation

We have encountered some of the issues surrounding the assessment of musical development earlier in the book. The psychometric approaches are mainly concerned with the assessment of the individual learner; with the measurement of aptitude for, achievement in, and attitudes towards music by means of standardised tests. In the U.K., the specialist music pupil's progress is thoroughly assessed by means of the graded Associated Board examinations, which are administered by music teachers. These fall most clearly into the second of the three categories above, though they probably fail to fulfil the psychometric criteria of the standardised musical achievement and literacy tests that were mentioned in Chapter 1. The non-specialist British schoolchild who is examined in music will in future take the new GCSE examinations at the age of sixteen. I indicated earlier in this chapter that these incorporate certain innovations, notably the assessment of composing alongside performing and listening. The HMI document acknowledges that some very difficult problems are inherent in the assessment of elusive qualities such as musicianship and creativity, but proposes nevertheless that assessment should be carried out for four reasons:

> cumulative information about a pupil's development of ideas, skills and concepts is essential in order to ensure the effectiveness of the music education being provided;
>
> when direct teaching has taken place, teachers need to know whether pupils have properly understood the work covered in relation to their ages, aptitudes and abilities;
>
> effective assessment of pupils' progress helps the teacher to adjust courses to match changing needs;
>
> systematic knowledge about individual progress is needed to inform pupils, parents and teachers.
>
> (1985, pp. 18–19)

In the British context, these could be regarded as recommendations for future implementation; in the U.S.A., evaluation and evaluation research are already very firmly established, in non-musical as well as in musical fields. The North American concept of evaluation is broader than the idea of 'assessment' described above; it encompasses the methods and curriculum of music instruction as well as the progress of the individual student (see e.g. Colwell, 1970b). We saw earlier that ongoing evaluation and assessment is an integral part of competency-based music education, which itself is highly compatible with the behavioural approach. In his Foreword to Madsen and Yarbrough's book *Competency-based music education*, Lee (1980) describes the teaching process as 'a continuing cycle of analysing the learning situation after taking data, designing a specific plan for teaching, evaluating the teaching-learning process, and re-analyzing the learning situation. The music teacher is viewed as an evaluator, designer and manager in developing a positive educational environment' (p. vii).

The evaluation of a course of music instruction is the process of determining whether or not its objectives have been attained; and this, of course, means specifying those objectives in detail. There are various guides to 'writing objectives' for music education programmes, and to the different evaluation techniques that are available: Boyle (1974) has catalogued these, and provided examples of the procedures used in various American states. The range of evaluation techniques is extensive, including information examinations, listening tests, student reports, interviews, performance tests, activity inventories, and attitude scales. It is presumably desirable to evaluate the effectiveness of teaching programmes in attaining all the educational objectives that were outlined in the last section – cognitive and affective as well as psychomotor – and Boyle's survey documents the progress that has been made in each of the three domains. A clear distinction has emerged between the evaluation of 'behavioural' and of 'non-behavioural' objectives, although Boyle argues that these should be regarded as opposite poles of a single continuum. Behavioural objectives are clearly and objectively spelt out in schemes such as Greer's PSI; in a sense, feedback from the evaluation is a built-in, ongoing part of the course of instruction. Non-behavioural objectives, for example, in the aesthetic and affective domains, are generally much more abstract and difficult to evaluate.

Although the emphasis on assessment and evaluation seems to be a peculiarly American one, the underlying philosophy of competency-based approaches may not be too dissimilar from the 'payment by results' scheme that was adopted in Victorian England – sixpence per head was paid for the rote learning of a specific number of songs, and a shilling for singing by sight! There are some signs of a shift back in this direction in Great Britain; the desirability of specifying 'absolute standards' in education, and of assessing these by means of criterion-referenced rather than the more commonly used norm-referenced tests is currently the subject of a considerable amount of educational debate, and indeed the Associated Board music examinations are sometimes cited as prime examples of criterion-referenced tests. It remains to be seen whether or not this trend will carry over into general, non-specialist music education.

Conclusion

I think it is clear that music education must have a firm foundation in developmental psychology. The specification of objectives for music education involves breaking down musical skills into their cognitive, affective, and psychomotor components, and the evaluation of these objectives draws heavily on psychological assessment procedures. Psychological theories and techniques have a central role to play in the formulation and evaluation of particular methods of music instruction, as well as in the theory and practice of music therapy. Research ought to enable us to investigate the interdependence of 'formal' and 'intuitive' musical skills, for example, as well as to assess the age levels at which different component skills are most appropriately taught.

I am by no means the first to make suggestions along these lines, of course: the Ann Arbor National Symposium on the Applications of Psychology to the Teaching and Learning of Music (MENC, 1981) was organised with precisely the same aims in mind. In spite of the immense potential for collaboration between workers in the two fields, which would be to their mutual benefit, the detailed connections remain largely unexplored. Swanwick (1977), writing from a British point of view, complains that 'To read through articles in the music education journals and to scan the books that advocate classroom practices is to enter a world that has apparently never assimilated the thinking of people who have influenced and still influence the climate of educational thought and practice' (p. 65). Although Swanwick's reference to educational theory is a broader one, his comment applies in particular to the influence of developmental psychology.

I have not viewed my task in writing this book as making explicit links between theory and practice, but rather as delineating and organising what the developmental psychological foundations of music education might be. Let me conclude by trying to summarise the main features that have emerged. First, it seems vital that the course of teaching and research must be guided by an adequate theory of development. Theories abound in developmental psychology, and those which have the potential for dealing with the problems of music were discussed in Chapter 1. It seems to me that the cognitive-developmental approach, of which Piaget's theory is the predominant representative, holds the most immediate promise in this respect. Although Piaget's theory has stimulated Pflederer Zimmerman and others to develop a research tradition around the concept of 'music conservation', and although it forms the theoretical background for the (albeit critical) research of the Harvard Project Zero group, it has nevertheless had no direct influence on the practice of music teaching.

Piagetian research could be thought of as a developmental part of the general trend towards a cognitive approach to the psychology of music. The concept of the cognitive scheme has cropped up at numerous points in the book, and there can be little doubt that the explanation of musical development must deal with the mental processes which underlie it. Here again, however, neither the cognitive psychological approach in general nor information-processing models in particular appear as yet to have had any direct influence upon the practice of music education. It is the behavioural approaches whose influence have been most direct, publicly observable, and quantifiable, especially on music education in North America. There is no doubt that these approaches are very effective in the teaching of lower-level musical skills, but their higher-level utility is less certain.

The growing recognition that the cognitive, social, and affective dimensions of development cannot be studied in isolation from one another is completely in tune with the needs of music education. Developmental psychologists are beginning to grapple with these interactions in empirical research, and this is precisely what is required in studying the mysteries and complexities of artistic behaviour. The level of theoretical and empirical sophistication demanded by the arts may well be greater than that required in any other area, and our current explanations are only just beginning to scratch the surface. I see the developmental psychology of music as a field in its infancy, with an enormous amount of as yet unfulfilled potential. There is plenty of work to be done, and I hope that this book's account of the infant will soon prove to be inadequate.

REFERENCES

Abeles, H.F. (1980). Responses to music, in *Handbook of music psychology*, ed. D. Hodges. Lawrence, Kansas: National Association for Music Therapy.

Abraham, O. (1901). Das absolute Tonbewusstein. *International Musikges*, 3, 1–86.

Adler, M.J. (1929). Music appreciation: an experimental approach to its measurement. *Archives of Psychology*, 110, 1–102.

Adorno, T.W. (1941). On popular music. *Zeitschrift für Sozialforschung*, 9, 17–49.

Aliferis, J. (1954). *Aliferis music achievement test*. Minneapolis: University of Minnesota Press.

Alpaugh, P.K. and Birren, J.E. (1977). Variables affecting creative contributions across the adult life span. *Human Development*, 20, 240–8.

Amabile, T.M. (1982). Social psychology of creativity: a consensual assessment technique. *Journal of Personality and Social Psychology*, 43, 997–1013.

Ambron, S.R. and Brodzinsky, D. (1979). *Lifespan human development*. New York: Holt, Rinehart & Winston.

Anastasi, A. (1958). Heredity, environment and the question 'How?' *Psychological Review*, 65, 197–208.

(1982). *Psychological testing* (5th edition). New York: Collier-Macmillan.

Anderson, C.C. and Cropley, A.J. (1966). Some correlates of originality. *Australian Journal of Psychology*, 18, 218–27.

Archer, J. and Lloyd, B. (1975). Sex differences: biological and social interaction, in *Child alive*, ed. R. Lewin. London: Temple Smith.

(1982). *Sex and gender*. Harmondsworth: Penguin.

Archibeque, C.P. (1966). Developing a taste for contemporary music. *Journal of Research in Music Education*, 14, 142–7.

Arnheim, R. (1952). Agenda for the psychology of art. *Journal of Aesthetics and Art Criticism*, 10, 310–14.

Asch, S.E. (1948). The doctrine of suggestion, prestige and imitation in social psychology. *Psychological Review*, 55, 250–76.

(1956). Studies of independence and conformity. A minority of one against a unanimous majority. *Psychological Monographs*, 70, No. 416.

Atkinson, R.C. and Schiffrin, R.M. (1968). Human memory: a proposed system and its control processes, in *Advances in the psychology of learning and motivation research and theory*, vol. 2, eds. K.W. Spence and J.T. Spence. New York: Academic Press.

Ausubel, D.P. (1968). *Educational psychology: A cognitive view*. New York: Holt, Rinehart & Winston.

Bachem, A. (1937). Various types of absolute pitch. *Journal of the Acoustical Society of America*, 9, 146–51.

Bahle, J. (1936). *Der musikalische Schaffensprozess*. Leipzig: Hirzel.

Bamberger, J. (1975). The development of musical intelligence: Children's representations of simple rhythms. Unpublished Artificial Intelligence Memo, 342, MIT.

(1978). Intuitive and formal musical knowing: parables of cognitive dissonance, in *The arts, cognition and basic skills*, ed. S.S. Madeja. St Louis, Missouri: Cemrel.

(1980). Cognitive structuring in the apprehension and description of simple rhythms. *Archives de Psychologie*, XLVIII-186, 171–97.

(1982). Revisiting children's drawings of simple rhythms: a function for reflection-in-action, in *U-shaped behavioral growth*, eds. S. Strauss and R. Stavy. New York: Academic Press.

Bandura, A. (1977). *Social learning theory*. Englewood Cliffs: Prentice-Hall.

Bandura, A. and Walters, R.H. (1963). *Social learning and personality development*. New York: Holt, Rinehart & Winston.

Bantock, G.H. (1968). *Culture, industrialisation and education*. London: Routledge & Kegan Paul.

Barker, R.G., Kounin, J.S. and Wright, H.F. (1943). *Child behavior and development*. New York: McGraw-Hill.

Barlow, H. and Morgenstern, S. (1948). *A dictionary of musical themes*. New York: Crown.

(1976). *A dictionary of opera and song themes* (revised edition). New York: Crown.

Barrett, M.D. and Light, P.H. (1976). Symbolism and intellectual realism in children's drawings. *British Journal of Educational Psychology*, 46, 198–202.

Barron, F. (1953). Complexity–simplicity as a personality dimension. *Journal of Abnormal and Social Psychology*, 48, 163–72.

(1955). The disposition towards originality. *Journal of Abnormal and Social Psychology*, 51, 478–85.

(1963). *Creativity and psychological health*. Princeton, N.J.: Van Nostrand.

(1965). The psychology of creativity, in *New directions in psychology*, vol. 2. New York: Holt, Rinehart & Winston.

Barron, F. and Welsh, G.S. (1952). Artistic perception as a factor in personality style: its measurement by a figure preference test. *Journal of Psychology*, 33, 199–203.

Bartlett, D.L. (1973). Effect of repeated listenings on structural discrimination and affective response. *Journal of Research in Music Education*, 21, 302–17.

Bartlett, J.C. (1984). Cognition of complex events: visual scenes and music, in *Cognitive processes in the perception of art*, eds. W.R. Crozier and A.J. Chapman. Amsterdam: Elsevier.

Bartlett, J.C. and Dowling, W.J. (1980). The recognition of transposed melodies: a key-distance effect in developmental perspective. *Journal of Experimental Psychology: Human Perception and Performance*, 6, 501–15.

Bartok, B. (1946). *For children*, vols. 1 and 2. New York: Boosey & Hawkes.

Baumann, V.H. (1960). Teen-age music preferences. *Journal of Research in Music Education*, 8, 75–84.

Bayley, N. (1968). Behavioral correlates of mental growth: birth to thirty-six years. *American Psychologist*, 23, 1–17.

Beebe-Center, J.G. (1932). *The psychology of pleasantness and unpleasantness*. New York: Van Nostrand.

Beloff, H. (ed.) (1980). A balance sheet on Burt. *Bulletin of the British Psychological Society Supplement*, **33**, 1–38.

Bem, S.L. (1974). The measurement of psychological androgyny. *Journal of Consulting and Clinical Psychology*, **42**, 155-62.

(1981). Gender schema theory: a cognitive account of sex typing. *Psychological Review*, **88**, 354–64.

Bench, J. (1969). Some effects of audio-frequency stimulation on the crying baby. *Journal of Auditory Research*, **9**, 122–8.

Benham, E. (1929). The creative activity. *British Journal of Psychology*, **20**, 59–65.

Bennett, S.N. and Jordan, J. (1975). A typology of teaching styles in primary schools. *British Journal of Educational Psychology*, **45**, 20–8.

Bentley, A. (1966). *Musical ability in children and its measurement*. London: Harrap.

(1968). *Monotones*. Music Education Research Papers No 1. London: Novello.

Berlyne, D.E. (1970). Novelty, complexity, and hedonic value. *Perception and Psychophysics*, **8**, 279–86.

(1971). *Aesthetics and psychobiology*. New York: Appleton-Century-Crofts.

(ed.) (1974). *Studies in the new experimental aesthetics: Steps toward an objective psychology of aesthetic appreciation*. New York: Halsted Press.

(1976). The new experimental aesthetics and the problem of classifying works of art. *Scientific Aesthetics*, **1**, 85–106.

(1977). Dimensions of perception of exotic and folk music. *Scientific Aesthetics*, **1**, 257–70.

Berlyne, D.E., Ogilvie, J.C. and Parham, L.C.C. (1968). The dimensionality of visual complexity, interestingness, and pleasingness. *Canadian Journal of Psychology*, **22**, 376–87.

Bernstein, B. (1971). *Class, codes and control*. London: Routledge & Kegan Paul.

Bernstein, L. (1976). *The unanswered question: Six talks at Harvard*. Cambridge, Mass.: Harvard University Press.

Bijou, S.W. and Baer, D.M. (1961). *Child development*, vol. 1. New York: Appleton-Century-Crofts.

Binet, A. (1903). *L'étude expérimentale de l'intelligence*. Paris: Schleicher.

Birch, T.E. (1963). Musical taste as indicated by records owned by college students with varying high school music experiences. *Dissertation Abstracts International*, **23**, 2, 545.

Birns, B., Blank, M., Bridger, W.H. and Escalona, S. (1965). Behavioral inhibition in neonates produced by auditory stimuli. *Psychosomatic Medicine*, **28**, 316–22.

Blacking, J. (1973). *How musical is man?* Seattle and London: Washington University Press.

(1967). *Venda children's songs*. Johannesburg: Witwatersrand University Press.

Blatt, S.J., Allison, J. and Feirstein, A. (1969). The capacity to cope with cognitive complexity. *Journal of Personality*, **37**, 269–88.

Blizek, W.L. (1974). An institutional theory of art. *British Journal of Aesthetics*, **14**, 142–50.

Bloom, B.S. (ed.) (1956). *Taxonomy of educational objectives: The classification of educational goals. Handbook 1: cognitive domain*. New York: McKay.

Boardman, E. (1964). An investigation of the effect of preschool training on the development of vocal accuracy in young children. Unpublished doctoral dissertation, University of Illinois.

Boden, M.A. (1979). *Piaget*. London: Fontana.

Bolton, N. (1972). *The psychology of thinking*. London: Methuen.

Booker, G.A. (1968). The disc jockey and his impact on teenage musical taste as reflected through a study in three north Florida cities. Unpublished doctoral dissertation, Florida State University.

Boselie, F. and Leeuwenberg, E. (1984). A general notion of beauty used to quantify the aesthetic attractivity of geometric forms, in *Cognitive processes in the perception of art*, eds. W.R. Crozier and A.J. Chapman. Amsterdam: Elsevier.

Botvin, G. (1974). Acquiring conservation of melody and cross-modal transfer through successive approximation. *Journal of Research in Music Education*, 22, 226–33.

Bourdieu, P. (1971). Intellectual field and creative project, in *Knowledge and control*, ed. M.F.D. Young. London: Collier-Macmillan.

Bower, G.H. and Hilgard, E.R. (1981). *Theories of learning* (5th edition). Englewood Cliffs: Prentice-Hall.

Bower, T.G.R. (1982). *Development in infancy* (2nd edition). San Francisco: W.H. Freeman.

Boyle, J.D. (ed.) (1974). *Instructional objectives in music: Resources for planning instruction and evaluating achievement.* Vienna, Virginia: MENC.

Boyle, J.D. (1982). A study of the comparative validity of three published, standardised measures of music preference. *Psychology of Music, Special Issue*, 11–16.

Brackbill, Y., Adams, G., Crowell, D.H. and Gray, M.L. (1966). Arousal level in neonates and preschool children under continuous auditory stimulation. *Journal of Experimental Child Psychology*, 4, 178–88.

Bradley, I. (1971). Repetition as a factor in the development of musical preferences. *Journal of Research in Music Education*, 19, 295–8.

(1972). Effect on student musical preference of a listening program in contemporary art music. *Journal of Research in Music Education*, 20, 344–53.

Brehmer, F. (1925). *Melodie Auffassung un melodische Begebung des Kinders*. Leipzig: J.A. Barth.

Bridger, W.H. (1961). Sensory habituation and discrimination in the human neonate. *American Journal of Psychiatry*, 117, 991–6.

Bridges, V.A. (1965). An exploratory study of the harmonic discrimination ability of children in kindergarten through grade three in two selected schools. Unpublished doctoral dissertation, Ohio State University.

Broadbent, D.E. (1958). *Perception and communication*. Oxford: Pergamon.

Brody, M. (1985). Reply to Serafine and to Marantz on Serafine. *Cognition*, 19, 93–8.

Bromley, D.B. (1956). Some experimental tests of the effects of age on creative intellectual output. *Journal of Gerontology*, 11, 74–82.

Bronfenbrenner, U. (1975). A theoretical perspective for research on human development, in *Social behaviour and experience*, eds. H. Brown and R. Stevens. London: Hodder & Stoughton.

Brown, G. (1983). Piaget's theory and educational psychology, in *Jean Piaget: An interdisciplinary critique*, eds. S. Modgil, C. Modgil, and G. Brown. London: Routledge & Kegan Paul.

Brown, G. and Desforges, C. (1979). *Piaget's theory: A psychological critique.* London: Routledge & Kegan Paul.

Brown, R. (1973). *A first language.* London: George Allen & Unwin.

Brown, R.L. and O'Leary, M. (1971). Pop music in an English secondary school system. *American Behavioral Scientist*, 14, 401–13.

Bruner, J.S (1966). *Toward a theory of instruction.* New York: Norton.

Bruner, J.S., Jolly, A. and Sylva, K. (eds.) (1966). *Play: Its role in development and evolution.* Harmondsworth: Penguin.

Bruner, J.S., Olver, R.R. and Greenfield, P.M. (eds.) (1966). *Studies in cognitive growth.* New York: Wiley.

Bryant, P.E. (1974). *Perception and understanding in young children.* London: Methuen.

(ed.) (1982). Piaget: Issues and experiments. *British Journal of Psychology*, 73, part 2.

Bryant, P.E. and Trabasso, T. (1971). Transitive inferences and memory in young children. *Nature*, 232, 456–8.

Bühler, K. (1930). *The mental development of the child.* London: Routledge & Kegan Paul.

Bullock, W.J. (1973). A review of measures of musico-aesthetic attitude. *Journal of Research in Music Education,* 21, 331–44.

Bullogh, E. (1921). Recent work in experimental aesthetics. *British Journal of Psychology,* 12, 76–99.

Burnett, M. (ed.) (1977). *Music education review,* vol. 1. London: Chappell.

Burnett, M. and Lawrence, I. (1979). *Music education review,* vol. 2. Slough: NFER.

Burt, C.L. (1961). Intelligence and social mobility. *British Journal of Statistical Psychology,* 14, 3–24.

Butcher, H.J. (1968). *Human intelligence: Its nature and assessment.* London: Methuen.

Butterworth, G. (ed.) (1977). *The child's representation of the world.* New York: Plenum Press.

Butterworth, G. and Light, P.H. (eds.) (1982). *Social cognition: Studies of the development of understanding.* Brighton: Harvester Press.

Cantor, G.N. (1968). Children's 'like–dislike' ratings of familiarized and non-familiarized visual stimuli. *Journal of Experimental Child Psychology,* 6, 651–7.

Cantor, G.N. and Kubose, S.K. (1969). Preschool children's ratings of familiarized and nonfamiliarized visual stimuli. *Journal of Experimental Child Psychology,* 8, 74–81.

Carlsen, J.C. and Williams, D.B. (1978). *A computer annotated bibliography: Music research in programmed instruction 1952–1972.* Reston, Virginia: MENC.

Carroll, J.D. and Chang, J.J. (1970). Analysis of individual differences in multi-dimensional scaling via an N-way generalisation of the 'Eckart–Young' decomposition. *Psychometrika,* 35, 283–319.

Carroll, J.D. and Wish, M. (1974). Multidimensional perceptual models and measurement methods, in *Handbook of perception,* vol. 2, eds. E.D. Carterette and M.P. Friedman. New York: Academic Press.

Castell, K.C. (1982). Children's sensitivity to stylistic differences in 'classical' and 'popular' music. *Psychology of Music, Special Issue,* 22–5.

(1984). Responses to music. Unpublished Ph.D. thesis, University of Leicester.

Castell, K.C. and Hill, E. (1985). The effects of stylistic information on ratings of ambiguous music. *Bulletin of the B.P.S.,* 38, A58.

Cattell, R.B. and Anderson, J.C. (1953). The measurement of personality and behavior disorders by the IPAT music preference test. *Journal of Applied Psychology,* 37, 446–54.

Cattell, R.B. and Cattell, M.D. (1969). *Handbook for the Junior-Senior High School Personality Questionnaire (HPSQ).* Champaign, Illinois: Institute for Personality and Ability Testing.

Cattell, R.B. and Drevdahl, J.E (1955). A comparison of the personality profile of eminent researchers with that of eminent teachers and administrators and of the general population. *British Journal of Psychology,* 46, 248–61.

Cattell, R.B., Eber, H.W. and Tatsuoka, M.M. (1970). *Handbook for the 16 Personality Factor Questionnaire (16PF).* Champaign, Illinois: Institute for Personality and Ability Testing.

Cattell, R.B. and Saunders, D.S. (1954). Musical preferences and personality diagnosis: I. A factorization of one hundred and twenty themes. *Journal of Social Psychology,* 39, 3–24.

Cermak, L.S. and Craik, F.I.M. (1979). *Levels of processing in human memory.* New York: Wiley.

Chang, H. and Trehub, S.E. (1977a). Auditory processing of relational information by young infants. *Journal of Experimental Child Psychology,* 24, 324-31.

(1977b). Infant's perception of temporal grouping in auditory patterns. *Child Development,* 48, 1666–70.

Chapman, A.J. and Williams, A.R. (1976). Prestige effects and aesthetic experiences: adolescents' reactions to music. *British Journal of Social and Clinical Psychology*, 15, 61–72.

Child, I.L. (1965). Personality correlates of esthetic judgment in college students. *Journal of Personality*, 33, 476–511.

(1969). Esthetics, in *Handbook of social psychology*, vol. 3, eds. G. Lindzey and E. Aronson. London: Addison-Wesley.

Choksy, L. (1974). *The Kodaly method: Comprehensive music education from infant to adult*. Englewood Cliffs: Prentice-Hall.

Clarke, P. (1970). Children's information seeking about the symphony. *Council for Research in Music Education Bulletin*, 19, 1–15.

Clarke-Stewart, A. (1982). *Day care*. London: Fontana.

Coker, W. (1972). *Music and meaning*. New York: Free Press.

Colman, A.M., Best, W.M. and Austen, A.J. (1986). Familiarity and liking: direct tests of the preference-feedback hypothesis. *Psychological Reports*, 58, 931–8.

Colman, A.M., Hargreaves, D.J. and Sluckin, W. (1981). Preferences for Christian names as a function of their experienced familiarity. *British Journal of Social Psychology*, 20, 3–5.

Colman, A.M., Sluckin, W. and Hargreaves, D.J. (1981). The effect of familiarity on preferences for surnames. *British Journal of Psychology*, 72, 363–9.

Colman, A.M., Walley, M.R. and Sluckin, W. (1975). Preferences for common words, uncommon words and non-words by children and young adults. *British Journal of Psychology*, 66, 481–6.

Colwell, R. (1967). Music education and experimental research. *Journal of Research in Music Education*, 15, 73–84.

(1970a). *Music achievement tests*. Chicago: Follett.

(1970b). *The evaluation of teaching and learning*. Englewood Cliffs: Prentice-Hall.

Cooke, D. (1959). *The language of music*. London: Oxford University Press.

Copland, A. (1939). *What to listen for in music*. New York: McGraw-Hill.

Copp, E.F. (1916). Musical ability. *Journal of Heredity*, 7, 297–305.

Costall, A. (1982). The relativity of absolute pitch. Paper presented to Conference of the Society for Research in Psychology of Music and Music Education, Roehampton, London.

Cotter, V. and Spradlin, J.E. (1971). A non-verbal technique for studying music preference. *Journal of Experimental Child Psychology*, 11, 357–65.

Cotter, V. and Toombs, S. (1966). A procedure for determining the musical preferences of mental retardates. *Journal of Music Therapy*, 3, 57–64.

Cox, M. (ed.) (1985). *The child's point of view: The development of cognition and language*. Brighton: Harvester.

Crickmore, L. (1973). A syndrome hypothesis of music appreciation. *Psychology of Music*, 1, 21–5.

Cropley, A.J. (1966). Creativity and intelligence. *British Journal of Educational Psychology*, 36, 259–66.

(1967). *Creativity*. London: Longmans, Green & Co.

Cross, P. Cattell, R.B. and Butcher, H.J. (1967). The personality pattern of creative artists. *British Journal of Educational Psychology*, 37, 292–9.

Crowther, R.D. (1985). A social psychological approach to adolescents' musical preferences (conference paper abstract). *Psychology of Music*, 13, 64.

Crowther, R.D. and Durkin, K. (1982). Sex- and age-related differences in the musical behaviour, interests and attitudes towards music of 232 secondary school students. *Educational Studies*, 8, 131–9.

Crowther, R.D., Durkin, K., Shire, B. and Hargreaves, D.J. (1985). Influences on the development of children's conservation-type responses to music. *Council for Research in Music Education Bulletin*, 85, 26–37.

Crozier, J. (1980). Absolute pitch. Paper presented at the International Society for Empirical Aesthetics, Montreal.

Crozier, J.B. (1974). Verbal and exploratory responses to sound sequences varying in uncertainty level, in *Studies in the new experimental aesthetics*, ed. D.E. Berlyne. New York: Wiley.

Crozier, W.R. and Chapman, A.J. (1981). Aesthetic preferences, prestige and social class, in *Psychology and the arts*, ed. D.O'Hare. Brighton: Harvester.

(eds.) (1984). *Cognitive processes in the perception of art*. Amsterdam: Elsevier.

Cupchik, G.C., Rickert, M. and Mendelson, J. (1982). Similarity and preference judgements of musical stimuli. *Scandinavian Journal of Psychology*, 23, 273–82.

Danziger, K. (1971). *Socialization*. Harmondsworth: Penguin.

Das, J.P., Rath, R. and Das, R.S. (1955). Understanding versus suggestion in the judgment of literary passages. *Journal of Abnormal and Social Psychology*, 51, 624–8.

Davidson, L. (1983). Tonal structures of children's early songs. Paper presented at the International Conference on Psychology and the Arts, Cardiff. *Bulletin of the British Psychological Society*, 36, A119–A120.

Davidson, L., McKernon, P., and Gardner, H. (1981). The acquisition of song: A developmental approach, in *Documentary report of the Ann Arbor symposium on the applications of psychology to the teaching and learning of music*. Reston, Virginia: MENC.

Davies, J.B. (1969). An analysis of factors involved in musical ability, and the derivation of tests of musical aptitude. Unpublished Ph.D. thesis, University of Durham.

(1978). *The psychology of music*. London: Hutchinson.

Dellas, M. and Gaier, E.L. (1970). Identification of creativity: the individual. *Psychological Bulletin*, 73, 55–73.

deMille, R. and Merrifield, P.R. (1962). Review of 'Creativity and Intelligence', by J.W. Getzels & P.W. Jackson. *Educational and Psychological Measurement*, 22, 803–8.

Denisoff, R.S. (1975). *Solid gold: The popular record industry*. New Brunswick, N.J.: Transaction Books.

Denisoff, R.S. and Levine, M. (1972). Brainwashing or background noise: the popular protest song, in *The sounds of social change*, eds. R.S. Denisoff and R.A. Peterson. Chicago: Rand McNally.

Dennis, W. (1966). Creative productivity between the ages of 20 and 80 years. *Journal of Gerontology*, 21, 1–8.

DES. (1985). *Music from 5 to 16*. Curriculum Matters 4. London: HMSO.

Deutsch, D. (ed.) (1982). *The psychology of music*. New York: Academic Press.

Dimaggio, P. and Useem, M. (1978). Social class and arts consumption: the origins and consequences of class differences in exposure to the arts in America. *Theory and Society*, 5, 141–61.

Dixon, R.D. (1981). Musical taste cultures and taste publics revisited: a research note of new evidence. *Popular Music and Society*, 8, 2–9.

(1982). LP chart careers: indices and predictors of ascent and descent in popularity. *Popular Music and Society*, 8, 19–43.

Dobbs, J. (ed.) (1982). *Tradition and change in music education*. 9th Yearbook of the International Society for Music Education. London: ISME.

Dollard, J. and Miller, N.E. (1950). *Personality and psychotherapy*. New York: McGraw-Hill.

Donaldson, M. (1978). *Children's minds*. London: Fontana/Open Books.

Donaldson, M., Grieve, R. and Pratt, C. (eds.) (1983). *Early childhood development and education*, Oxford: Basil Blackwell.

Dorow, L.G. (1977). The effect of teacher approval/disapproval ratios on student music selection behavior and concert attentiveness. *Journal of Research in Music Education*, 25, 173–9.

Dowling, W.J. (1982). Melodic information processing and its development, in *The psychology of music*, ed. D. Deutsch. New York: Academic Press.

(1984). Development of musical schemata in children's spontaneous singing, in *Cognitive processes in the perception of art*, eds. W.R. Crozier and A.J. Chapman. Amsterdam: Elsevier.

Dowling, W.J. and Bartlett, J.C. (1981). The importance of interval information in long-term memory for melodies. *Psychomusicology*, 1, 30–49.

Dowling, W.J. and Goedecke, M. (in press). *The impact of a Suzuki-based instrumental music program on auditory information-processing skills of inner-city school children.*

Drexler, E.N. (1938). A study of the ability to carry a melody at the preschool level. *Child Development*, 9, 319–32.

Duerksen, G.L. (1968). A study of the relationship between the perception of musical processes and the enjoyment of music. *Council for Research in Music Education Bulletin*, 16, 1–8.

(1972). Some effects of expectation on evaluation of recorded musical performance. *Journal of Research in Music Education*, 20, 268–72.

Duncker, K. (1945). On problem solving. *Psychological Monographs*, 58, No. 270.

Dunkling, L. (1977). *First names first*. London: Dent.

Dunn, J. & Kendrick, C. (1982). *Siblings: Love, envy and understanding*. London: Grant McIntyre.

Dunn-Rankin, P. (1983). *Scaling methods*. Hillsdale, New Jersey: Lawrence Erlbaum.

Durkin, K. and Crowther, R.D. (1982). Language in music education: research overview. *Psychology of Music*, 10, 59–61.

Eisenberg, R.B. (1976). *Auditory competence in early life*. Baltimore: University Park Press.

Eisenstein, S.R. (1976). A successive approximation procedure for learning musical symbol names. *Journal of Music Therapy*, 13, 173–9.

Eiser, J.R. (1980). *Cognitive social psychology*. Maidenhead: McGraw-Hill.

Elliott, C.D., Murray, D.J. and Pearson, L.S. (1978). *British Ability Scales*. Windsor: NFER.

Eng, H. (1931). *The psychology of children's drawings*. London: Routledge & Kegan Paul.

Eysenck, H.J. (1940). The general factor in aesthetic judgements. *British Journal of Psychology*, 31, 94–102.

(1967). Intelligence assessment: a theoretical and experimental approach. *British Journal of Educational Psychology*, 37, 81–98.

Farnsworth, P.R. (1949). Rating scales for musical interests. *Journal of Psychology*, 28, 245–53.

(1954). A study of the Hevner Adjective List. *Journal of Aesthetics and Art Criticism*, 13, 97–103.

(1969). *The social psychology of music* (2nd edition). Ames: Iowa State University Press.

Farnsworth, P.R. and Beaumont, H. (1929). Suggestion in pictures. *Journal of General Psychology*, 2, 362–6.

Faw, T.T. and Pien, D. (1971). The influence of stimulus exposure on rated preference: effects of age, pattern of exposure, and stimulus meaningfulness. *Journal of Experimental Child Psychology*, 11, 339–46.

Fay, P.J. and Middleton, W.C. (1941). Relationship between musical talent and preference for different types of music. *Journal of Educational Psychology*, 32, 573–83.

Fechner, G.T. (1876). *Vorschule der äesthetik*. Leipzig: Breitkopf & Hartel.

Fishbein, M. (1967). Attitude and the prediction of behavior, in *Readings in attitude theory and measurement*, ed. M. Fishbein. New York: Wiley.

Fisher, R.L. (1951). Preferences of different age and socioeconomic groups in unstructured musical situations. *Journal of Social Psychology*, 33, 147–52.

Flavell, J.H. (1963). *The developmental psychology of Jean Piaget*. Princeton, N.J.: Van Nostrand.

Fletcher, H. and Walker, R. (1970). *Mathematics for schools: An integrated series*. Level I, Books 1–7. London: Addison-Wesley.

Foley, E.A. (1975). The effects of training in conservation of tonal and rhythmic patterns on second-grade children. *Journal of Research in Music Education*, 23, 240–8.

Forsythe, J.L. (1975). The effect of teacher approval, disapproval, and errors on student attentiveness: Music versus classroom teachers, in *Research in music behavior: Modifying music behavior in the classroom*, eds. C.K. Madsen, R.D. Greer and C.H. Madsen. New York: Teachers College Press.

Fox, W.S. and Williams, J.D. (1974). Political orientation and music preferences among college students. *Public Opinion Quarterly*, 38, 352–71.

Fox, W.S. and Wince, M.H. (1975). Musical taste cultures and taste publics. *Youth and Society*, 7, 198–224.

Francès, R. (1963). Limites et nature des effets de prestige – I. L'attention et la mémoire. *Journal de Psychologie*, 60, 271–91.

   (1967). Communication persuasive et communication esthétique. *Journal de Psychologie*, 4, 415–30.

Fransella, F. and Bannister, D. (1977). *A manual for repertory grid technique*. London: Academic Press.

Freeman, J., Butcher, H.J. and Christie, T. (1971). *Creativity: A selective review of research* (2nd edition). London: SRHE.

Freeman, N.H. (1972). Process and product in children's drawing. *Perception*, 1, 123–40.

   (1975). Do children draw men with arms coming out of the head? *Nature*, 254, 416–17.

   (1976). Children's drawings – cognitive aspects. *Journal of Child Psychology and Psychiatry*, 17, 345–50.

   (1980). *Strategies of representation in young children*. London: Academic Press.

Freud, S. (1910). *Leonardo da Vinci: A study in psychosexuality*. New York: Random House, 1947.

Fullard, W.G. (1975). Pitch discrimination in elementary-school children as a function of training procedure and age, in *Research in music behavior: Modifying music behavior in the classroom*, eds. C.K. Madsen, R.D. Greer and C.H. Madsen. New York: Teachers College Press.

Gagné, R.M. (1977). *Conditions of learning* (3rd edition). New York: Holt, Rinehart & Winston.

Galton, M. and Simon, B. (eds.) (1980). *Progress and performance in the primary classroom*. London: Routledge & Kegan Paul.

Gans, H.J. (1974). *Popular culture and high culture*. New York: Basic Books.

Gardner, H. (1970). Children's sensitivity to painting styles. *Child Development*, 41, 813–21.

   (1971). Children's duplication of rhythmic patterns. *Journal of Research in Music Education*, 19, 355–60.

   (1972a). Style sensitivity in children. *Human Development*, 15, 325–38.

   (1972b). The development of sensitivity to figural and stylistic aspects of paintings. *British Journal of Psychology*, 63, 605–15.

(1973a). *The arts and human development*. New York: Wiley.

(1973b). Children's sensitivity to musical styles. *Merrill-Palmer Quarterly*, 19, 67–77.

(1979). Development psychology after Piaget: An approach in terms of symbolization. *Human Development*, 22, 73–88.

(1982). The prodigies' progress, in *Art, mind and brain*, ed. H. Gardner. New York: Basic Books.

Gardner, H. and Gardner, J. (1971). Children's literary skills. *Journal of Experimental Education*, 39, 42–6.

Gardner, H., Winner, E. and Kircher, M. (1975). Children's conceptions of the arts. *Journal of Aesthetic Education*, 9, 60–77.

Gardner, P.A.D. and Pickford, R.W. (1944). Relation between dissonance and context. *Nature*, 154, 274–5.

Gaston, E.T. (1958). *A test of musicality: Manual of directions*. Lawrence, Kansas: Odell's Instrumental Service.

Geiger, T. (1950). A radio test of musical taste. *Public Opinion Quarterly*, 14, 453–60.

Geringer, J.M. (1976). Tuning preferences in recorded orchestral music. *Journal of Research in Music Education*, 24, 169–76.

(1977). An assessment of children's musical instrument preferences. *Journal of Music Therapy*, 14, 172–9.

(1982). Verbal and operant music listening preferences in relationship to age and musical training. *Psychology of Music, Special Issue*, 47–50.

Geringer, J.M. and Madsen, C.K. (1981). Verbal and operant discrimination – preference for tone quality and intonation. *Psychology of Music*, 9, 26–30.

Geringer, J.M. and McManus, D. (1979). A survey of musical taste in relationship to age and musical training. *College Music Symposium*, 19, 69–76.

Gesell, A. (1940). *The first five years of life*. New York: Harper and Row.

Gesell, A. and Ilg, F. (1943). *The infant and child in the culture of today*. London: Hamilton.

(1946). *The child from five to ten*. New York: Harper.

Getzels, J.W. and Czikszentmihalyi, M. (1976). *The creative vision: A longitudinal study of problem finding in art*. New York: Wiley.

Getzels, J.W. and Jackson, P.W. (1962). *Creativity and intelligence: Explorations with gifted students*. New York: Wiley.

Ghiselin, B. (ed.) (1952). *The creative process*. Cambridge: Cambridge University Press.

Gibson, E.J. (1969). *Principles of perceptual learning and development*. New York: Appleton-Century-Crofts.

Gilbert, G.M. (1942). Sex differences in musical aptitude and training. *Journal of General Psychology*, 26, 19–33.

Goldschmid, M.L. (1968). *The role of experience in the acquisition of conservation*. Proceedings of the 76th Annual Convention of the American Psychological Association.

Goodnow, J. (1971). Auditory-visual matching: modality problem or translation problem? *Child Development*, 42, 1187–201.

(1977). *Children's drawing*. London: Fontana/Open Books.

Gorder, W.D. (1980). Divergent production abilities as constructs of musical creativity. *Journal of Research in Music Education*, 28, 34–42.

Gordon, E. (1965). *Musical aptitude profile manual*. Boston: Houghton Mifflin.

(1971). *Iowa tests of music literacy*. Iowa City: Bureau of Educational Research and Service, University of Iowa.

Gough, H.G. (1960). The adjective check list as a personality assessment technique. *Psychological Reports*, Monograph Supplement 2, 6, 107–22.

Greer, R.D. (1978). *An operant approach to motivation and affect: Ten years of research in music learning.* Paper presented at the National Symposium for the Application of Learning Theory to Music Education, Ann Arbor, Michigan. Reston, Virginia: MENC, 1981.

(1980). *Design for music learning.* New York: Teachers College Press.

Greer, R.D. and Dorow, L.G. (1976). *Specializing education behaviorally.* Dubuque, Iowa: Kendall-Hunt.

Greer, R.D., Dorow, L.G. and Hanser, S. (1973). Music discrimination training and the music selection behavior of nursery and primary level children. *Council for Research in Music Education Bulletin,* 35, 30–43.

Greer, R.D., Dorow, L.G. and Randall, A. (1974). Music listening preferences of elementary school children. *Journal of Research in Music Education,* 22, 284–91.

Greer, R.D., Dorow, L.G., Wachhaus, G. and White, E.R. (1973). Adult approval and students' music selection behavior. *Journal of Research in Music Education,* 21, 345–54.

Greer, R.D., Dorow, L.G. and Wolpert, R.S. (1978). *The effect of taught musical affect on the learning ability of young children at cognitive musical tasks.* Paper presented at the Music Educators National Conference, Chicago.

Greer, R.D., Randall, A. and Timberlake, C. (1971). The discriminate use of music listening as a contingency for improvement in vocal pitch acuity and attending behavior. *Council for Research in Music Education Bulletin,* 26, 10–28.

Guilford, J.P. (1967). *The nature of human intelligence.* New York: McGraw-Hill.

Guilford, J.P. and Hoepfner, R. (1966). Sixteen divergent-production abilities at the ninth-grade level. *Multivariate Behavioral Research,* 1, 43–64.

Haack, P.A. (1980). The behavior of music listeners, in *Handbook of music psychology,* ed. D.A. Hodges. Lawrence, Kansas: National Association for Music Therapy.

Haag, E. van den (1959). Of happiness and despair we have no measure, in *Mass culture,* eds. B. Rosenberg and D. White. Glencoe, Illinois: The Free Press.

Haddon, F.A. and Lytton, H. (1968). Teaching approach and the development of divergent thinking abilities in primary schools. *British Journal of Educational Psychology,* 38, 171–80.

Hair, H.I. (1977). Discrimination of tonal direction on verbal and nonverbal tasks by first grade children. *Journal of Research in Music Education,* 25, 197–210.

Hampson, S.E. (1982). *The construction of personality: An introduction.* London: Routledge & Kegan Paul.

Hanslick, E. (1891). *The beautiful in music.* London: Novello.

Hare, F.G. (1975). The identification of dimensions underlying verbal and exploratory responses to music through multidimensional scaling. Unpublished doctoral dissertation, University of Toronto.

(1977). Dimensions of music perception. *Scientific Aesthetics,* 1, 271–80.

Hargreaves, D.H. (1967). *Social relations in a secondary school.* London: Routledge & Kegan Paul.

Hargreaves, D.J. (1974). Psychological testing: current perspectives and future developments. *Educational Review,* 27, 26–33.

(1978). Psychological studies of children's drawing. *Educational Review,* 30, 247–54.

(1979). Sex roles and creativity, in *Sex role stereotyping,* eds. O. Hartnett, G. Boden and M. Fuller. London: Tavistock.

(1982a). The development of aesthetic reactions to music. *Psychology of Music,* Special Issue, 51–4.

(1982b). Preference and prejudice in music: a psychological approach. *Popular Music and Society,* 8, 13–18.

(1982c). The development of ideational fluency: some normative data. *British Journal of Educational Psychology*, **52**, 109–12.

(1984). The effects of repetition on liking for music. *Journal of Research in Music Education*, **32**, 35–47.

(1986). Psychological theories of sex-role stereotyping, in *The psychology of sex roles*, eds. D.J. Hargreaves and A.M. Colley. London: Harper & Row.

Hargreaves, D.J. and Bolton, N. (1972). Selecting creativity tests for use in research. *British Journal of Psychology*, **63**, 451–62.

Hargreaves, D.J. and Castell, K.C. (1986). Development of liking for familiar and unfamiliar melodies. Paper presented at the Eleventh International Seminar of the International Society for Music Education, Frankfurt, West Germany.

Hargreaves, D.J., Castell, K.C. and Crowther, R.D. (in press). The effects of stimulus familiarity on conservation-type responses to tone sequences: a cross-cultural study. *Journal of Research in Music Education*.

Hargreaves, D.J. and Colman, A.M. '1981). The dimensions of aesthetic reactions to music. *Psychology of Music, 9*, 15–20.

Hargreaves, D.J., Jones, P.M. and Martin, D. (1981). The air gap phenomenon in children's landscape drawings. *Journal of Experimental Child Psychology*, **32**, 11–20.

Hargreaves, D.J., Messerschmidt, P. and Rubert, C. (1980). Musical preference and evaluation. *Psychology of Music*, **8**, 13–18.

Hargreaves, H.L. (1927). The 'faculty' of imagination. *British Journal of Psychology Monograph Supplement*, No. 3.

Harlen, W. (1975). *Science 5–13: A formative evaluation*. Schools Council Research Studies. London: Macmillan.

Harris, D.B. (1963). *Children's drawings as measures of intellectual maturity*. New York: Harcourt, Brace & World.

Hart, L.M. and Goldin-Meadow, S. (1984). The child as a nonegocentric art critic. *Child Development*, **55**, 2122–9.

Hattie, J.A. (1977). Conditions for administering creativity tests. *Psychological Bulletin*, **84**, 1249–60.

Heingartner, A. and Hall, J.V. (1974). Affective consequences in adults and children of repeated exposure to auditory stimuli. *Journal of Personality and Social Psychology*, **29**, 719–23.

Helmholtz, H.L.F. von (1962). *On the sensations of tone* (4th edition). London: Longmans, Green & Co., 1912.

Herron, R.E. and Sutton-Smith, B. (eds.) (1971). *Child's play*. New York: Wiley.

Hevner, K. (1935). The affective character of the major and minor modes in music. *American Journal of Psychology*, **47**, 103–18.

Heyduk, R.G. (1975). Rated preference for musical composition as it relates to complexity and exporure frequency. *Perception of Psychophysics*, **17**, 84–91.

Hirsch, P. (1969). *The structure of the popular music industry*. Ann Arbor: Survey Research Center, University of Michigan.

(1971). Sociological approaches to the pop music phenomenon. *American Behavioral Scientist*, **14**, 371–88.

Hodges, D. (ed.) (1980). *Handbook of music psychology*. Lawrence, Kansas: National Association for Music Therapy.

Hoffer, C.R. (1983). *Teaching music in the secondary schools* (3rd edition). Belmont, California: Wadsworth.

Horn, J.L. and Stankov, L. (1982). Auditory and visual factors in intelligence. *Intelligence*, **6**, 165–85.

Hovland, C.I., Janis, I.L. and Kelley, H.H. (1953). *Communication and persuasion*. New Haven: Yale University Press.

Howell, P., Cross, I. and West, R. (eds.) (1985). *Musical structure and cognition.* London: Academic Press.

Hudson, L. (1966). *Contrary imaginations.* Harmondsworth: Penguin.

(1968). *Frames of mind.* Harmondsworth: Penguin.

Igaga, J.M. and Versey, J. (1977). Cultural differences in rhythmic perception. *Psychology of Music,* 5, 23–7.

(1978). Cultural differences in rhythmic performance. *Psychology of Music,* 6, 61–4.

Imberty, M. (1969). *L'acquisition des structures tonales chez l'enfant.* Paris: Klincksieck.

Inglefield, H.G. (1968). The relationship of selected personality variables to conformity behavior reflected in the musical preferences of adolescents when exposed to peer group leader influences. Unpublished doctoral dissertation, Ohio State University.

Inhelder, B., Sinclair, H. and Bovet, M. (1966). On cognitive development. *American Psychologist,* 21, 160–4.

Jackson, P.W. and Messick, S. (1965). The person, the product and the response: conceptual problems in the assessment of creativity. *Journal of Personality,* 33, 309–29.

Jaquish, G.A. (1983). Intra-individual variability in divergent thinking in response to audio, visual and tactile stimuli. *British Journal of Psychology,* 74, 467–72.

Jaquish, G.A. and Ripple, R.E. (1981). Cognitive creative abilities and self-esteem across the adult life-span. *Human Development,* 24, 110–19.

Johnstone, J. and Katz, E. (1957). Youth and popular music: a study of the sociology of taste. *American Journal of Sociology,* 62, 563–8.

Jolly, H.D. (1967). Popular music: A study in collective behavior. Unpublished doctoral dissertation, Stanford University.

Kahneman, D. (1973). *Attention and effort.* Englewood Cliffs, N.J.: Prentice-Hall.

Kavolis, V. (1963). A role theory of artistic interest. *Journal of Social Psychology,* 60, 31–7.

Kellogg, R. (1969). *Analysing children's art.* Palo Alto, California: National Press.

Kemp, A.E. (1981a). The personality structure of the musician: I. Identifying a profile of traits for the performer. *Psychology of Music,* 9, 3–14.

(1981b). Personality differences between the players of string, woodwind, brass and keyboard instruments, and singers. *Council for Research in Music Education Bulletin,* 66, 33–8.

(1981c). The personality structure of the musician: II. Identifying a profile of traits for the composer. *Psychology of Music,* 9, 69–75.

(1982a). Personality traits of successful student music teachers. *Psychology of Music, Special Issue,* 72-5.

(1982b). The personality structure of the musician: III. The significance of sex differences. *Psychology of Music,* 10, 48–58.

(1982c). The personality structure of the musician: IV. Incorporating group profiles into a comprehensive model. *Psychology of Music,* 10, 3–6.

(1984). Psychological androgyny in musicians. *Council for Research in Music Education Bulletin,* 85, 102–8.

Kessen, W., Levine, J. and Wendrich, K.A. (1969). The imitation of pitch in infants. *Infant Behavior and Development,* 2, 93–9.

Keston, M.J. (1954). An experimental value of two methods of teaching music appreciation. *Journal of Experimental Education,* 22, 215–26.

Keston, M.J. and Pinto, I.M. (1955). Possible factors influencing musical preference. *Journal of Genetic Psychology,* 86, 101–13.

Kimble, G.A. (1961). *Hilgard and Marquis' conditioning and learning* (2nd edition). New York: Appleton-Century-Crofts.

Klahr, D. and Wallace, J.G. (1976). *Cognitive development: An information-processing view.* Hillsdale, N.J.: Erlbaum.

Koestler, A. (1964). *The act of creation.* London: Hutchinson.

Kohlberg, L. (1966). A cognitive developmental analysis of children's sex role concepts and attitudes, in *The development of sex differences*, ed. E.E. Maccoby. Stanford: Stanford University Press.

(1976). Moral stages and moralization: The cognitive-developmental approach, in *Moral development and behavior*, ed. T. Lickona. New York: Holt, Rinehart & Winston.

Konečni. V.J. (1975). The mediation of aggressive behavior: arousal level vs. anger and cognitive labeling. *Journal of Personality and Social Psychology*, 32, 706–12.

(1979). Determinants of aesthetic preference and effects of exposure to aesthetic stimuli: social, emotional and cognitive factors, in *Progress in experimental personality research*, vol. 9, ed. B.A. Maher. New York: Academic Press.

(1982). Social interaction and musical preference, in *The psychology of music*, ed. D. Deutsch. New York: Academic Press.

(1984). Elusive effects of artists' 'messages', in *Cognitive processes in the perception of art*, eds. W.R. Crozier and A.J. Chapman. Amsterdam: Elsevier.

Konečni, V.J., Crozier, J.B. and Doob, A.N. (1976). Anger and expression of aggression: effects on aesthetic preference. *Scientific Aesthetics*, 1, 47–55.

Konečni, V.J. and Sargent-Pollock, D. (1976). Choice between melodies differing in complexity under divided-attention conditions. *Journal of Experimental Psychology: Human Perception and Performance*, 2, 347–56.

Krathwohl, D.R., Bloom, B.S. and Masia, B.B. (1964). *Taxonomy of educational objectives. Handbook II: Affective domain.* New York: McKay.

Krech, D., Crutchfield, R.S. and Ballachey, E.L. (1962). *Individual in society.* New York: McGraw-Hill.

Kris, E. (1950). On preconscious mental processes. *Psychoanalytic Quarterly*, 19, 540–60.

Krugman, H.E. (1943). Affective response to music as a function of familiarity. *Journal of Abnormal and Social Psychology*, 38, 388–92.

Krumhansl, C.L. (1983). Perceptual structures for tonal music. *Music Perception*, 1, 24–58.

Krumhansl, C.L. and Castellano, M.A. (1983). Dynamic processes in musical perception. *Memory and Cognition*, 11, 325–34.

Kubie, L.S. (1958). *Neurotic distortion of the creative process.* Lawrence, Kansas: University of Kansas Press.

Kuhn, T.L. (1981). Instrumentation for the measurement of music attitudes. *Contributions to Music Education*, 8, 2–38.

Kuhn, T.L., Sims, W.L. and Shehan, P.K. (1981). Relationship between listening time and like–dislike ratings on three music selections. *Journal of Music Therapy*, 18, 181–92.

Langer, S. (1953). *Feeling and form.* New York: Scribner.

Lazarsfeld, P.F. and Stanton, F. (1944). *Radio research 1942-43.* New York: Duell, Sloane & Pearce.

LeBlanc, A. (1980). Outline of a proposed model of sources of variation in musical taste. *Council for Research in Music Education Bulletin*, 61, 29–34.

Lehman, H.C. (1953). *Age and achievement.* Princeton, N.J.: Princeton University Press.

Leonhard, C. and House, R.W. (1972). *Foundations and principles of music education* (2nd edition). New York: McGraw-Hill.

Lerdahl, F. and Jackendoff, R. (1983). *A generative theory of tonal music.* Cambridge, Mass.: MIT Press.

Lerner, R.M. (1976). *Concepts and theories of human development*. Reading, Mass.: Addison-Wesley.

Levin, I. (1978). Creativity and two modes of associative fluency: chains and stars. *Journal of Personality*, 46, 426–37.

Lewin, K. (1942). Field theory and learning, in *41st Yearbook, National society for the study of education*, part 2. Bloomington: Public School Publishing.

Liberman, A. (1960). *The artist in his studio*. New York: Viking Press.

Light, P. (1983). Social cognition and Piaget: a case of negative transfer? In *Jean Piaget: An interdisciplinary critique*, eds. S. Modgil, C. Modgil and G. Brown. London: Routledge & Kegan Paul.

Lipps, T. (1885). *Psychologische studien*. Heidelberg: Weiss.

Long, N.H. (1965). *Indiana-Oregon music discrimination tests*. Bloomington, Indiana: Midwest Music Tests.

Longuet-Higgins, H.C. (1978). The perception of music. *Interdisciplinary Science Review*, 3, 148–56.

Lowenfeld, V. and Brittain, W.L. (1975). *Creative and mental growth* (6th edition). New York: Macmillan.

Lucquet, G.H. (1927). *Le dessin enfantin*. Paris: Alcan.

Lundin, R.W. (1967). *An objective psychology of music* (2nd edition). New York: Ronald.

Machotka, P. (1966). Aesthetic criteria in childhood: justifications of preference. *Child Development*, 37, 877–85.

(1982). Esthetic judgement warm and cool: cognitive and affective determinants. *Journal of Personality and Social Psychology*, 42, 100–7.

McGarrigle, J. and Donaldson, M. (1975). Conservation accidents. *Cognition*, 3, 304–10.

McKellar, P. (1957). *Imagination and thinking*. London: Cohen & West.

McKernon, P.E. (1979). The development of first songs in young children, in *Early symbolization*, eds. H. Gardner and D. Wolf. San Francisco: Jossey-Bass.

MacKinnon, D.W. (1962). The nature and nurture of creative talent. *American Psychologist*, 17, 484–95.

McMullen, P.T. (1974). Influence of number of different pitches and melodic redundancy on preference responses. *Journal of Research in Music Education*, 22, 198–204.

(1980). Music as a perceived stimulus object and affective responses as an alternative theoretical framework, in *Handbook of music psychology*, ed. D.A. Hodges. Lawrence, Kansas: National Association for Music Therapy.

McMullen, P.T. and Arnold, M.J. (1976). Preference and interest as functions of distributional redundancy in rhythmic sequences. *Journal of Research in Music Education*, 24, 22–31.

McPherson, J.H. (1963). A proposal for establishing ultimate criteria for measuring creative output, in *Scientific creativity: Its recognition and development*, eds. C.W. Taylor and F. Barron. New York: Wiley.

Madsen, C.K., Dorow, L.G., Moore, R.S. and Womble, J.U. (1976). Effect of music lessons via television as reinforcement for correct mathematical responses. *Journal of Research in Music Education*, 24, 50–9.

Madsen, C.K. and Forsythe, J.L. (1973). Effect of contingent music listening on increases of mathematical responses. *Journal of Research in Music Education*, 21, 176–81.

Madsen, C.K., Greer, R.D. and Madsen, C.H. (eds.) (1975). *Research in music behavior: Modifying music behavior in the classroom*. New York: Teachers College Press.

Madsen, C.K. and Kuhn, T.L. (1978). *Contemporary music education*. Arlington Heights, Ill.: Harlen Davidson.

Madsen, C.K. and Moore, R.S. (eds.) (1978). *Experimental research in music: Workbook in design and statistical tests.* Raleigh, North Carolina: Contemporary Publishing Co.

Madsen, C.K. and Yarborough, C. (1980). *Competency-based music education.* Englewood Cliffs: Prentice-Hall.

Marantz, A. (1985). 'Cognition in music': reply to Serafine. *Cognition*, 19, 73–86.

Mark, M.L. (1978). *Contemporary music education.* New York: Schirmer.

Martin, G. (ed.) (1983). *Making music.* London: Pan.

Marx, M.H. and Goodson, F.E. (eds.) (1976). *Theories in contemporary psychology* (2nd edition). New York: Macmillan.

Mashkin, K.B. and Volgy, T.J. (1975). Socio-political attitudes and musical preferences. *Social Science Quarterly*, 56, 450–9.

Mednick, S.A. (1962). The associative basis of the creative process. *Psychological Review*, 69, 220–32.

MENC (1981). *Documentary report of the Ann Arbor symposium.* Reston, Virginia: MENC.

Meyer, L.B. (1956). *Emotion and meaning in music.* Chicago: University of Chicago Press.

(1967). *Music, the arts, and ideas.* Chicago: University of Chicago Press.

Miller, G.A. (1956). The magical number seven plus or minus two: some limits on our capacity for processing information. *Psychological Review*, 63, 81–97.

Miller, P.H. (1983). *Theories of developmental psychology.* San Francisco: W.H. Freeman.

Miller, S.A. (1976). Non-verbal assessment of Piagetian concepts. *Psychological Bulletin*, 83, 405–30.

Mills, E. and Murphy, St T.C. (eds.) (1974). *The Suzuki concept.* New York: Diablo Press.

Minsky, M. (1977). Frame-system theory, in *Thinking: Readings in cognitive science*, eds. P.N. Johnson-Laird and P.C. Wason. Cambridge: Cambridge University Press.

Modgil, S. (ed.) (1974). *Piagetian research: A handbook of recent studies.* Slough: NFER.

Modgil, S., Modgil, C., and Brown, G. (eds.) (1983). *Jean Piaget: An interdisciplinary critique.* London: Routledge & Kegan Paul.

Moog, H. (1976). *The musical experience of the pre-school child.* Trans. C. Clarke. London: Schott.

Moore, H.T. (1914). The genetic aspect of consonance and dissonance. *Psychological Monographs*, 17, No. 73.

Moorhead, G.E. and Pond, D. (1978). *Music of young children.* Santa Barbara, California: Pillsbury Foundation, 1941–51.

Morgan, B.J. and Lindsley, O.R. (1966). Operant preference for stereophonic over monophonic music. *Journal of Music Therapy*, 3, 135–43.

Morison, P. and Gardner, H. (1978). Dragons and dinosaurs: the child's capacity to differentiate fantasy from reality. *Child Development*, 49, 642–8.

Mueller, J.H. and Hevner, K. (1942). *Trends in musical taste.* Indiana University Publishers.

Mull, H.K. (1957). The effect of repetition upon the enjoyment of modern music. *Journal of Psychology*, 43, 155–62.

Munro, T. (1963). The psychology of art: past, present, future. *Journal of Aesthetics and Art Criticism*, 21, 264–82.

Murdock, G. and Phelps, G. (1973). *Mass media and the secondary school.* London: Schools Council/Macmillan.

Murray, K.C. (1972). The effect of teacher approval/disapproval on the performance level, attentiveness, and attitude of high school choruses. Unpublished doctoral dissertation, Florida State University.

Myers, C.S. (1922). Individual differences in listening to music. *British Journal of Psychology*, 13, 52–71.

(1927). Individual differences in listening to music, in *The effects of music*, ed. M. Schoen. New York: Harcourt Brace.

Myers, C.S. and Valentine, C.W. (1914). A study of the individual differences in attitude towards tones. *British Journal of Psychology*, 7, 68–111.

Neisser, U. (1963). The multiplicity of thought. *British Journal of Psychology*, 54, 1–14.

(1976). *Cognition and reality: Principles and implications of cognitive psychology.* San Francisco: W.H. Freeman.

Nettl, B. (1956). *Music in primitive culture.* Cambridge, Mass.: Harvard University Press.

Nicholls, J.G. (1972). Creativity in the person who will never produce anything original and useful: the concept of creativity as a normally-distributed trait. *American Psychologist*, 27, 717–27.

Noll, V.H. and Scannell, D.P. (1972). *Introduction to educational measurement.* Boston: Houghton Mifflin.

Nordenstreng, K. (1968). A comparison between the semantic differential and similarity analysis in the measurement of musical experience. *Scandinavian Journal of Psychology*, 9, 89–96.

Nuffield Foundation (1972). *Nuffield mathematics project.* Edinburgh: Chambers.

Nye, R.E. and Nye, V.T. (1977). *Music in the elementary school* (4th edition). Englewood Cliffs: Prentice-Hall.

Oakes, W.F. (1951). An alternative interpretation of 'absolute pitch'. *Transactions of the Kansas Academy of Science*, 54, 396–406.

Ogden, R.M. (1924). *Hearing.* New York: Harcourt, Brace & World.

O'Hare, D. (1979). Multidimensional scaling representations and individual differences in concept learning of artistic style. *British Journal of Psychology*, 70, 219–30.

Orff, C. and Keetman, G. (1958). *Orff-Schulwerk music for children.* (trans. M. Murray). London: Schott.

Ortmann, O. (1927). Types of listeners: genetic considerations, in *The effects of music*, ed. M. Schoen. New York: Harcourt Brace.

Ostwald, P. (1973). Musical behavior in early childhood. *Developmental Medicine and Child Neurology*, 15, 367–75.

Paisley, W.J. (1964). Identifying the unknown communicator in painting, literature and music: the significance of minor encoding habits. *Journal of Communication*, 14, 219–37.

Pantle, J.E. (1978). The effect of teacher approval of music on music selection and music verbal preference. Paper presented at Music Educators National Conference, Chicago.

Parke, R.D. (1981). *Fathering.* London: Fontana.

Parsons, M. (1981). A suggestion concerning the development of aesthetic experience in children. *Journal of Aesthetics and Art Criticism*, 34, 305–14.

Parsons, M., Johnston, M. and Durham, R. (1978). Developmental stages in children's aesthetic responses. *Journal of Aesthetic Education*, 12, 83–104.

Patrick, C. (1935). Creative thought in poets. *Archives of Psychology*, 26, 1-74.

(1937). Creative thought in artists. *Journal of Psychology*, 4, 35–73.

(1955). *What is creative thinking?* New York: Philosophical Library.

Patterson, C.H. (1977). *Foundation for a theory of instruction and educational psychology.* New York: Harper and Row.

Payne, E. (1967). Musical taste and personality. *British Journal of Psychology*, 58, 133–8.

Paynter, J. (1977). The role of creativity in the school music curriculum, in *Music education review*, vol. 1, ed. M. Burnett. London: Novello.

(1982). *Music in the secondary school curriculum*. Cambridge: Cambridge University Press.

Pedersen, F.A. (ed.) (1980). *The father–infant relationship*. New York: Praeger.

Pettigrew, T.F. (1958). The measurement and correlates of category width as a cognitive variable. *Journal of Personality*, 26, 532–44.

Petzold, R.G. (1966). *Auditory perception of musical sounds by children in the first six grades*. Cooperative Research Project No. 1051, University of Wisconsin.

Piaget, J. (1951). *Play, dreams and imitation in childhood*. London: Routledge & Kegan Paul.

(1966). Response to Brian Sutton-Smith. *Psychological Review*, 73, 111–12.

Piaget, J. and Inhelder, B. (1969). *The psychology of the child*. London: Routledge & Kegan Paul.

Pine, F. and Holt, R.R. (1960). Creativity and primary process: a study of adaptive regression. *Journal of Abnormal and Social Psychology*, 61, 370–9.

Pflederer, M. (1964). The responses of children to musical tasks embodying Piaget's principle of conservation. *Journal of Research in Music Education*, 12, 251–68.

(1967). Conservation laws applied to the development of musical intelligence. *Journal of Research in Music Education*, 15, 215–23.

Pflederer, M. and Sechrest, L. (1968). Conservation-type responses of children to musical stimuli. *Council for Research in Music Education Bulletin*, 13, 19–36.

Pflederer Zimmerman, M. and Sechrest, L. (1970). Brief focused instruction and musical concepts. *Journal of Research in Music Education*, 18, 25–36.

Plomp, R. and Levelt, W.J.M. (1965). Tonal consonance and critical bandwidth. *Journal of the Acoustical Society of America*, 38, 548–60.

Pond, D., Shelley, S.J. and Wilson, B.D. (1978). The Pillsbury Foundation School revisited. Paper presented to the Music Educators 26th National Conference, Chicago.

Pressing, J. (1984). Cognitive processes in improvisation, in *Cognitive processes in the perception of art*, eds. W.R. Crozier and A.J. Chapman. Amsterdam: Elsevier.

Radocy, R.E. (1975). A naive minority of one and deliberate majority mismatches of tonal stimuli. *Journal of Research in Music Education*, 23, 120–33.

(1976). Effects of authority figure biases on changing judgments of musical events. *Journal of Research in Music Education*, 24, 119–28.

(1982). Preference for classical music: a test for the hedgehog. *Psychology of Music*, Special Issue, 91–5.

Radocy, R.E. and Boyle, J.D. (1969). *Psychological foundations of musical behavior*. Springfield, Ill.: C.C. Thomas.

Rainbow, E.L. (1965). A pilot study to investigate the constructs of musical aptitude. *Journal of Research in Music Education*, 13, 3–14.

(1977). A longitudinal investigation of the rhythmic abilities of pre-school aged children. *Council for Research in Music Education Bulletin*, 50, 55–61.

Rainbow, E.L. and Owen, D. (1979). A progress report on a three year investigation of the rhythmic ability of pre-school aged children. *Council for Research in Music Education Bulletin*, 59, 84–6.

Ramsey, J.H. (1981). An investigation of the effects of age, singing ability, and experience with pitched instruments on the melodic perception of preschool children. Unpublished doctoral dissertation, University of Iowa.

Rasch, R.A. and Plomp, R. (1982). The perception of musical tones, in *The psychology of music*, ed. D. Deutsch. New York: Academic Press.

Regelski, T.A. (1975). *Principles and problems of music education*. Englewood Cliffs: Prentice-Hall.

Reimers, D. (1927). Unterschungen uber die Entwickelung des Tonalitätgefühls, cited in *La perception de la musique*, by R. Francès. Paris: Vrin, 1958.

Revesz, G. (1913). *Zur Grundlegung der Tonpsychologie*. Leipzig: Veit.

(1925). *The psychology of a musical prodigy*. New York: Harcourt Brace.

(1954). *Introduction to the psychology of music*. Norman, Oklahoma: University of Oklahoma Press.

Richards, M.P.M. (ed.) (1974). *The integration of a child into a social world*. Cambridge: Cambridge University Press.

Ridgeway, C.L. (1976). Affective interaction as a determinant of musical involvement. *The Sociological Quarterly*, 17, 414–28.

Rigg, M.G. (1948). Favorable versus unfavorable propaganda in the enjoyment of music. *Journal of Experimental Psychology*, 38, 78–81.

Robinson, J.P. and Hirsch, P.M. (1969). Teenage response to rock and roll protest songs. Paper presented to Annual Meeting of the American Sociological Association, San Francisco.

(1972). Teenage response to rock and roll protest songs, in *The sounds of social change*, eds. R.S. Denisoff and R.A. Peterson. Chicago: Rand McNally.

Roe, A. (1951). A psychological study of eminent biologists. *Psychological Monographs*, 64, No. 14.

(1952). *The making of a scientist*. New York: Dodd, Mead.

(1953). A psychological study of eminent psychologists and anthropologists and a comparison with biological and physical scientists. *Psychological Monographs*, 67, no. 2.

Rogers, V.R. (1957). Children's musical preferences as related to grade level and other factors. *Elementary School Journal*, 57, 433–5.

Romaniuk, J.G. and Romaniuk, M. (1981). Creativity across the life span: a measurement perspective. *Human Development*, 24, 366–81.

Rosentiel, A., Morison, P., Silverman, J. and Gardner, H. (1978). Critical judgement: a developmental study. *Journal of Aesthetic Education*, 12, 95–107.

Ross, M. (ed.) (1982). *The development of aesthetic experience*. Oxford: Pergamon.

Rousseau, J.J. (1762). *Emile, or On education*. London: Dent.

Rubin, Z. (1980). *Children's friendships*. London: Fontana.

Rubin-Rabson, G. (1940). The influence of age, intelligence and training on reactions to classic and modern music. *Journal of General Psychology*, 22, 413–29.

Rural Schools Music Association (1977). *The Suzuki investigation in Hertfordshire*. London: Bedford Square Press.

Russell, P.A. (1982). Relationships between judgements of the complexity, pleasingness and interestingness of music. *Current Psychological Research*, 2, 195–202.

Salk, L. (1962). Mother's heartbeat as imprinting stimulus. *Transactions of the New York Academy of Science*, 24, 753–63.

Schaffer, H.R. (1971). *The growth of sociability*. Harmondsworth: Penguin.

Schaie, K.W. (1965). A general model for the study of developmental problems. *Psychological Bulletin*, 64, 92–107.

Schoen, M. (1940). *The psychology of music*. New York: Roland.

Schoen, M. and Gatewood, E.L. (1927). The mood effects of music, in *The effects of music*, ed. M. Schoen. New York: Harcourt Brace.

Schroder, H.M., Driver, M.J. and Streufert, S. (1967). *Human information processing*. New York: Holt, Rinehart & Winston.

Schuckert, R.F. and McDonald, R.M. (1978). An attempt to modify the musical preferences of preschool children. *Journal of Research in Music Education*, 16, 39–45.

Schuessler, K.F. (1948). Social background and musical taste. *American Sociological Review*, 13, 330–5.

Schultz, C. and Lang, G. (1963). The reliability of music preferences under varying mood conditions. *Journal of Clinical Psychology*, **19**, 506.

Schwardon, A.A. (1967). *Aesthetics: Dimensions for music education*. Washington, D.C.: MENC.

Schwebel, M. and Raph, J. (eds.) (1973). *Piaget in the classroom*. New York: Basic Books.

Scott, W.A. (1963). Conceptualising and measuring structural properties of cognition, in *Motivation and social interaction: Cognitive determinants*, ed. O.J. Harvey. New York: Ronald.

Sears, R.R., Maccoby, E.E. and Levin, H. (1957). *Patterns of child rearing*. New York: Harper and Row.

Seashore, C.E. (1919). *Seashore measures of musical talents*. Chicago: Stoelting.

  (1938). *Psychology of music*. New York: McGraw-Hill.

  (1960). *Seashore measures of musical talents* (2nd revision). New York: The Psychological Corporation.

Serafine, M.L. (1975). A measure of metre conservation in music, based on Piaget's theory. Unpublished doctoral dissertation, University of Florida.

  (1980). Piagetian research in music. *Council for Research in Music Education Bulletin*, **62**, 1–21.

  (1983). Cognition in music. *Cognition*, **14**, 119–83.

  (1985). Brief reply to Brody. *Cognition*, **19**, 99.

Serafine, M.L., Crowder, R.G. and Repp, B.H. (1984). Integration of melody and text in memory for songs. *Cognition*, **16**, 285–303.

Sergeant, D.C. (1969). Experimental investigation of absolute pitch. *Journal of Research in Music Education*, **17**, 135–43.

  (1979). Vocalisation as a substructure for discriminatory and cognitive functioning in music: a pilot study. *Council for Research in Music Education Bulletin*, **59**, 98–101.

Sergeant, D.C. and Boyle, J.D. (1980). Contextual influences on pitch judgement. *Psychology of Music*, **8**, 3–15.

Sergeant, D.C. and Roche, S. (1973). Perceptual shifts in the auditory information processing of young children. *Psychology of Music*, **1**, 39–48.

Sergeant, D.C. and Thatcher, G. (1974). Intelligence, social status and musical abilities. *Psychology of Music*, **2**, 32–57.

Shepard, R.N. (1965). Approximation to uniform gradients of generalization by monotone transformations of scale, in *Stimulus generalization*, ed. D.I. Mostovsky. Stanford: Stanford University Press.

  (1982). Structural representations of musical pitch, in *The psychology of music*, ed. D. Deutsch. New York: Academic Press.

Shepherd, J. (1977a). The 'meaning' of music, in *Whose music? A sociology of musical languages*, eds. J. Shepherd , P. Virden, G. Vulliamy and T. Wishart. London: Latimer.

  (1977b). The musical coding of ideologies, in *Whose music? A sociology of musical languages*, eds. J. Shepherd, P. Virden, G. Vulliamy and T. Wishart. London: Latimer.

Sherif, M. (1935). An experimental study of stereotypes. *Journal of Abnormal and Social Psychology*, **29**, 371–5.

Shotwell, J. (1979). Counting steps, in *Early symbolization*, eds. H. Gardner and D. Wolf. San Francisco: Jossey-Bass.

Shuter, R. (1964). An investigation of hereditary and environmental factors in musical ability. Unpublished Ph.D. Thesis, University of London.

  (1968). *The psychology of musical ability*. London: Methuen.

Shuter-Dyson, R. and Gabriel, C. (1981). *The psychology of musical ability* (2nd edition). London: Methuen.

Siegel, J. and Siegel, W. (1977). Categorical perception of tonal intervals: musicians can't tell *sharp* from *flat*. *Perception and Psychophysics*, **21**, 399–407.

Silverman, J., Winner, E., Rosenstiel, A. and Gardner, H. (1975). On training sensitivity to painting styles. *Perception*, **4**, 373–84.

Simon, C.R. and Wohlwill, J.F. (1968). An experimental study of the role of expectation and variation in music. *Journal of Research in Music Education*, **16**, 227–38.

Simon, T. and Smith, P.K. (1983). The study of play and problem solving in pre-school children: Have experimenter effects been responsible for previous results? *British Journal of Developmental Psychology*, **1**, 289–98.

Simonton, D.K. (1977). Creative productivity, age, and stress: a biographical time-series analysis of 10 classical composers. *Journal of Personality and Social Psychology*, **35**, 791–804.

(1980a). Thematic fame and melodic originality: a multivariate computer-content analysis. *Journal of Personality*, **48**, 206–19.

(1980b). Thematic fame, melodic originality, and musical zeitgeist: A biographical and transhistorical content analysis. *Journal of Personality and Social Psychology*, **39**, 972–83.

(1983). Esthetics, biography, and history in musical creativity, in *Documentary report on the Ann Arbor symposium on the application of psychology to the teaching and learning of music*. Reston, Virginia: MENC.

(1984). *Genius, creativity and leadership*. Cambridge, Mass: Harvard University Press.

Simpson, K. (ed.) (1976). *Some great music educators*. London: Novello.

Skinner, B.F. (1972). A lecture on having a poem, in *Cumulative record*, ed. B.F. Skinner (3rd edition). New York: Appleton-Century-Crofts.

Skipper, J.K. (1975). Musical tastes of Canadian and American college students: an examination of the massification and Americanization theses. *Canadian Journal of Sociology*, **1**, 49–59.

Sloboda, J.A. (1985). *The musical mind: The cognitive psychology of music*. Oxford: Oxford University Press.

Sluckin, W., Hargreaves, D.J. and Colman, A.M. (1982). Some experimental studies of familiarity and liking. *Bulletin of the British Psychological Society*, **35**, 189–94.

(1983). Novelty and human aesthetic preferences, in *Exploration in animals and humans*, eds. J. Archer and L. Birke. London: Van Nostrand Reinhold.

Smith, P.K. (1978). Play is only one way to learn. *New Society*, **45**, no. 825, 180–2.

(ed.) (1984). *Play in animals and humans*. Oxford: Basil Blackwell.

Smith, P.K. and Syddall, S. (1978). Play or non-play tutoring in pre-school children: is it play or tutoring which matters? *British Journal of Educational Psychology*, **48**, 315–25.

Spearman, C.E. (1927). *The abilities of man*. London: Macmillan.

(1930). *Creative mind*. London: Nisbet.

Spotts, J.V. and Mackler, B. (1967). Relationships of field-dependent and field-independent cognitive styles to creative test performance. *Perceptual and Motor Skills*, **24**, 239–68.

Stambak, M. (1951). Le problème du rythme dans le développement de l'enfant et dans les dyslexies d'évolution. *Enfance*, **4**, 480–502.

(1960). Trois épreuves de rythme, in *Manuel pour l'examen psychologique de l'enfant*, ed. R. Zazzo. Paris: Delachaux & Niestlé.

Standifer, J.A. (1970). Effects on aesthetic sensitivity of developing perception of musical expressiveness. *Journal of Research in Music Education*, **18**, 112–25.

Steck, L. and Machotka, P. (1975). Preference for musical complexity: effects of context. *Journal of Experimental Psychology: Human Perception and Performance*, **104**, 170–4.

Steenberg, N.J. (1959). IPAT music preference test of personality, in *The fifth mental measurements yearbook*, ed. O.K. Buros. Highland, N.J.: Gryphon.

Storr, A. (1972). *The dynamics of creation*. Harmondsworth: Penguin.

Strong, E.K. (1945). *Vocational interest blank for men*. Stanford, California: Stanford University Press.

Stumpf, C. (1883). *Tonpsychologie*. Leipzig: Herzel.

(1898). Konsonanz and Dissonanz. *Beitrage zur Akustic und Musikwissenschaft* 7, 1–108.

Sudnow, D. (1978). *Ways of the hand: The organization of improvised conduct*. London: Routledge & Kegan Paul.

Sundberg, J. and Lindblom, B. (1976). Generative theories in language and music descriptions. *Cognition*, 4, 99–122.

Sutton-Smith, B. (1966). Piaget on play: a critique. *Psychological Review*, 73, 104–10.

Suzuki, S. (1969). *Nurtured by love: A new approach to education*. New York: Exposition Press.

Swanwick, K. (1968). *Popular music and the teacher*. Oxford: Pergamon.

(1977). Belief and action in music education, in *Music education review*, vol. 1, ed. M. Burnett. London: Chappell.

(1979). *A basis for music education*. Windsor: NFER.

(1982). Problems of a sociological approach to pop music – a case study, in *9th ISME Yearbook*, ed. J. Dobbs. London: ISME.

Szemere, A. (1982). The role of folk music in young people's life, in *9th ISME Yearbook*, ed. J. Dobbs. London: ISME.

Szonyi, E. (1973). *Kodaly's principles in practice*. London: Boosey & Hawkes.

Taft, R. (1971). Creativity: hot and cold. *Journal of Personality*, 39, 345–61.

Tanner, F.D. (1976). The effect of disc jockey approval of music and peer approval of music on music selection. Unpublished doctoral dissertation, Columbia University.

Taylor, C.H. (1963). Techniques for the evaluation of musical status. *Journal of Research in Music Education*, 11, 55–62.

Taylor, D. (1979). *Music now*. Milton Keynes: Open University Press.

Teplov, B.M. (1966). *Psychologie des aptitudes musicales*. Paris: Presses Universitaires de France.

Terhardt, E. (1976). Ein psychoakustisch begründetes Konzept der musikalischen Konsonanz. *Acustica*, 36, 121–37.

Thackray, R. (1972). *Rhythmic abilities in children*. London: Novello.

Thomas, R.M. (1985). *Comparing theories of child development* (2nd edition). Belmont, California: Wadsworth.

Torrance, E.P. (1962). *Guiding creative talent*. Englewood Cliffs: Prentice-Hall.

(1967). *Understanding the fourth grade slump in creative thinking*. U.S. Office of Education Report.

Trehub, S.E., Bull, D. and Thorpe, L.A. (1984). Infants' perception of melodies: the role of melodic contour. *Child Development*, 55, 821–30.

Tuckman, B.W. (1966). Integrative complexity: its measurement and relation to creativity. *Educational and Psychological Measurement*, 26, 369–82.

Tunks, T.W. (1980). Applications of psychological positions on learning and development to musical behavior, in *Handbook of music psychology*, ed.D. Hodges. Lawrence, Kansas: National Association for Music Therapy.

Tysoe, M. (1984). You don't have to be mad, but . . . *New Society*, 70, 244–6.

Updegraff, R., Heileger, L. and Learned, J. (1938). The effect of training upon the singing ability and musical interest of three-, four- and five-year-old children. *University of Iowa Studies in Child Welfare*, 14, 83–121.

Valentine, C.W. (1962). *The experimental psychology of beauty*. London: Methuen.

Van Alstyne, D. and Osborne, E. (1937). Rhythm responses of negro and white children two to six. *Monographs of the Society for Research in Child Development*, 2, 4.

Varma, V.P. and Williams, P. (eds.) (1976). *Piaget, psychology and education*. London: Hodder & Stoughton.

Vater, H. (1934). Musikalische produktion. *Archiv fuer die Gesamte Psychologie*, 90, 1–60.

Vaughan, M.M. (1977). Musical creativity: its cultivation and measurement. *Council for Research in Music Education Bulletin*, 50, 72–7.

Vaughan, M.M. and Myers, R.E. (1971). An examination of musical process as related to creative thinking. *Journal of Research in Music Education*, 19, 337–41.

Vernon, P.E. (1979). *Intelligence: Heredity and environment*. San Francisco: W.H. Freeman.

Verveer, E.M., Barry, H. and Bousfield. W.A. (1933). Changes in affectivity with repetition. *American Journal of Psychology*, 45, 130–4.

Vidor, M. (1931). *Was ist musikalität?* Munich: Beck.

Vitz, P.C. (1966). Affect as a function of stimulus variation. *Journal of Experimental Psychology*, 71, 74–9.

Vulliamy, G. (1977). Music and the mass culture debate, in *Whose music? A sociology of musical languages*, eds. J. Shepherd, P. Virden, G. Vulliamy and T. Wishart. London: Latimer.

(1980). Music education and music languages. *Australian Journal of Music Education*, 26, 25–8.

Vulliamy, G. and Lee, E. (eds.) (1976). *Pop music in school*. Cambridge: Cambridge University Press.

Walker, E.L. (1980). *Psychological complexity and preference: A hedgehog theory of behavior*. Monterey, California: Brooks-Cole.

Wallach, M.A. (1970). Creativity, in *Carmichael's manual of child psychology*, ed. P.H. Mussen. New York: Wiley.

Wallach, M.A. and Kogan, N. (1965). *Modes of thinking in young children*. New York: Holt, Rinehart & Winston.

Wallach, M.A. and Wing, C.W. (1969). *The talented student: A validation of the creativity-intelligence distinction*. New York: Holt, Rinehart & Winston.

Wallas, G. (1926). *The art of thought*. London: Watts.

Wapnick, J. (1976). A review of research on attitude and preference. *Council for Research in Music Education Bulletin*, 48, 1-20.

Ward, W.D. and Burns, E.M. (1982). Absolute pitch, in *The psychology of music*, ed. D. Deutsch. New York: Academic Press.

Watson, J.B. (1924). *Behaviorism*. New York: Norton.

Watson, K.B. (1942). The nature and measurement of musical meanings. *Psychological Monographs*, 54, no. 244.

Webster, P.R. (1979). Relationship between creative behavior in music and selected variables as measured in high school students. *Journal of Research in Music Education*, 27, 227–42.

Webster, P. and Zimmerman, M. (1983). Conservation of rhythmic and tonal patterns of second through sixth grade children. *Council for Research in Music Education Bulletin*, 73, 28–49.

Wedin, L. (1972). A multidimensional study of perceptual-emotional qualities in music. *Scandinavian Journal of Psychology*, 13, 241–57.

Weick, K.E., Gilfillan, D.P. and Keith, T.A. (1973). The effect of composer credibility on orchestra performance. *Sociometry*, 36, 435–62.

Welch, G.F. (1979). Poor pitch singing: a review of the literature. *Psychology of Music*, 7, 50–8.

Werner, H. (1961). *Comparative psychology of mental development*. New York: Science Editions.

Werner, H. and Kaplan, B. (1963). *Symbol formation – An organismic-developmental approach to language and the expression of thought.* New York: Wiley.

Wertheimer, M. (1945). *Productive thinking.* New York: Harper.

Wiebe, G. (1940). The effect of radio plugging on students' opinions of popular songs. *Journal of Applied Psychology*, 24, 721–7.

Wilensky, H.L. (1964). Mass society and mass culture: interdependence or independence? *American Sociological Review*, 29, 173–97.

Williams, D.B. (1981). Editorial statement. *Psychomusicology*, 1, 3.

Williams, F.E. (1976). Rediscovering the fourth-grade slump in a study of children's self-concept. *Journal of Creative Behavior*, 10, 15–28.

Williams, H.M., Sievers, C.H. and Hattwick, M.S. (1933). The measurement of musical development. *University of Iowa Studies in Child Welfare*, 7, no. 191.

Williams, R.O. (1972). Effects of musical aptitude, instruction, and social status on attitudes toward music. *Journal of Research in Music Education*, 20, 362–9.

Wing, H.D. (1968). Tests of musical ability and appreciation (2nd edition). *British Journal of Psychology*, Monograph Supplement No. 27.

Winn, M. (1979). The pleasures and perils of being a child prodigy. *New York Times Magazine*, 23 December, pp. 12–17, 38–45.

Winner, E. (1982). *Invented worlds: The psychology of the arts.* Cambridge, Mass.: Harvard University Press.

Winner, E., Rosenblatt, E., Windmueller, G., Davidson, L. and Gardner, H. (1986). Children's perception of 'aesthetic' properties of the arts: Domain-specific or pan-artistic? *British Journal of Developmental Psychology*, 4, 149–160.

Winner, E., Rosenstiel, A., and Gardner, H. (1976). The development of metaphor understanding. *Developmental Psychology*, 12, 289–97.

Wishart, T. (1977). Musical writing, musical speaking, in *Whose music? A sociology of musical languages*, eds. J. Shepherd, P. Virden, G. Vulliamy and T. Wishart. London: Latimer.

Witkin, H.A., Dyk, R.B., Faterson, H.F., Goodenough, D.R. and Karp, S.A. (1962). *Psychological differentiation: Studies of development.* New York: Wiley.

Wright, D.F. (1975). Musical meaning and its social determinants. *Sociology*, 9, 419–35.

Yamamoto, K. (1965). 'Creativity' – a blind man's report on the elephant. *Journal of Counselling Psychology*, 12, 428–34.

Zajonc, R.B. (1968). Attitudinal effects of mere exposure. *Journal of Personality and Social Psychology*, 9, Monograph Supplement 2, 1–21.

(1980). Feeling and thinking: preferences need no inferences. *American Psychologist*, 35, 151–75.

Zenatti, A. (1969). *Le développement génétique de la perception musicale.* Paris: CNRS.

Zenatti, A. (1974). Perception et appréciation de la consonance musicale par l'enfant entre 4 et 10 ans. *Sciences de l'Art*, 9, 74–61.

(1975). Melodic perception and tonal acculturation: a comparative study of normal children and mental defectives. *Journal of Research in Music Education*, 23, 41–52.

(1976a). Jugement esthétique et perceptive de l'enfant, entre 4 à 10 ans, dans des épreuves rythmiques. *Année Psychologique*, 76, 93–125.

(1976b). Influence de quelques variables socio-culturelles sur le développment musical de l'enfant. *Psychologie Française*, 21, 185–90.

(1983). The role of perceptual-discrimination ability in tests of memory for melody, harmony and rhythm. Paper presented at the International Conference on Psychology and the Arts, Cardiff.

AUTHOR INDEX

SUBJECT INDEX